SHAKESPEARE AND THE PRINCE OF LOVE

Shakespeare and the Prince of Love

The Feast of Misrule in the Middle Temple

by
ANTHONY ARLIDGE

dlm

First published in 2000
by Giles de la Mare Publishers Limited
53 Dartmouth Park Hill, London NW5 1JD

Typeset by Tom Knott
Printed in Great Britain by
Hillman Printers (Frome) Limited
All rights reserved

© Anthony Arlidge 2000

Anthony Arlidge is hereby identified as author of
this work in accordance with Section 77 of the
Copyright, Designs and Patents Act 1988

A CIP record of this book is available
from the British Library

ISBN 1–900357–19–4 paperback

Contents

Illustrations

Preface

by Anne Barton, Professor of English at Cambridge University

On 6th February 1998, I had the good fortune to be present in the Hall of the Middle Temple when a version of Benjamin Rudyerd's text for the 1598 Candlemas revels in honour of that year's Prince D'Amour was presented by students of the Inn. It was a wonderful and also very illuminating performance: vigorous, fresh, funny, beautifully acted, directed, danced and sung. As Anthony Arlidge observes in this book, the text leapt off the page and to an extent that few members of its late-twentieth-century audience could have foreseen. In doing so, it suddenly rendered an ancient and almost forgotten tradition of Yuletide revelling and festive misrule in London's Inns of Court not only comprehensible but arrestingly contemporary.

Arlidge himself was the prime instigator and motivating force behind the entire 1998 enterprise. In the course of his researches, however, he had become fascinated by what he discovered about the more general importance of the Middle Temple between 1598 and 1602 in London's literary scene. *Shakespeare and the Prince of Love* assembles much material about individual students, Benchers, Serjeants and Judges associated with this Inn at the time. It chronicles the students' (sometimes rather disreputable) doings, their excursions into literature, even the taverns and ordinaries they frequented, where they jested, drank and argued with each other when they should have been dining (and simultaneously practising their legal skills) in 'Commons' in Hall. It all sheds a good deal of light upon Rudyerd's text – which Arlidge has now made easily available for readers in Appendix II. It also, as Arlidge came to recognize, raises some very interesting possibilities about Shakespeare's connection with the Middle Temple.

That Shakespeare, although never formally associated with one of the Inns of Court, nevertheless seems familiar in his plays with legal processes and terminology more readily explicable in John Marston or John Ford – both of them dramatists with Inns of Court backgrounds – has long been recognized. By uncovering Shakespeare's long-standing Warwickshire connection with Thomas Greene, a final-year student at the Middle Temple in 1602, Arlidge is able to suggest how this might have come about and, even more provocatively, to raise the possibility that Shakespeare was personally acquainted with the 'literary' luminaries of the Inn, had drunk and talked with them, knew about the Epiphany revels, and had been inside the great Hall. Was the performance of *Twelfth Night* at the Middle Temple, recorded by student John Manningham in his diary for 2nd February 1602, in fact the first night of a play specially commissioned by John Shurley, then Treasurer of the Inn? Arlidge argues that it was, and that this play (like *Troilus and Cressida*) should be restored to an initial Inns of Court context that makes sense not only of its title but of a number of its more puzzling allusions. There is as yet no concrete proof, but the idea is tantalizing – and considerably more persuasive than Leslie Hotson's argument in 1954 for a first night at Court. Anyone interested not only in this particular play but in Shakespeare and the non-dramatic as well dramatic literature of the period will find a good deal that is stimulating and also informative in this book.

Foreword

by Sir Louis Blom-Cooper Q.C.

Anthony Arlidge, in this fascinating work, has established – at least on a balance of probabilities, appropriately for a common-law practitioner not too imbued with the exacting if not irksome standard of proof in the criminal process – that *Twelfth Night* had its premiere in Middle Temple Hall on 2nd February 1602. As we approach the quatercentenary of that thespian event, which celebrated the seasonal revelries and topsy-turvydom of those Elizabethan times, it is pertinent to posit the perennial question: what prompted William Shakespeare to have this comic play performed in the heartland of the legal profession?

No doubt can be cast upon Shakespeare's more than nodding acquaintance with the law and with lawyers. The plays and sonnets are replete with legal references. In *The Quotable Lawyers* (1986) no fewer than 62 out of 2,600 best quotes in the law, from ancient times to the present, are ascribed to Shakespeare's plays and sonnets. It is astonishing that judicial utterances alluding to the Bard's works do not match Shakespearean allusions to the law. Any collection of the few Shakespearean quotations from the Law Reports should not, however, overlook Lord (then Mr Justice) Diplock's description of *Shylock versus Antonio* in *Tsakiroglou & Co. Ltd. versus Noblee Thorl GmbH* (1960) 2 Q.B. 318, 329, as 'a case which might have been decided on grounds of public policy but, in fact, turned on pure questions of construction'. Portia, having failed in her moving plea for money, entangled Shylock into a strict construction of the bond of a pound of flesh, holding in reserve its illegality (the attempt on the life of a citizen by spilling blood), which, if Shylock had foreseen it, would have led him rapidly to accept Bassanio's tender of six times the sum of money lent. It is Shylock's harshness which goes far to render his defeat dramatically acceptable to modern audiences. But then Shylock was pursuing an approach adopted by lawyers who had always been more prone than merchants to cling to the letter of the contract. No doubt today Article 3 of the European Convention on Human Rights would instinctively deflect Shylock from enforcing his inhuman, if not degrading, bargain. But I digress.

Twelfth Night has no court-room scene, though it does have a number of legal allusions. At heart it is a play about a servant 'sick of self-love and taste with a distempered appetite' amid, as Arlidge describes, the mad behaviour of lovers and gender inversion. But there is a sub-plot in the play in which Feste and his fellow servants taunt the imprisoned Malvolio for aspiring to marry above his station. Misled into thinking that a letter calling on him to appear before Olivia 'cross-gartered and yellow-stockinged' came from the Countess, Malvolio exhibits, by his bizarre dress, 'a very midsummer madness'. Feste observes that the 'whirligig of time brings in its revenges', at which Malvolio explodes: 'I'll be revenged on the whole pack of you.' Olivia's conclusion is that Malvolio has been 'most notoriously abused'. Revenge is thus featured as a practical joke, but nevertheless unsympathetically.

Shakespeare's exposure of the natural if intrinsically uncivilized act of revenge may be more directly displayed in other plays. A quarter of a century later, Francis Bacon expressed it in terms that have a direct and profound meaning in British society today:

> Revenge is a kind of wild justice, which the more man's nature runs to, the more ought law to weed it out ...

Acknowledgements

For some years I have been Master of the Entertainments in the Middle Temple and in that capacity I began preparing the celebration of the quatercentenary of the performance of *Twelfth Night* in the Inn. Some chance discoveries appeared to connect the text with the Inn and led finally to this modest volume. Having set out on a lit. hist., I swiftly became aware of my own inadequacies; I turned to men and above all women who knew. My long list of thanks includes: Janet Pennington, the archivist at Lancing College, who was of invaluable assistance in researching the Sherleys of Wiston; Christopher Whittock, of the East Sussex Record Office, who put me in touch with her and helped with the background to the Shurleys of Isfield; Sarah-Jane Tillard of Isfield Place and Harry Goring of Wiston Hall for the opportunity to visit their houses and reproduce photographs of them; Christopher Christodoulou for taking these and other pictures; Jane Beevers, a professional genealogist from Warwick, and Jack Lyes, archivist of the Bristol Law Society, who helped with research into the life of Thomas Greene, Shakespeare's 'cousin'; Janet Edgell, the Middle Temple Librarian who sadly has since died; Angela Knox, of the library staff, who located a copy of the script of the Middle Temple Revels of 1597/8, and particularly Lesley Whitelaw, the Middle Temple archivist, who has given constant support, including deciphering original records in the Star Chamber and letters by relevant Elizabethans; my son Matthew for help in researching the names of characters in *Twelfth Night*; most particularly Professor Anne Barton of Trinity College, Cambridge, who has twice read the manuscript, saved me from some appalling errors and helped with some positive criticism – great generosity to an obvious amateur; the National Trust, the Marquess of Bath, and the British Museum for permission to produce photographs and text; Doreen Ayling for proof-reading, a lot of word-processing and indexing; Tracy Ayling for photographs of the performance of the 1597/8 Revels in 1998; last but by no means least my publisher Giles de la Mare – after many years as an editor with and director of Faber and Faber, Giles set up his own small publishing house: his huge expertise was truly invaluable even if my attempts to satisfy him proved nearly fatal. None of the above bear any responsibility for what follows. Any errors are mine and nobody else's.

Page from the diary of John Manningham recording the performance of *Twelfth Night* in Middle Temple Hall. The year 1601 here would have been 1602 according to the modern calendar. *Reproduced by kind permission of the British Library*

Introduction:
The Detective Trail

At the beginning of 1602, John Manningham was a fourth-year student at the Middle Temple in London, one of the four major Inns of Court where young lawyers studied. He kept a diary[1] and on 2nd February made the following entry:

> at our feast wee had a play called Twelve Night or What You Will. much like the commedy of errors or Menechmi in plautus but most like and neere to that in Italian called *Inganni* a good practise in it to make the Steward beleeve his Lady widdowe was in Love with him by countarfeyting a letter as from his Lady in generall tearmes, telling him what shee liked best in him and prescribing his gesture in smiling, his apparaile &c. And then when he came to practise making him beleeve they tooke him to be mad.

The year recorded in the diary is 1601, but at that time the New Year commenced in March, so the modern equivalent is 1602. Although he makes no mention of the author, the title he records and the description of the plot leave no doubt that this is Shakespeare's play. Manningham was not too sure of the title because he started to write Mid and then crossed it out and wrote Twelve. This might indicate the play was of recent authorship. He was right about its similarity to *The Comedy of Errors*, for which *The Menechmi* was a source. *Inganni* does bear some similarity to *Twelfth Night*, although Shakespeare may not have known of it directly. Manningham had not followed the plot with complete attention because Olivia is not a widow, but a maid. She does not mourn a husband, but a brother. The mistake is understandable. Many of the students in the Middle Temple were upwardly mobile socially and one sure way to wealth and rank was to marry a rich widow.

While he does not name Shakespeare as the author, Manningham plainly knew of him. On 13th March 1602 he recounted a story told him by another student:

> Upon a tyme Burbidge playd Richard III there was a citizen grone soe farr in liking with him that before shee went from the play shee appointed him to come that night unto hir by the name of Richard III. Shakespeare over-

hearing their conclusion went before, was intertained and at his game ere
Burbidge came. Then message being brought that Richard the Third was at
the dore, Shakespeare caused return to be made that William the Conqueror
was before Richard the Third. Shakespeare's name was William.[2]

He knew of others in the literary set for he recorded that 'Ben Jonson the
poet now lives upon one Townsend and scornes the world.'[3] He also noted
that 'Dunne is undonne; he was lately secretary to the Lord Keeper and cast
of because he would match himselfe to a gentlewoman against his Lord's
pleasure.'[4] The diary refers as well to a story which is alluded to in *Twelfth
Night*. At the beginning of Act V, Feste enters with Malvolio's letter protesting about his imprisonment and ill-treatment. The following dialogue
ensues:

> FABIAN: Now, as thou lov'st me, let me see his letter.
> FESTE: Good Master Fabian, grant me another request.
> FABIAN: Anything!
> FESTE: Do not desire to see this letter.
> FABIAN: This is to give a dog, and in recompense desire my dog again.

In March 1602 Manningham recorded the story upon which Fabian's line
must have been based:

> Mr. Francis Curle told me howe one Dr Bullein, the Queenes kinsman,
> had a dog which he doted on, soe much that the Queen understanding of it
> requested he would graunt hir one desyre, and he should have what soever
> he would aske. Shee demaunded his dogge; he gave it, and 'Nowe, Madam,'
> quoth he, 'you promised to give me my desyre.' 'I will,' quoth shee. 'Then
> I pray you give me my dog againe.'[5]

It has long been accepted that Manningham recorded a very early performance of *Twelfth Night*, but his diary entry leaves many questions un-
answered. Why was it performed to an audience of law students? Is there
any significance in the date? Who performed it? What does the title mean?
Why is this almost the only one of Shakespeare's plays to have a double
title? What was the playwright's connection with the Middle Temple? The
search for the answers to these questions turned into a literary detective
story. Although the diary entry has been known about since the early
nineteenth century, no detailed research seems to have been made in the
archives of the Middle Temple into the background to the performance.
Preserved records of entertainment commence only in 1609, but they show
that plays were frequently performed on great feast days in the Inn,
particularly at Candlemas. The Inn was and is governed by senior members
called Benchers. They meet periodically in a 'parliament' and elect one of
their number annually to serve as their head, under the title of Treasurer.

Minutes of the parliament and admission registers helped to establish some apparent references in the text of the play to the Inn and people associated with it. Taken together these are sufficient to present a strong case that the play was commissioned for performance in the Inn – for 2nd February being indeed a first night.

The scent of the trail was picked up from two vital pieces of evidence. The first related to the date of the performance. In Elizabethan times, festivities at the year's end combined the celebration of Christmas and a medieval tradition of misrule. Twelfth Night marked the end of the Christian festival, but judging by contemporary accounts it also seems to have been a high point of the period of misrule. Records of student revels showed them electing a Prince of Misrule whose reign ended at Candlemas on 2nd February. In the Middle Temple he was called the Prince of Love. Love and misrule are important themes in *Twelfth Night* and link the text to the date of performance. Moreover, the feast at Candlemas was one of the two most important dates in the Inn calendar, when members of the Inn who had gained professional preferment were sumptuously entertained. The play was a perfect vehicle for such an occasion.[6] The second important piece of evidence was the identity of the Treasurer in 1602, one John Shurley. There are two jokes in the text that seem to relate to his family[7] and so point to a special compliment paid to him. If this were an 'inn-joke', there might be others.

Revels, which included both formal and informal entertainment, played an important part in Elizabethan life and understandably feature in several of Shakespeare's plays, including *Twelfth Night*.[8] Malvolio's zeal in try-ing to dampen the revelry of Sir Toby Belch and his friends forms the principal part of the sub-plot. There had been particularly famous revels in the Middle Temple in the Christmas period 1597/8. Extracts from them are found in commonplace books of the period, and it is likely that Shakespeare had heard of them. In 1660, when the period of Common-wealth rule ended, a publisher in Fleet Street felt that they were still suf-ficiently commercial for a copy of the script to be printed. In his preface he harked back to a golden era of fun at the turn of the previous century. With the help of the Inn librarian, a copy of this script was located at Harvard. It was performed by students of the Inn again in 1998. Although the text was supplemented with some anachronisms, the original humour – not unlike a modern end of term revue – survived remarkably and on occasion brought the house down. The spirit of the original, particularly the notion of misrule, came through strongly. A copy of the 1660 text is included in an appendix. If some of it seems rather stiff on the printed page, it leapt from it in performance. The Elizabethan costumes made modern lawyers seem very dull dogs indeed. It throws a fascinating light on the background to *Twelfth Night*.

Leslie Hotson's researches in the 1950s and 1960s revealed some personalities who were important in the creation of the play.[9] He suggested a
member of the Royal Court as a plausible model for the character of
Malvolio, and he also discovered detailed accounts of a visit by the real life
Orsino, Duke of Bracciano, to the court of Elizabeth I on Twelfth Night
1601. On that occasion the Company in which Shakespeare held a
share, the Lord Chamberlain's Men, performed a play, though none of the
accounts of the day name it. The coincidence of the date and Orsino's visit
led Hotson to suggest that this occasion was the first night of *Twelfth
Night*. The inferential leap was considerable and recent editors have consistently rejected the thesis. The new findings set out in this book confirm
that they are right to do so. Nevertheless, the coincidence of the name and
night is sufficient to suggest that here at least is the germ of an idea for the
play. The reports of Orsino's visit also demonstrate the importance of
Twelfth Night in the Christmas festivities.

Other plays by Shakespeare were performed in the Inns of Court too.
The Comedy of Errors was produced in Gray's Inn amongst the student
revels at Christmas 1594. The Earl of Southampton, to whom Shakespeare
addressed *Venus and Adonis*, and the Lord Chamberlain, Lord Hunsdon,
who patronized his Company, were both members of the Inn. There is
evidence that *Troilus and Cressida* was also first performed in an Inn.
The students of the Inns were theatre mad. Everard Gilpin,[10] a member of
Gray's Inn and a friend of some Middle Templars, described their life in his
Fifth Satire:

> Here may I sit, yet walke to Westminster
> And hear Fitzherbert, Plowden, Brooke and Dyer
> Canvas a law case: or if my dispose
> Perswade me to a play I'le to the Rose
> Or Curtaine, one of Plautus Comedies
> Or the Pathetique Spaniard's Tragedies.

These legal names were all law reporters who were frequently cited in the
courts.

There are good reasons why the offer of a commission might have
been attractive to Shakespeare's Company. An indoor winter venue obviously enabled the play to go on. Additionally the Company had become
connected with the failed Essex rebellion in January 1601. Ostensibly the
Earl of Essex was seeking to preserve the protestant succession through
James VI of Scotland, although the sceptical thought that he was seeking
the throne for himself. Either event might have required Elizabeth to
abdicate. On Saturday 7th February a party of the Earl's supporters, led by
a member of the Middle Temple called Sir Charles Percy, crossed the
Thames and offered the Lord Chamberlain's Men special payment to

perform *Richard II*, because it showed an abdication. When the rebellion failed, one of Shakespeare's partners was summoned before the Privy Council to explain why they had performed it and he explained the background.[11] No action appears to have been taken, but the following August the Queen confided in the keeper of the Tower, William Lambarde: 'I am Richard II, know ye not that.'[12] The Earl of Southampton, who was a member of Gray's Inn, was implicated in the rebellion and the government party had strong influence in that Inn. An offer in mid 1601 to perform away from the Royal Court and Gray's Inn might have had its attractions.

Whilst there is no record of those who attended the feast on 2nd February 1602, it is possible to deduce from the admission registers and minutes of the Inn parliaments who was likely to have been there. The Judges and the Serjeants certainly would have attended. At this time there were three common law courts which sat in Westminster Hall – the Queen's Bench, Exchequer and Common Pleas. In 1602 the heads of two of these were former members of the Middle Temple: Chief Justice Popham of the Queen's Bench and Chief Baron Perriam of the Exchequer. Middle Temple records establish that they were present at the feast which marked the beginning of the Christmas festivities on All Hallow's Eve 1601, together with Mr Justice Fenner, Mr Baron Savile and Serjeants Harris and Williams. Unless they were indisposed they would certainly have been present at Candlemas as well. At the other end of the pecking order would have been students such as John Manningham and his friends. Manningham mentions in his diary performing a moot with John Bramstone, who was later to become Chief Justice of the Queen's Bench. His portrait still hangs in the Inn with that of Baron Perriam. When Manningham was admitted to the Inn, one of his sureties or supporters was John Hoskins, who was a prominent member of the literary set and already famed for his oratory. Hoskins' close friend was Richard Martin, who had been Prince of Misrule when the revels were last held in 1597/8. There is clear evidence that these two, together with a Bencher called Edward Phillips, attended meetings of the so-called Mermaid Club on Friday nights. This was a group of young writers, including Jonson and Donne, who met in the Mermaid Tavern to the east of St Paul's to drink and read poetry. Another prominent performer in the 1597/8 revels was John Davies. He appears to have been jealous of Martin's success in the role of the Prince, for shortly afterwards he savagely assaulted Martin in Hall and was expelled from the Inn. Trying to impress in order to secure his return to the Inn, he became a poet of substance and renown. In his poem *Orchestra or a Poeme of Dauncing* he describes in detail the dances in which Sir Andrew Aguecheek claims expertise. Davies was readmitted to the Inn on All Hallow's Eve 1601 and would have wanted to be present at Candlemas. Eventually he was appointed Lord Chief Justice of Ireland.

The final-year students, as might be expected, played a leading role in organizing the light-hearted side of the revels. Amongst them in 1602 was a Warwickshire man called Thomas Greene. Not long after, he was living in Stratford upon Avon with the Shakespeare family, and in his diary he called Shakespeare his cousin. When the exact nature of their relationship was pursued, it was discovered that the two men were at least distantly related by marriage and possibly more closely linked illegitimately. Thomas Greene had some modest literary ambitions. John Marston, who was a student of the Middle Temple, had already made a considerable reputation and amongst others had written a play called *What You Will*, probably performed earlier the same year. As Shakespeare used the same words as his subtitle for *Twelfth Night*, there is another teasing link between the play and the venue. There were other younger students, such as John Ford and John Webster, who would make a literary name for themselves. The latter joined the Inn in 1597, close in time to Manningham, and had his first dramatic work accepted by Philip Henslowe in 1602. A few years later he was to write *The Duchess of Malfi* about a duchess who marries her steward, and *The White Devil* about the Orsini family. Ford was the son of a Bencher of the Middle Temple, as was Marston. These young men must have been in the audience.

It is clear then that in 1602 the Middle Temple was at the heart of the London literary scene. The students were rushing into poetry, satire and epigram. Woe betide the young man who could not write a sonnet to his mistress' eyebrow. Shakespeare recognized the problem in *Much Ado About Nothing*. Once convinced he is in love with Beatrice, Benedick feels obliged to write her a love poem. He acknowledges his effort is feeble:

> a whole bookful of these quondam carpet-mongers, whose names yet run smoothly in the even road of a blank verse, why, they were never so truly turned over and over as my poor self in love. Marry, I cannot show it in rhyme, I have tried; I can find out no rhyme to 'lady' but 'baby' – an innocent rhyme; for 'scorn', 'horn' – a hard rhyme; for 'school', 'fool' – a babbling rhyme; very ominous endings! No I was not born under a rhyming planet, nor I cannot woo in festival terms.[13]

Later when the Prince mocks his change of heart towards marriage he says:

> I'll tell thee what Prince; a college of wit-crackers cannot flout me out of my humour. Dost thou think I care for a satire or any epigram? No; if a man will be beaten with brains, 'a shall wear nothing handsome about him. In brief, since I do purpose to marry, I will think nothing to any purpose that the world can say against it.[14]

The Middle Temple was a college of witcrackers. They were adept at festival terms. Their satires and epigrams give a vivid picture of the lives of a very important segment of Shakespeare's audience. Unsurprisingly his plays are dotted with legal jokes. The performance of *Twelfth Night* in the Middle Temple offers a unique snapshot of high-life in Elizabethan London. The inception of the play is an end in itself, but also a starting point; investigation of its background will sometimes take the action away from the immediate context of the play to the broader picture of life in the Inns of Court. When all the pieces of evidence about the performance have emerged, an assessment will be made of the contention that this was indeed a first night.

It was also a last night. For some of those present, their student days were about to end. Richard Martin, the Prince of Love, was called to the Bar the following night. *Twelfth Night* is also a play about ending. It concludes with Feste's sad refrain about the rain raining every day. Now his misrule is over. The theme of the song is the passage from youth to maturity. Youthful swaggering is left behind. The Middle Temple was full of young swaggerers who would soon have to change to sober lawyers.

Before relating the play to the particular context of the Inns of Court, it is important to understand its broader social background. This is a subject which embraces not only contemporary events, such as the visit of a true-life Orsino to London and the current War of the Theatres, but also the custom of misrule. Although this will involve some detail, it can be conveniently centred on the double title of the play, which provides important clues to the history of the first night. Additionally, the true identity of the Yeoman of the Wardrobe is discovered.

CHAPTER ONE

'Twelfth Night or What You Will'

DUKE ORSINO

At first sight *Twelfth Night* seems an odd title for a play which on a superficial level is not about Christmas at all, for little textual information is provided as to when in the year the action is set. There is one reference to December, when Sir Toby sings in Malvolio's presence 'O' the twelfth day of December', presumably a drunken mistake for the twelfth day of Christmas.[1] Other than that there are some possible references to summer. Orsino bids his attendants to go 'away before me to sweet beds of flowers',[2] and Maria says that Malvolio has been 'yonder i' the sun practising behaviour to his own shadow this half hour'.[3] Some scenes are set in Olivia's garden. The only wintry reference is Feste's song at the end of the play.

The title must nevertheless have been chosen for a reason. As we have seen, Leslie Hotson first noted the coincidence that Orsino, Duke of Bracciano, visited the court of Queen Elizabeth I on Twelfth Night in 1601, when the Lord Chamberlain's Men performed a play.[4] After the death of his parents when he was young, the duke had been brought up at the Medici court in Florence. Florence at this time was opposed to the influence of both the Papacy and Spain and so Queen Elizabeth was anxious to court an important visitor from that city. Duke Ferdinando of Florence had recently arranged the marriage of his niece Maria to Henry of Navarre, the new king of France and an ally of England. The marriage was celebrated by proxy in Florence on 5th October 1600. Don Virginio Orsino was Maria's childhood companion. He was present at her proxy wedding and was chosen to accompany her on the journey to the French court to join her husband.

Pope Clement VIII came from the Aldobrandini family who were bitterly opposed to the Medicis. It was the Pope's powerful nephew, Cardinal Aldobrandini, who had come to Florence in 1600 to celebrate the marriage of Maria to Henry of Navarre. Virginio was sent to meet him and became involved in a bitter confrontation as to who should take precedence in entering Florence. This confrontation was reported to a Middle Templar, Sir John Popham, the Chief Justice of the Queen's Bench we have mentioned. John Hanam wrote to him on 17th October 1600 and he would almost certainly have passed on the information to the Government. The confrontation meant that it was politic for Don Virginio to remain out of Italy for a while. Earlier in 1600 he had entertained William Cecil, son of the second Lord Burghley, in the Pitti Palace. Don Virginio accompanied Maria by galley to Marseilles. It was only after their departure that Virginio wrote to Duke Ferdinando telling him of his intention to make a journey through France and the Low Countries to England.

On 20th November 1600 one Winwood wrote to Sir Henry Neville stating Virginio's intention to come to England.[5] This letter did not reach Neville until Christmas Day. It was followed shortly by another saying that a member of Virginio's party had asked Winwood to seek access for him to the Queen. He crossed the Channel on 1st January and arrived in London, according to his correspondence with his wife, on the 3rd.

Meanwhile, in London preparations were in hand to celebrate Twelfth Night. It was to be an important occasion, for the principal guest was the Muscovite Ambassador sent to London by Tsar Boris Godunov. Lord Hunsdon, the Lord Chamberlain, was responsible for the arrangements. He made a record of his preparation, which survives.[6] He notes that he is

> to confer with my Lord Admirall and the Master of the Revells for takeing order generally with the players to make choyse of [a] play that shalbe best furnished with rich apparell, have greate variety and change of Musicke and daunces, and of a Subiect that may be most pleasing to her Majestie.

The Lord Chamberlain's Men were subsequently paid for performing the play on that occasion. There is no record of its name. Lord Hunsdon's pre-scription of a play with rich apparel and frequent changes of music and dance does not match *Twelfth Night*. Olivia's household is after all in mourning.

There are other arguments which militate against Hotson's argument that the play was *Twelfth Night*. Although Don Virginio's intended visit had been communicated to England, the extant letters contain no indi-cation of when he was going to arrive. It seems unlikely that the Court knew of the precise date of his arrival before he sent a message to the Queen on 3rd January asking for an audience. A play for Twelfth Night would have been selected long before that. This might leave the possibility that Shakespeare was to change the name of his romantic hero to compli-ment the guest. Hotson suggests that the Queen was meant to see Orsino's love for Olivia as paralleled by Virginio's for her. Virginio was at this time a married man with six children. It would have been a risky course to picture love between two parties who had never met before, one of whom Shakespeare himself is unlikely to have encountered in advance. Further-more, the point is made early in the play that Orsino is a bachelor.[7] It might also have seemed insulting to picture the Duke of Bracciano as the Duke of Illyria, a country with a somewhat unsavoury reputation. Antonio the sea-captain who accompanies Sebastian says that he has many enemies at Orsino's court.[8] Later he explains:

> Once in a seafight 'gainst the Count his galleys
> I did some service – of such note indeed
> That, were I ta'en here, it would scarce be answered.[9]

Don Virginio had in fact been defeated in a sea-fight by Turkish galleys – he would hardly want to be reminded of it. An oblique reference once he was back home would add an Italianate air to the fictional court without risk of incurring displeasure. We shall see that there is a textual allusion in *Twelfth Night* that appears to refer to a play which was not staged until later in 1601.[10] All in all, it seems unlikely that the play performed before Don Virginio was *Twelfth Night*. The coincidence of the date and his name, however, may well have provided the germ of the idea for the play.

Nevertheless, descriptions of Don Virginio's visit certainly demonstrate the importance of Twelfth Night in the Christmas Festivities. A number of accounts of the day still exist.[11] Virginio wrote twice to his wife Flavia over this period and his letters are preserved in the family archives.[12] In one of them he describes how on the morning of the twelfth day after Christmas he was collected by William Cecil and driven to the Palace at Whitehall. In due course he was admitted to a withdrawing Chamber where he found

> all the officers of the Crown and Knights of the Garter, all dressed in white
> – as was the whole Court that day – but with so much gold and jewels,
> that it was a marvellous thing. These all came to greet me, the most part
> speaking Italian, many French, and some Spanish. I answered all as well as
> I knew how, in the tongue which I heard spoken; and I am sure that at the
> least I made myself understood. I found no more than two gentlemen who
> knew no other tongue than the English; and with these I employed other
> gentlemen as interpreters. All these brought me near the door where the
> Queen was to enter. Over against me was the Muscovite Ambassador,
> who had come as an Extraordinary to 'compliment' with her Majesty.
> The Queen came to the door and I presently approached in all humility
> to do her reverence; and she drew near me with most gracious cheer,
> speaking Italian so well, uttering withal such fine conceits, that I can
> maintain I might have been taking lessons from Boccaccio or the Academy.
> Her Majesty was dressed all in white, with so many pearls, broideries, and
> diamonds, that I am amazed how she could carry them. When I had done
> her reverence, Signore Giolio and Signore Grazia did the like; and then all
> the Court set forward in order towards the chapel. The order is such that
> I am having the whole noted in writing; nor do I believe I shall ever see a
> court which, for order surpasses this one. I attended her Majesty to a room
> next the chapel, where I stayed, in company with many gentlemen; and as
> we stood in excellent conversation, we heard a wondrous music.

At dinner (about noon) he did not eat in the same chamber as the Queen, that honour being reserved for the Ambassador, but when the meal was concluded he was summoned again to meet her, when she conversed with him and the Ambassador. He then retired to the Earl of Worcester's chambers where he was entertained with music 'played on instruments never heard in Italy, but miraculous'[13] and then supped. After supper he was conducted to a hall in the palace where the Queen came in

> and commanded me to go along discoursing with her. Her Majesty mounted the stairs, amid such sounding of trumpets that methought I was on the field of war, and entered a public hall, where all round about were rising steps with ladies and diverse consorts of music. As soon as her Majesty was set at her place, many ladies and knights began a Grand Ball. When this came to an end, there was acted a mingled comedy, with pieces of music and dances ('una commeddia mescolata con musiche e balli') and this too I am keeping to tell by word of mouth. The Muscovite Ambassador was not present.
> I stood ever near her Majesty, who bade me be covered, and withal caused a stool to be fetched for me; and although she willed me a thousand times to sit, I would however never obey her. She conversed continually with me; and when the comedy was finished, I waited on her to her lodgings.

By the time Virginio returned home it was two in the morning.

MISRULE

Twelfth Night, of course, marked the end of the Twelve Days of Christmas and the Feast of the Epiphany celebrating the visit of the wise men to the child Jesus. The festivities, however, on that night were also the high point of a pagan tradition. Stow in his *Survey of London* in 1592 described it thus:

> in the feaste of Christmas there was in the King's house, wheresoever hee was lodged, a Lord of Misrule or Maister of merry disports and the like had yee in the house of every noble man of honor or good worshippe were he spirituall or temporall. Amongst the which the Mayor of London and eyther of the Shiriffes had their severall Lords of Misrule ever contending without quarrell or offence who should make the rarest pastimes to delight the Beholders. These Lordes beginning their rule on Alhollon Eve continued the same till the morrow after the Feast of the Purification commonlie called Candlemas day. In all which space there were fine and subtle disguisings, Maskes and Mummeries, with playing at Cardes for Counters, Nayles, and pointes in evry house more for pastimes than for gaine.[14]

The description *misrule* was deliberate. The Lord of Misrule was usually elevated from a lowly position and his entertainments associated with the spirit of saturnalian disorder. It is a commonplace that Shakespeare's plays reflect the themes of order and disorder. Elizabethan society, whilst still upholding medieval order, was under constant pressure to change, through population growth, the transfer of wealth, inflation and religious reformation. The contrast between rule and misrule reflects the general concern for order, whilst acknowledging the delights of disorder. Misrule appears most obviously where there is literal usurpation. Usurpers are found not only in Shakespeare's histories and tragedies, but also in his comedies, such as *The Tempest* and *As You Like It*. The misrule in *A Midsummer Night's Dream* is caused and cured by magic. The disorder in *Twelfth Night* stems from accident or human contrivance.

C. L. Barber in *Shakespeare's Festive Comedy*[15] demonstrated how his plays from *Love's Labour's Lost* to *Twelfth Night* reflect the spirit of saturnalia. Medieval leisure was organized around feast days, including Twelfth Night and Candlemas. Apart from eating and drinking, the celebrations included music-making, dancing, disguisings and play-acting.[16] Shakespeare assumed his audience's familiarity with this tradition. For instance, in *All's Well That Ends Well* the Clown Lavache makes a comparison that is 'as fit as ten groats is for the hand of an attorney ... as a pancake for Shrove Tuesday, a morris for May Day, a nail to his hole.'[17] The plays do not merely reflect the tradition of misrule, but are organized around it; the chaos which springs from it ends with a final release and harmony, much as the celebrations of the ordinary man released him from the ardours of his everyday life. This parallel is most obvious in *A Midsummer Night's Dream*.[18] It seems probable that this play was not first performed on the day to which the title alludes, but in February 1596.[19] The text nevertheless has a large number of summer references, which even if they do not refer literally to the time of the action, call upon various folk traditions that are associated both with the morning of May Day and Midsummer's Eve. In the characters of Titania and Oberon there are echoes of the May King and Queen. The actions of the young lovers echo the tradition of bringing summer home from the country. Their behaviour in the woods near Athens evokes comparisons with the popular concept of midsummer madness. The action of the play is built around the idea of summer festivals, with the rejoicing and disorder they traditionally brought. When Oberon streaks Titania's eyes with the juice of love in idleness, he utters a charm so that waking she falls in love with an ass, an obvious disturbance of the natural order. Puck, sent to work similar magic on one of the young Athenian lovers, mistakes his man and the allegiances of the lovers undergo a sudden reversal that produces total disorder.

Similarly *Twelfth Night* can be seen as thematically built round the disorder traditionally associated with misrule at Christmas and the mad behaviour that produces.[20] The text is pre-occupied with madness. When Malvolio appears in his yellow stockings and cross-gartered, Olivia says 'this is very midsummer madness.'[21] He is later treated as a madman by Feste.[22] When Sir Andrew arrives with his challenge to Cesario, Fabian observes: 'More matter for a May morning.'[23] When Malvolio interrupts the revelry of Sir Toby and his friends he exclaims 'my masters are you mad' and describes their behaviour as 'this uncivil rule'.[24] When Olivia is told of Malvolio's 'madness', she describes herself (in the thrall of her love for Cesario):

> I am as mad as he
> If sad and merry madness equal be.[25]

When Sebastian is assaulted by Sir Andrew Aguecheek, he asks 'are all the people mad?'[26]

The plot draws substantially on two associated ideas – the mad behaviour of lovers and the gender inversion often occurring during saturnalia. The sexual world is turned upside down when Viola disguises herself as Cesario to gain access to Orsino's court. As a result, a woman falls in love with a woman disguised as a man, a man with a boy who is a disguised girl. Orsino is immediately attracted to Cesario, as Valentine attests when he speaks of the favours Orsino has shown his new page after only three days.[27] For her part, Viola immediately falls in love with Orsino. Ironically, she is sent on behalf of the man she loves to woo his mistress:

> a barful strife!
> Who'er I woo, myself would be his wife.[28]

When Malvolio describes Cesario to Olivia he says he is

> not yet old enough for a man, nor young enough for a boy; as a squash is before 'tis a peascod, or a codling when 'tis almost an apple. 'Tis with him in standing water, between boy and man. He is very well-favoured, and he speaks very shrewishly. One would think his mother's milk were scarce out of him.[29]

Olivia falls as swiftly in love with Cesario as Viola did with Orsino and sends Cesario a token of her love. Viola/Cesario comments on the frailty of women's affections:

> What will become of this? As I am man,
> My state is desperate for my master's love.
> As I am woman – now, alas the day! –
> What thriftless sighs shall poor Olivia breathe.[30]

When she describes the object of her love to Orsino in the guise of her sister's love, he questions her about what became of her sister. Viola/Cesario replies:

> I am all the daughters of my father's house,
> And all the brothers too.[31]

She does not know that her brother Sebastian is still alive and, when he arrives, the confusion is compounded when he marries Olivia who thinks he is Cesario. That marriage, however, frees Viola to reveal her true identity to Orsino and the plot then resolves. Throughout Orsino's relationship with Viola/Cesario there is a subtle sense that there is a closeness between them beyond ordinary male bonding. Orsino seems to recognize this when Cesario is revealed to be a woman:

> Your master quits you; and, for your service done him
> So much against the mettle of your sex,
> So far beneath your soft and tender breeding,
> And since you called me master for so long,
> Here is my hand, you shall from this time be
> Your master's mistress.[32]

There is also misrule in the Malvolio sub-plot. Sir Toby and his followers are an obviously unruly element in Olivia's household. They treat a sane man as mad. More particularly Malvolio seeks to upset the established order by marrying above his station. In Webster's *Duchess of Malfi*, written three years after *Twelfth Night* was performed, the Duchess takes her steward Antonio as her lover. Seeking to enter her bed, he says:

> ANTONIO: I must lie here.
> DUCHESS: Must! You are a lord of misrule.
> ANTONIO: Indeed my rule is only at night.[33]

A similar link between love and misrule is found in Lyly's *Endimion*, which was a source for *A Midsummer Night's Dream*. The main comic character, Sir Tophas, falls in love with a witch. Several times he links his grotesque love to the notion of misrule and at one point specifically to misrule at Christmas:

> Love hath justled my liberty from the wall and taken the upper hand of my
> reason ... Love is a lord of misrule and keepeth Christmas in my corps.[34]

When Feste adopts a disguise to taunt the imprisoned Malvolio, he says he is Sir Topas.

The name of the clown, who orchestrates much of the action, underscores the festival terms of the play. 'Feste' derives from the Italian 'feste', plural of 'festa', meaning feast or more generally festivity. This in turn derives from the Latin 'festum', with the plural 'festa'. The use of the plural underlines that this is not a reference to a single occasion, but a festive period. In any event, both the Italian and the Latin terms bear the overtone of festival or festivity, so that even the singular does not simply convey a meal. Christmas festivities in the Inns of Court were peppered with feasts. An audience there would readily have accepted allusions to the period of misrule as a method of unifying a number of comic and romantic devices.

We shall see that there is evidence that the play was written in a hurry. It is refreshing to think of the playwright creating a new sitcom to a deadline, thinking of new twists to a tried formula.

'THE WAR OF THE THEATRES'

If *Twelfth Night* foreshadows the themes of the play, what is the point of adding *What You Will*? This is almost the only example in the canon of a sub-title. It seems to continue the tradition of *As You Like It* or *Much Ado About Nothing* and suggest another situation comedy in the vein of the preceding plays. There is, however, a further reason for its addition. *Twelfth Night* was written during the so-called 'War of the Theatres', when playwrights inserted in their texts jokes at the expense of their competitors. It has already been noted that John Marston wrote a separate play called *What You Will*.[35] John was a student member of the Inn and lived in chambers there. By 1602 he had already had several plays performed, mainly in the small private theatres that had grown up near the Temple. There is clearly a relationship between his plays and Shakespeare's. *Jack Drum's Entertainment* and *Antonio and Mellida* appear to ring variations on the theme of *Romeo and Juliet*, and *Antonio's Revenge* bears a strong resemblance to *Hamlet*. In the case of these plays Shakespeare's version probably appeared first, so that Marston would have been making use of his material. He did the same by naming the hero in his later play, *The Malcontent*, Malevole. Although it is difficult to date the first performances of all these plays, his *What You Will* is generally supposed to have preceded Shakespeare's *Twelfth Night*. In this case Marston may have been mocking Shakespeare's earlier titles.

Competition in this period had grown between the private indoor venues and the common or public playhouses on the South Bank. Two prominent Companies of boy actors based on the choirs of St Paul's and the Chapel Royal were especially popular in the private theatres. The Children of St Paul's performed *Jack Drum's Entertainment* and the *Antonio* plays. From Michaelmas 1600, the Children of the Chapel Royal were installed in the Blackfriars Theatre. Probably in that year Ben Jonson's *Cynthia's Revels* was performed there, followed in the spring of 1601 by his *Poetaster*. In both plays Jonson made jokes at the expense of the common theatres. In the latter play, for instance, reference is made to the professional actors growing cold as snakes in the winter.[36] Later in 1601, Thomas Dekker responded in his play *Satiromastix*, apparently modelling a humorous poet called Horace on Jonson and mocking the latter's use of the word 'element'. Shakespeare makes an apparent reference to this in *Twelfth Night*. In Act III, Scene 1, Feste speaks to Viola about announcing her to Olivia:

> I will conster to them whence you come. Who you are and what you would are out of my welkin – I might say 'element', but the word is overworn.[37]

Dekker's play was registered on 11th November 1601. This would appear to date *Twelfth Night* late in 1601. By 1603 Marston's interest in the Children of the Chapel Royal was such that he bought shares in that Company. Shakespeare makes reference to an established Company of players facing competition from a Company of boys in *Hamlet*. When the travelling players arrive at Elsinore the following dialogue ensues:

> HAMLET: ...What players are they?
>
> ROSENCRANTZ: Even those you were wont to take such delight in, the tragedians of the city.
>
> HAMLET: How chances it they travel? Their residence, both in reputation and profit, was better both ways.
>
> ROSENCRANTZ: I think their inhibition comes by the means of the late innovation.
>
> HAMLET: Do they hold the same estimation they did when I was in the city? Are they so followed?
>
> ROSENCRANTZ: No, indeed are they not.
>
> HAMLET: How comes it? Do they grow rusty?
>
> ROSENCRANTZ: Nay, their endeavour keeps in the wonted pace. But there is, sir, an eyrie of children, little eyases, that cry out on the top of question and are most tyrannically clapped for't. These are now the fashion, and so berattle the common stages – so they call them – that many wearing rapiers are afraid of goose quills and dare scarce come thither ... there has been much to-do on both sides ...
>
> HAMLET: Do the boys carry it away?
>
> ROSENCRANTZ: Ay, that they do, my lord – Hercules and his load too.[38]

That Shakespeare is referring to contemporary events is confirmed by the reference to Hercules' load, for he carried the Globe. The reference to the late innovation has caused some controversy, some saying it relates to the advent of the boy players and others suggesting that it refers to the Essex rebellion.

THE YEOMAN OF THE WARDROBE

Shakespeare makes a joke about those concerned with the Children of the Chapel Royal in *Twelfth Night*. To unravel its meaning required patient research. The result goes to the heart of the War of the Theatres, and may have a homosexual innuendo. Malvolio seeks to justify his social ambition to marry the Countess Olivia, to whom he is steward, in these terms: 'There is example for't. The Lady of the Strachy married the yeoman of the wardrobe.'[39] There was a contemporary William Strachey who was a partner in the Blackfriars Theatre.[40] He was born the son of a draper in the Essex market town of Saffron Walden. He was educated at Emmanuel College, Cambridge, and from there joined Gray's Inn.[41] He had direct connections with members of the Middle Temple and the London literary set. Richard Martin wrote to him in 1610, speaking of their ancient acquaintance. John Donne wrote at a later date to Henry Wotton, also a Middle Templar, commending Strachey as 'allwayes my good friend'. In 1603 Jonson's *Sejanus* was performed at the Globe with Shakespeare in the cast. When it was published in November 1604, Strachey was one of a number of writers who contributed verses to preface the edition. Thomas Campion, a fellow member of Gray's Inn, wrote an epigram about Strachey in which he described him making elegant little verses. He appears to have led a lively life for shortly before his death he wrote some penitential verses in which he declared:

I have sinned against Earth and heaven
Early by date, late in the even,
All manner sinnes, all manner wayes,
I have committed in my daies.[42]

In 1595 he married Frances Forster, from Crowhurst in Surrey. By 1605 he seems to have been in some financial difficulty. Maybe this led to his later involvement in expeditions to the Levant and Virginia. Most importantly for our purposes, one of his partners in the Blackfriar's Theatre was the Yeoman of the Wardrobe.

On 2nd September 1597 one Henry Evans took a lease for twenty-one years on the Blackfriars Theatre from Burbage. From then on, in association with Nathaniel Giles who held a royal patent as Master of the Children and Gentlemen of the Chapel Royal, he produced plays performed entirely by boy actors at that theatre. The Master of the Children of the Chapel Royal had the right to impress children to sing in the choir. Evans seems to have used this power to force children to perform in his Company. In 1601 a man called Clifton complained to the Star Chamber about the abduction of his son by Evans.[43] He argued that the power to impress boys was only for the choir; his son had no singing ability and had been forced to act in plays. The end result of the action was that Evans was censured and all assurances made to him declared void. The decree has not survived,[44] but judging by a reference in a later action, it seems to have been made at the end of 1601 or early in 1602. After the action Evans left London for a period. He seems to have anticipated that the decision might go against him, because in October 1601 he transferred the lease on the theatre to his son-in-law Alexander Hawkins. Moreover, on 20th April 1602 Evans and Hawkins entered into a deed of co-partnership with William Rastell, a merchant, Thomas Kendall a haberdasher and Edward Kirkham. It seems likely that these arrangements were to deal with Evans' difficult situation after the decree.

Edward Kirkham was first employed in the Royal Wardrobe in the early 1580s, probably as a tailor. It was situated just off Carter Lane near the Blackfriars playhouse (both sites can still be identified from street names). Under the control of the Master of the Revels, it created costumes for pageants and masques. In 1586 Kirkham was granted a royal patent:

> Know ye that wee in consideration of the diligent service of our well-beloved subject Edward Kirkham who hath done virtuous service in the office of our Revells ... doe give and graunte unto the said Kirkham the Office of yeoman or keeper of our vestures or apperrell of all and singular our Masked Revells and disguisings ... and further we doe give unto the said Edward Kirkham yearly during his said life one livery coate such as the yeoman Officers of our household have of us to be yearly had and received att our Great Wardrobe.[45]

It would appear, therefore, that by 1602 there were at least five partners in the Blackfriars Theatre Company, one of them the Yeoman of the Royal Wardrobe. In 1606 a further action occurred in the Court of Chancery arising from a dispute between these partners concerning payment for dilapidations to the theatre building. One of the witnesses was William Strachey, whose signed deposition still exists.[46] In it he states that

> He hath sene a bill of the particular reparacons of the sd howse which hath bene delyvered by or from one Burbidg who ys brother to him that ys Landlord of the sayd howse wherby Henry Evans one of the defts (defendants) hath bene required to doe those reparacons and he further saith that he verely thinketh that the sd Evans hath done such reparacions accordingly for the he this dept (deponent) haveing some interest in the busynes belonging to the sd howse hath payd a sixth parte of the sd charge delyvered to this dept ... and that he this dept hath heretofore sene a bill or account of the defts whereby they charged the complts severally with a sixth parte of the charge for reparacions done uppon the sd howse and he saith that he hath herd ... that two of the complts namely Kyrkham and Rastall ... paye each of them their sixth parte of the said charge as this

dept hath done but they say they cannot gett the other complt Kendall to paye his sixth parte of the sd charge.

He went on to depose that he, together with Kirkham, Rastall and Kendall, had a sixth share of the profits from the Company and that the latter three had a view and inventory of the Company's costumes. Strachey was not named in the partnership deed of 1602, but his evidence plainly shows he had a sixth share in the Company, even if only on an informal basis. None of the actions relating to the Company make any mention of any later partnership deed. As all the shares were equal it seems likely that they were partners from the beginning. Maybe no formal document was required from Strachey as he was a gentleman. Although the partnership deed just postdates the performance of *Twelfth Night*, it also seems likely, given the Star Chamber proceedings against Evans, that arrangements were being put in place before this date.

All of this evidence supports the view that the Malvolio's line is an in-joke. If the line is just a piece of nonsense, it would seem odd for Shakespeare to pick on a relatively unusual name like Strachey, and an extraordinary coincidence that someone of that name would be well known to the audience and connected with the Yeoman of the Wardrobe. The omission of the 'e' in the name is of no significance, since in some contemporary documents in the Essex Record Office the family name is spelt as Shakespeare spells it. But who was the Lady of the Strachey? The marriages of the ladies in the Strachey family are accounted for with none marrying a Kirkham.[47] An illicit relationship seems ruled out since the whole point of the joke is marriage as a means of social advancement. The Elizabethans did use yeoman in an ironic sense – thus the yeoman of the collar was the hangman.[48] One possibility is that the Lady of the Strachey was Strachey himself. It would not have been unusual to refer to a man who was effeminate or dressed extravagantly as a woman. It is tempting to look for a homosexual interest, particularly as Middleton (a fellow Gray's Inn student) wrote, in *Father Hubbard's Tales*, of a gallant that if his humour so serve him he could 'call in at the Blackfriars, where he would see a nest of boys able to ravish a man.' According to one suggestion, this line mirrors Shakespeare's description of the boy players in *Hamlet* where he names them as 'an eyrie of children, little eyases'.[49] Literally this means a nest of eaglets, but eyases would be pronounced the same as eye-arses.[50] Strachey's confession that he had sinned all ways might embrace homosexual conduct. Another explanation might be that the joke is similar to the modern usage of partners or companies 'going to bed together' in the sense of merging for business purposes. It would have had the added advantage of being a jibe against a business competitor.

All of this brings the argument back to the sub-title *What You Will*. John

Finkelpearl, in *John Marston of the Middle Temple*, makes a plausible case that John Marston started the War of the Theatres in a play performed during the Middle Temple revels in 1597/8. If Marston had pre-empted Shakespeare with the title *What You Will*, the latter could simply have entitled his play *Twelfth Night*. That he used the sub-title almost uniquely in his work suggests there was a purpose. Maybe he simply saw no reason not to use it (since writers frequently borrowed from others) and wanted to advise the reader not to place too much consequence on the main title. Yet he did not feel it necessary to do this with *A Midsummer Night's Dream*. Maybe he wanted to reclaim his own genre of title. Maybe he wanted to suggest that his play was better than Marston's. Shakespeare plainly had a special sensitivity to competition from the theatre where Marston's plays were performed, and this does strengthen the contention that he was trying to make an in-joke to an Inn audience.

If the sub-title *What You Will* and the joke about William Strachey were 'inn-jokes', then the possibility must be considered whether there are other similar jokes in the text. The following chapter reveals the first of these – a joke about Olivia's house being very light. The description of the room exactly matches Middle Temple Hall. But what was the Middle Temple? Who studied there? What lives did they lead? The following chapter seeks to answer those questions, and incidentally chances upon a bribe offered by the Treasurer to obtain advancement.

CHAPTER TWO

Mad Days

INNS OF COURT

When *Every Man Out of his Humour* was re-published in 1616, the author
Ben Jonson appended a preface in which he referred to the Inns of Court
as 'the noblest nourseries [nurseries] of humanity, and liberty in the
kingdome', adding that 'when I wrote this Poeme, I had friendship with
divers in your societies'. The first performance of the play was in 1599.
Others took a more jaundiced view. In 1633 the puritan pamphleteer
William Prynne wrote in his *Histriomastix*:

> That Innes of Court men were undone but for Players, that they are their
> chiefest guests and imployment, and the sole busines that makes them
> afternnoons men[1] and this is one of the first things they learne as soone
> as they are admitted, to see Stage-plays.

There were four major Inns – the Inner and Middle Temples, Lincoln's
Inn and Gray's Inn – and some ten minor Inns or Inns of Chancery.[2] Some
students spent three years in these preparatory Inns; others came straight
from university to the major Inns, where a minimum of seven years was
required for qualification. The original name adopted by qualified prac-
titioners was 'apprentice of the law'. This term was still used at the end
of the sixteenth century, but was gradually being replaced by the title
'barrister'.[3] The title seems to have derived from a bar in court from which
advocates pleaded, or a notional barrier in mock trials in the Inns behind
which the qualified barristers stood. The apprentices of the law appeared in
the Temple in the fourteenth century. They occupied the church, halls and
chambers formerly the property of the Knights Templar, that order having
been dissolved by the Pope in 1311. The magnificent round twelfth-century
church still houses the effigies of the knights. From the start the lawyers
seem to have organized themselves into two separate societies, the Inner
and Middle Temples, the first reference to the latter being in 1404, when
a member left money to the steward. The Temple was conveniently sited
between the commerce of the City and the common law courts, which sat in
Westminster Hall.

The Inns housed practising barristers and students, the former instructing the latter. Teaching was largely oral. Each term a barrister member of the Inn was appointed Reader to oversee the education of the students. Dining in Hall was a collegiate duty and during and after dinner legal points were argued as part of the education process. Manningham in his diary gives an example:

> Mr Fleetwood, after he was gone from supper, remembred a case to the purpose he was talking of before he went, and came againe to tell us of it, which Mr Bramston said was as yf a reveller when he had made a legg at the end of his galliard, should come againe to shewe a tricke which he had forgotten.[4]

Litigation since the Norman Conquest had been conducted in French, or later in a bastard version of it called law French, made up of a mixture of English and French. One celebrated example is found in a case where a judge was assaulted by a prisoner 'que puis son condemnation ject un brickbat a le dit justice que narrowly mist.'[5] The English judges developed a method of working from practical example to practical example rather than from a general code of laws in the Roman form. The precedents were reported in Year Books written in law French. At the universities of Oxford and Cambridge the teaching was in Latin and so could not accommodate this native law. About 1470 Sir John Fortescue, a former Chief Justice of the King's Bench, explained the result which (in translation) reads:

> Since the laws of England are learned in these three languages, they could not be conveniently learned or studied in the Universities, where the Latin language alone is used. But those laws are taught and learned in a certain public academy, more convenient and suitable for their apprehension than any University. For this academy is situated near the king's courts, where these laws are pleaded and disputed from day to day, and judgements are rendered in accordance with the judges, who are grave men, mature, expert and trained in these laws. So those laws are read and taught in these courts as if in public schools, to which students of the law flock every day in term time. That academy also is situated between the site of those courts and the City of London, which is the richest of all the cities and towns of that realm in all the necessaries of life. And that academy is not situated in the city, where the tumult of the crowd could disturb the students quiet, but is a little isolated in a suburb of the city, and nearer to the aforesaid courts, so that the students are able to attend them daily at pleasure without inconvenience or fatigue.[6]

The legal historian, F. W. Maitland, regarded the establishment of this national school of law as the chief distinction between medieval England and its continental counterparts.[7] It was known as the Third University.

Native customary law in Europe had gradually succumbed to the dominant influence of Roman law. In England it became the object of national pride that this had not occurred. The development of English law became a symbol of national identity and vigour.

By the sixteenth century there was a strong movement in Europe, prompted by the new humanism, for the introduction of systems of law to replace both national customary law and the medieval accretions which had built up around classical Roman law. This is known to continental jurists as 'the Reception'.[8] Classical Roman law systems were in particular 'received' in Scotland and Germany. Attempts were made to do the same in England as well. In the 1520s Henry VIII's cousin Reginald de la Pole was advocating the reception of a Roman law system into England. One in his employ, Thomas Starkey, wrote:

> Thys ys no dowte but that our law and ordur thereof ys over-confuse. Hyt ys infynyte and without ordur or end. There ys no stabyl grounde therein, nor sure stay; but every one that can coloure reson makyth a stope to the best law that ys before tyme devysyd. The suttylty of one sergeant schal enerte and destroy al the jugementys of many wyse men before tyme receyvyd. There is no stabyl ground in our commyn law to leyne unto … Therefor, to remedy thys mater roundly, hyt was necessary, in our law, to use the same remedy that Justynyan[9] dyd in the law of the Romanynys, to bryng thys infynyte processe to certaynn endys, to cut away thys long lawys and by the wysdome of some polytyke and wyse men instytute a few and bettur lawys and ordynancys.

The King himself was influenced by these views and endowed chairs of civil or Roman law at Oxford and Cambridge. The government also used the Court of Chancery and newly established prerogative courts of Requests and Star Chamber to bypass the common law courts. The King even considered establishing a national school of civilian law.[10] This never came to fruition, but the new courts did take work from the common law courts. In 1537 the reporting of legal decisions in the Year Books ceased. In 1547 students of the common law petitioned the King's Privy Council complaining about the inroads that the Court of Chancery was making into the common law. Stow in his *Annals of England* reported in 1557:

> This yeere in Michaelmas terme men might have seene in Westminster hall at the Kinges bench barre not two men of law before the justices; there was but one named Forstar, who looked about and had nothing to do and the judges looking about them.[11]

The common lawyers, however, fought back. New law reporters appeared to fill the gap left by the Year Books. A new generation of able lawyers arose including Edward Coke, later to be Attorney-General and

After my harty commendacon, I send
yor first [letter?] forewith [being?] sent for to
be imployed on the [glasse?] howse worke
ye be the... of my master...
... of the ... sample... appointed
... assigned to the buyldyng... a new
... in the [glasse?] howse, beyng the
[glasse?] howse [worke?]... and
... neybors at the... the do not
... in... request... all or howse,
... appoyntaor will...
yor... for yor... in this behalf.
... that you will signyfye unto... yor
good... [certain?]. ... that you will
... the... yor good will from...
... poynt by... forewith... I
am the more... to request... that yor
... of the said howse. ... al though
you in the said... I... [request?]... agreit
gentlemen shall... occasion... and...
to gyve to you... [faythfully?]... in yor
... forewith to be attempted...
... desire forewith, beyng bold
to wryte to you, and to crave yor...
... to who [th]effect of my desyre will
you at the... forewith to fare well. fare
... the... of June 1562
   yor frend to [use?]
   [Edmund Plowden?]

After my harty commendacons: Lewis your servant berer heroff beyng sent for to be employed on the Quene's highnes works ys by the mediacon of my Masters and felowes of the Myddle Temple appoynted and assigned to the buylding of a newe halle in the said howse being the Quene's highnes howse and worke and I beying Treasorer at this tyme do most hartly in the behoeffe of all our howse and they yor acqueytance will herafter particularly desire you, wee may have yor favor for yor man in this behelffe and that you will signyfye unto him yor good contencon herein and that you will not withdrawe yor good will from hym in ony point by meanes hereoff wherfor I am the more earnest to request for that yor councell be of the said howse and althoghe some of the howse (as I myselffe) be agenst you in some things yet hereafter this yor gentlenes shall occacyon me and my felowes to give to you our fryndly furtherance in yor matters hereafter to be attempted or begone. This upon deserte beyng bolde to wryte to you and to crave yor gentilnes hopyng to receve the effect of my desire bidde you at this present hartly to farewell.

From Shiplake the
XXIII of June 1562
Yor frynde to use or comande
Edmund Plowden

Note: the work and the house are the Queens, because the Crown owned the land upon which the Hall was built.

Letter from Edmund Plowden to the Marquess of Bath recording the use of an employee of the Marquess in the building of Middle Temple Hall; and transcription. *Photograph by Christopher Christodoulou; reproduced by kind permission of the Marquess of Bath, Longleat House, Warminster, Wilts, GB*

Chief Justice of the King's Bench under James I, who saw the common law as Fortescue saw it – a bulwark against absolute monarchy. The courts were to be the first battleground of the English Revolution.

The fresh confidence of the Inns of Court was no doubt exemplified by the building of the new Middle Temple Hall.[12] Astonishingly, there is comparatively little information about the project in the Inn records. The first mention of it is a minute of parliament in 1562 which directs that until the completion of the new Hall each member shall bear the cost of repair of his own chamber.[13] Edmund Plowden was one of the most distinguished lawyers of his day. He made reports of cases for his own use from 1537, which he was eventually persuaded to publish: they were the first modern law reports. He was elected Treasurer of the Middle Temple in June 1561 and remained in this office until May 1567. On his retirement the minutes of the Inn parliament record that he is to remain promoter for the building of the new Hall and for making collections. Its construction is a tribute to the Inn's confidence in its relations with the Sovereign, since at this time the land on which it was built belonged to the Crown. It was paid for by levies on and forced loans from members of the Inn.[14] Those who did not pay up lost their chambers. The date 1570 is inserted in the east window and 1573 appears with Plowden's coat of arms displayed in the south window. Presumably the building was completed about that time. It is a magnificent late Gothic hall, measuring about thirty-five metres in length and thirteen metres in width, except in the two bay-windows at the western end, where it is wider. The long side-walls face north and south respectively, the southern facing the river Thames; each has a clerestory of glazed windows, the lower half of the wall being brick with internal panelling. The windows are now filled with stained glass, but in 1602 they were largely clear glass. The Hall is topped with a superb double hammer-beam roof, supported by external buttresses. There was a double hammer-beam roof in Westminster Hall that had been built in 1399. Single hammer-beam roofs had been built in the royal palaces at Eltham (1481) and Hampton Court (1530). When it was built, the roof of the Middle Temple Hall must have been the finest in the kingdom in a domestic building. It provided a model for later roofs at Trinity College, Cambridge, and Knole House in Kent. At the east end there is a finely-carved screen. It has two wide entrances with a gallery above.

When Malvolio is imprisoned as a madman, Feste comes to torment him in the guise of the priest Sir Topas. Malvolio complains that he has been laid in hideous darkness. The dialogue continues:

FESTE: Sayst thou that house is dark?
MALVOLIO: As hell, Sir Topas.
FESTE: Why, it hath bay windows transparent as barricadoes, and the

clerestories towards the south-north are as lustrous as ebony. And yet
complainest thou of obstruction.

MALVOLIO: I am not mad, Sir Topas. I say to you, this house is dark.

FESTE: Madman, thou errest. I say, there is no darkness but ignorance, in
which thou art more puzzled than the Egyptians in their fog.

MALVOLIO: I say this house is as dark as ignorance, though ignorance were
as dark as hell.[15]

The reference to the glass would have had a particular significance. The
Reverend William Hall writing in his *Description of England in 1577*
records how in early Tudor times windows had been filled with wicker
or fine rifts of oak in chequer wise, but now only clear glass was used.
Early in Elizabeth's reign artisans from Normandy and Lorraine had emi-
grated to England and greatly improved the native glass industry, enabling
it to supply window glass for lattice windows.[16] The Middle Temple Hall
must have been amongst the first major buildings to use this new technology. A 'barricado' was a line of stakes – a barricade. It would not be
completely transparent; nor would ebony, though here the reference is to
lustre rather than clarity. Nevertheless Feste is dwelling on the lightness
of the room. References in the Inn records demonstrate the importance
attached to the windows in the Hall. In the 1597/8 Revels there was a mock
trial of a discontented lover. One charge laid against him was that he had
'swallowed Garlick, and that without allay or qualification ... that the
strength of it brake some fewer than fifty Panes of our glass windows.'
Early seventeenth-century records describe watchmen being employed during revels to ensure that the windows were not broken. There may have
been other halls that would have fitted the description in the text, but the
older medieval halls, such as that at Whitehall Palace, had far less window
space. The geographical placing of the walls quoted in the play does suggest
that Shakespeare was referring to a particular building and therefore
making an in-joke to his audience. The building is plainly not a theatre and
the description matches Middle Temple Hall, which has clerestories in the
south and north walls, and bay-windows, and is exceptionally light for a
building of its kind.

The new Hall was at the centre of London life. According to tradition the
High Table, at which the Benchers still dine, was made from a single oak
from Windsor Great Park, a gift from Queen Elizabeth. The Inn records of
entertainments during her reign have been destroyed, but she must have
visited the new Hall, which was built on her land. The young men of the
Inn certainly entertained her at the Royal Court. The great and the good
were members of the Inn. Sir Walter Raleigh was admitted in 1574.[17] The
explorer Frobisher, who tried to find the north-west passage to the Indies,
was made an honorary member in 1592. So in the following year was Sir

John Hawkins, who was Treasurer of the Navy and held a command under Drake when the Armada was repelled in 1588. There is no record of Drake being admitted a member, but the minutes do record that on 4th August 1586 he came to the Hall when the society were dining having recently returned from a voyage.[18] He had disembarked at Plymouth in July after a voyage to America suppressing the Spanish colonies there and returning some of the Virginia colonists to England.[19] He was greeted in the Inn with great joy and congratulated on his happy return. He is described as one of the fellowship of the Middle Temple ('unus de Consortio Medii Templi') and as a longstanding friend ('antiquam familiaritatem et amicitiam cum consortio'). Many members of the Inns of Court were also members of Parliament, and from 1580 to the end of Elizabeth's reign the Hall was frequently assigned as a meeting place for committees of the House of Commons.

THE STUDENTS

The students in the Inns led a more rumbustious life than their elders. Many of them had no intention of practising at the bar or even qualifying for it. They came to the Inns as a sort of finishing school. A survey of four major Inns in 1574 reveals they contained some 176 practising barristers, but 593 other gentlemen.[20] The breakdown for the Middle Temple was 11 Benchers, 40 barristers and 139 other gentlemen. In 1614 an edict of the Privy Council acknowledged the extent to which life in the Inns had been deflected from its original purpose:

> For that the institution of these Societies was ordained chiefly for the profession of the law and in the second degree for the Education of the sons and youth of riper years of the Nobility and Gentry of this Realm, and in no sort for the lodging or abode of the Gentlemen of the Country, which if it should be suffered were to disparage the said Societies, and to turn them from hospitia to diversoria.[21]

Shakespeare was very familiar with this livelier side of student life. In *Henry IV, Part II*, Shallow and Silence, now Justices of the Peace in Gloucestershire, reminisce:

SHALLOW: I dare say my cousin William is become a good scholar. He is at Oxford still is he not?

SILENCE: Indeed sir, to my cost.

SHALLOW: 'A must then to the inns o'court shortly. I was once of Clement's Inn,[22] where I think they will talk of mad Shallow yet.

SILENCE: You were called 'lusty Shallow' then, cousin.

SHALLOW: By the mass I was called anything; and I would have done anything indeed too and roundly too. There was I, and Little John Doit of Staffordshire, and Black John Barnes and Francis Pickbone and Will Squele, a Cotswold man; you had not four such swinge-bucklers in all the inns of court again; and I may say to you, we knew where the bona robas[23] were and had the best of them all at commandment. Then was Jack Falstaff, now Sir John, a boy and page to Thomas Mowbray, Duke of Norfolk.

SILENCE: This Sir John, cousin, that comes hither anon about soldiers?

SHALLOW: The same Sir John, the very same. I saw him break Skogan's head at the court gate, when 'a was a crack not thus high; and the very same day did I fight with one Sampson Stockfish, fruiterer, behind Gray's Inn. Jesu, Jesu, the mad days that I have spent.[24]

The minutes of Middle Temple parliaments show the Benchers inveighing against the students' failure to attend to their studies or at church, against their playing dice and cards in Hall, and the length of their hair and the extravagance of their dress.[25] In 1574 the Benchers ordered:

None hereafter admitted shall enjoy any Chambers or be in Commons[26] unless he doth Exercise moots, and other Exercises for learning within three yeares after his admission, and be allowed a Student or Inner Barrister by the Bench.[27]

Ten years later they tried to restrain the students' extravagance of dress:

Imprimis that noe great ruffes be worne; secondly that no white colour dublett or hose be worne; thirdly that noe facinge of velvett be worne in gownes but by such as are of the Bench; fowerthly that no gentillmen shall walk the streets in their cloaks but in thir gowns; fyfthly that noe hatt or longe curled haire be worne; syxthly that noe gownes shal be worne but such as be of a sad colour.[28]

Contemporary literature indicates that this order was doomed to failure. John Davies of the Middle Temple wrote in 1594 of a 'new fangled youth made for these times':[29]

The fine youth Ciprius is more tierse and neate,
Then the new garden of th'olde Temple is,
And stil the newest fashion he doth get,
And with the time doth chaunge from that to this,
He weares a hat now of the flat crown-block,
The treble ruffes, long cloake and doublet French:
He takes Tobacco, and doth weare a locke
And wastes more time in dressing than a wench.

The verses written by the students of the Middle Temple describe the many temptations open to the young men of the Temple, among them the Paris Garden on the south bank of the Thames opposite the City where bear-baiting took place. Davies writes of various students. One he calls Publius:

> Publius student at the common law,
> Oft leaves his bookes, and for his recreation:
> To Paris Garden doth himself Withdrawe,
> Where he is ravisht with such delectation
> As downe amonst the dogges and beares he goes,
> Where whilst he skipping cries To head, To head,
> His Satten doublet and his velvet hose,
> Are all with spittle from above be-spread.
> Then is he like his Fathers cuntrey hall,
> Stinking with dogges, and muted all with haukes.
> And rightly too on him this filth doth fall,
> Which for such filthie sports his bookes forsakes,
> Leaving olde Ployden, Dier and Brooke alone,
> To see olde Harry Hunkes and Sacarson.

Bear-baiting was a popular sport, though not with everyone. We are told in *Twelfth Night* that Malvolio brought Fabian out of favour with his lady about a bear-baiting.[30] In the same area were to be found both brothels and theatres. Davies describes

> Faustus not lord, nor knight, nor wise, nor olde,
> To every place about the towne doth ride,
> He rides into the fields, Playes to behold ...
> He rides unto the house of bawderie too.
> Thither his horse so often doeth him carry,
> That shortlie he wil quite forget to go.

Davies pictures a similar conjunction of interests in a certain courtier:

> Rufus the Courtier, at the theater,
> Leaving the best and most conspicuous place,
> Doth eyther to the stage himselfe transferre,
> Or through a grate, doth shew his doubtful face,
>
> For that the clamorous frie of Innes of court,
> Filles up the privat roomes of greater price:
> And such a place where all may have resort,
> He in his singularitie doth despise.
>
> Yet doth not his particuler humour shun
> The common stewes and brothells of the towne,

Though all the world in troops do thither run,
Cleane and uncleane, the gentle and the Clowne.

Then why shoulde Rufus in his pride abhore,
A common seat that loves a common whoore.

Another poet, Francis Lenton, published a poem in 1629 called *The Young Gallants Whirligigg* in which he described the habit of the Inns of Court men themselves sitting on the stage to show off their clothes, although he acknowledges that this display frequently put them into debt:

Your Theaters hee daily doth frequent[31]
(Except the intermitted time of Lent)
Treasuring up within his memory
The amorous toyes of every Comedy...
The Cockpit[32] heretofore would serve his wit,
But now upon the Fryers[33] stage hee'll sit,
It must be so, though this expensive foole
Should pay an angell for a paltry stoole ...
His silken garments and his sattin robe
That hath so often visited the Globe,
And all his spangled rare perfum'd attires
Which once so glistred in the Torchy Fryers,
Must to the Broakers to compound his debt.

THE DRAMA

The students' love of the theatre extended to performing themselves and as a result the Inns became the cradle of modern British drama.[34] By the middle of the sixteenth century the new humanism had penetrated their walls. Something like half the students in the Inns had first been educated at the universities of Oxford and Cambridge,[35] where the classics were studied. In the 1560s and 1570s about half those translating from the classics into English were members of the Inns of Court.[36] Jasper Heywood's preface to his translation of Seneca's *Thyestes* states:

In Lyncolnes Inne and temples twayne
    Grayes Inne and other mo,
Thou shalt them fynde whose paynfull pen
    thy verse shall florishe so,
That Melpomen thou wouldst well weene
    had taught them for to wright
And all their woorks with stately style,
    and goodly grace t'endight.

He then lists a large number of translators working in the Inns. Among them were two members of the Inner Temple, Thomas Sackville and Thomas Norton, who in 1561 wrote a play first entitled *Ferrex and Porrex*, later *Gorboduc*. It was the first tragedy to be written in English about an English subject (Gorboduc was supposedly an early English king) and it was written in blank verse. Its plot bears some similarity to that of *King Lear*, and its message is that divided rule produces civil war and total disorder. The play was first performed in the Inner Temple on Twelfth Night 1562 and then on 18th January at Whitehall before the Queen. In 1566 George Gascoigne of Gray's Inn wrote a tragedy called *Jocasta*, largely based on Euripides' *Phoenician Women*, again in blank verse; in the same year he wrote a comedy called *The Supposes* translated from the Italian play by Ariosto called *Gli Suppositi*. Both were performed in Gray's Inn. Another tragedy based on an Italian model called *Tancred and Gismund* was presented in the Inner Temple in 1568. One part-author may have been Christopher Hatton, whom Queen Elizabeth first spotted for his dancing and eventually promoted to be her Lord Chancellor. In 1588 the gentlemen of Gray's Inn produced *The Misfortunes of Arthur*, a tragedy on the Senecan model, but based on English mythology and written in blank verse. On 28th December 1594 the members of the Inner Temple were invited to a Revel in Gray's Inn. They went in large numbers attended by ladies and led by an ambassador on behalf of Frederick Templarius. There were elaborate ceremonial greetings between the ambassador and the Prince of Purpoole, the Prince of Misrule in Gray's Inn. Such disorder ensued that the entertainment arranged for the ambassador had to be abandoned. He returned to the safety of the Inner Temple. Thereafter 'it was thought good not to offer any thing of account, saving dancing and revelling with gentlewomen; and after such sports a Comedy of Errors (like to Plautus his Menechmus) was played by the players. So that night was begun and continued to the end in nothing but confusion and errors; whereupon, it was ever afterwards called the Night of Errors.'[37] It is generally accepted that this referred to Shakespeare's play, which had been performed earlier the same day at the Royal Court at Greenwich. On Twelfth Night an 'ambassador for the mighty Empire of Russia and Muscovy' arrived in Russian attire with accompanying gentlemen and an entertainment was held. The next morning His Highness the Prince of Purpoole took a journey towards Russia and 'there remained until Candlemas, at which time after his glorious conquests abroad His Excellency retired.' The visit of the Russians has been suggested as the inspiration for the Muscovite masque in Act V of *Love's Labour's Lost*. The earlier plays such as *Gorboduc* were performed before the establishment of permanent theatres – Burbage was to build his theatre in Shoreditch in 1576. There was a thriving interest in the new drama in the Inns and an extensive tradition of amateur performance.

THE SERJEANTS' FEAST

There were two days in the year when all the members of the Inn were expected to dine in Hall. These were the feasts of All Saints on 1st November
and Purification, or Candlemas, on 2nd February,[38] when as already noted
the Serjeants and Judges were present. The office of Serjeant had its origins
in the fourteenth century.[39] Chaucer, in his prologue to *the Canterbury
Tales*, describes one of the pilgrims, who is a Serjeant at Law, as knowing
all the decisions in cases from the time of William the Conqueror and all
statutes by heart. He was

> ... full of rich excellence.
> Discreet he was and of greet reverence –
> He semed swich, his wordes weren so wise.
> Justice he was full often in assise,
> By patente and pleyn commissioun.[40]
> For his science and for his heigh renoun
> Of fees and robes hadde he many oon.
> So greet a purchasour[41] was nowher noon:
> Al was fee symple[42] to hym in effect,
> His purchasyng myghte nat been infect.
> Nowher so bisy a man as he there nas
> And yet he semed bisier than he was.

Twice in the passage Chaucer hints that what the Serjeant seems to be is not
what he actually is. No doubt like many modern lawyers he was rather full
of himself and liked to give the impression his practice was larger than it
was in fact. Most Serjeants were knighted, but by the end of the sixteenth
century some were claiming that the rank was superior to that of knight. It
was never finally settled, but within the law courts precedence depended on
seniority as a Serjeant, not on the additional grant of a knighthood. On
appointment it became customary for the new Serjeant to give gold rings
engraved with his motto to his friends and associates. Thus Fortescue[43]
describes how on the day of his appointment the new Serjeant customarily
gives three hundred gold rings to his friends and to persons of note, and
how he must give a feast and entertainment such as are held at the coronation of a king lasting for seven days. He continues (in translation):

> Nor is there any advocate in the whole world who enriches himself by
> reason of his office as much as the serjeant ... and as a sign that all justices
> have so graduated each of them, when seated in the court of the king, will
> wear a coif of white silk, which is the primary and principal of the sartorial
> insignia with which serjeants-at-law are decorated at their creation. Nor
> shall a justice or serjeant-at-law ever doff this coif, so that his head is

entirely uncovered, even in the presence of the king even though he is
talking to His Highness.

The coif was a white silk head-covering which sat on the hair like a bonnet
and was secured underneath the chin. By the late sixteenth century it was
usually worn under a black skull-cap. The Serjeants wore a variety of
gowns, the principal one being parti-coloured, one colour shot through
with another. Originally the colours of the principal gown varied, but by
Tudor times they were fixed as murrey (purple-red) and blue. In addition
the Serjeants had scarlet robes, very like Judges, which they wore on grand
days in the Inns of Court, and violet robes which they wore to Readers'
feasts. By the end of the sixteenth century, the seven days of feasting required from the new Serjeant had been reduced to one and the number of
gold rings that had to be given had also been reduced. Nevertheless, the
appointment was still a grand one.

There is no account of the Feast of Candlemas in 1602 other than the
entry in Manningham's diary. There is, however, a description of such
a feast in a document prepared by Master Brerewood in 1638 when he
laments the decline in dancing skills.[44] He makes it plain that the feast is
ceremonial and magnificent. Of more significance is the entertainment after
dinner at mid-day. Brerewood describes how one of the Readers (a barrister
in charge of the students' education) led the members of the Inn in solemn
measures:

> Theise measures were wont to be truelie danced, it beinge accounted a
> shame for an Innes of Court man not to have learned to dance, especially
> the measures, but nowe their dancing is tourned into bare walkinge.

At the close of the solemn dancing, the Reader invited a member of Hall
to commence a psalm in which the rest of the company joined. After this
ceremonial part of the evening more light-hearted entertainment followed:

> Likewise besides the solempne Revells or measures aforesaid they were
> wont to be comonlie entertayned either with Post Revells performed by
> the better sorte of the younger gentlemen of the Societie with galliards,
> corantos and other dances or els with stage plaies.

Enter Sir Toby, who proposes a galliard, a coranto, a jig and revels.[45]

Serjeants were not appointed annually, but as the need arose; in some years
several were promoted in a group call. In 1594 ten were created, in 1595
one, and one again in 1601. By the end of that year it was apparent that
there was a shortage of Serjeants; moreover some of the Judges were becoming old and infirm and replacements were needed. There must have
been gossip in the Inns about when the next preferments would occur.

For some reason the Queen was reluctant to appoint too many Serjeants. On 27th January 1603, by which time there had been no further preferments, Sir Robert Cecil wrote a letter to Thomas Windebank, clerk to the signet:

> I have conferred with my lord keeper, and my Lord chiefe Justice, concerninge the Election of Sergiants, and have told them her majestys unwillingness to choose soe many as ten, and yet that (in respect of the reasons which they have used) she is contented, hopinge that this shal be a better call then the former, whereunto they protest, that they did hope, that her majesty would rather have choosen, the whoale paper, then have left out any, exceptinge those two her attorneys, wherein only their peculiar places may be alleged for an excuse. Theise beinge reasons which they desyred might be reiterated unto her. First the Adge and infirmityes of three of the learnedst Judges in the kingdome, viz the two chief Justices and Justice Walmeseley, who hath of late the Goute and the Palsye. Next the Chiefe Baron and Baron Clerke beeing allsoe to be put to his Pention, and Justice Fennour, one that will never runn mad with so much learning. Then there remayneth but Justice Gaudye and Justice Kyngmill and Justice Yelverton, who are noone of the strongest nether, and the yongest threescore years ould. Now Sir this is what they say, that all theise places are to be supplyed with Sergiants, and being well knowne to most of theise, whoe are all great Gayners (which they must leave if they be called to be Judges herafter) there is few of them named, but would be contented to be left out.[46]

He goes on to suggest that Mr Barker and Mr Dodderidge (of the Middle Temple) were worthy to be added to the list. Manningham in his diary records how the Treasurer in 1603 sought to obtain promotion:

> It is said Mr Snig offers £800 to be Sergeant, whereupon Mr Sergeant Harris said that he doubted not but he should shortly salut his deare brother Mr Snig.[47]

John Shurley, Treasurer of the Middle Temple in 1602, made a similar, but more circumspect approach. He wrote to Sir Michael Hickes, secretary to Sir Robert Cecil, about his possible appointment. Hickes was a very influential man, having been formerly in the service of Lord Burghley. He was also a literary patron, having commissioned verses from, amongst others, John Davies of the Middle Temple.[48] Davies had been expelled from the Inn, but was reinstated by Shurley during his Treasurership. Hickes was a member of Lincoln's Inn. In 1568 it is recorded that he was charged £3 6s 8d 'for victuals for many gentlemen of the Middle Temple, who came here to dance the Post Revels with the gentlemen of this Inn.'[49] Shurley at this date was a third-year student in the Middle Temple, so it is possible that the two men knew one another from this time. Shurley's letter asserts they were old friends. It is dated 2nd December, without stating the year. The probability is that it was December 1602. It reads:[50]

> Sir in respecte of the olde acquayntance and friendship betweene us I am so bold to pray yor helpe and furtherance unto Mr. Secretary on my behalfe, for his honours favour and furtherance for the obtyninge of a serjeants place. I was first named in the middell temple by the Judges and so delivered unto my Lord Keeper, how my name standeth now I know not. I have and do desyre to relye upon his honours favour therein at the last call my name being in the byll I was beholdinge unto the last Lord Treasurer ... the bearer hereof wyll at more large talke with you herein, I pray you gyve him your best advise and furtherance. And for any good you shall do me herein I wyll be verie thankful unto you for it and always ready to pleasure you what I may.

The letter gives a broad hint that some reward in kind will be forthcoming and no doubt the bearer of the letter explained more fully what could not be committed to writing. It would be unfair to regard either Snigge or Shurley as particularly corrupt. The Tudor monarchs paid their officers little or nothing, leaving them to make a living (indeed a prosperous one) from the patronage they could exercise. At any event John Shurley's desire for promotion could only have been furthered by impressing the existing Serjeants and the Judges with the entertainment at the feast at Candlemas.

If there were reasons for the Treasurer to commission a play, were there any existing connections between Shakespeare and the Middle Temple, which would have made his Company the likely candidate? The next chapter reveals Shakespeare's close association with a final-year student in the Inn and the playwright's knowledge of Plowden's law reports.

CHAPTER THREE

Temple Connections

LEGAL JOKES

Shakespeare's plays are packed with legal references and *Twelfth Night* has its share of legal jokes. Thus when Fabian is trying to persuade Sir Andrew that Olivia's favours to Cesario demonstrate her love of Sir Andrew, he says he will prove it legitimate upon the oaths of judgement and reason.[1] Sir Toby adds that they (judgement and reason) have been grandjurymen since before Noah was a sailor. The grand jury preferred the bill of indictment which the petty jury tried – a procedure still followed in the United States. When Sir Toby proposes more fun at Malvolio's expense, he says to Maria:

> Come, we'll have him in a dark room and bound. My niece is already in the belief that he's mad. We may carry it thus for our pleasure and his penance till our very pastime, tired out of breath, prompt us to have mercy upon him; at which time, we will bring the device to the bar, and crown thee for a finder of madmen.[2]

The coroner's (or crowner's) jury adjudicated on an allegation of madness before the madman could be confined. The coroner appears earlier when Olivia speaks to Feste about her drunken cousin, Sir Toby:

> OLIVIA: What's a drunken man like, fool?
> FESTE: Like a drowned man, a fool, and a madman. One draught above heat makes him a fool, the second mads him, and a third drowns him.
> OLIVIA: Go thou and seek the crowner, and let him sit o' my coz, for he's in the third degree of drink – he's drowned.[3]

Slightly more detailed legal knowledge is revealed when Sir Andrew Aguecheek brags after his 'duel' with Cesario:

> I'll go another way to work with him. I'll have an action of battery against him, if there be any law in Illyria – though I struck him first, yet it's no matter for that.[4]

The joke involves knowing not only the distinction between battery and assault, battery being a completed assault, and assault being merely a threatened battery, but also that a man may strike first in self-defence to prevent a threatened attack. His description of the duel, of course, in no way matches Sir Andrew's feeble attempt to fight Cesario (who is in any event a woman), so that the joke has several layers of humour. Earlier it is Fabian who gives Sir Andrew legal advice about his challenge to Cesario. The challenge reads:

> Youth whatsoever thou art, thou art but a scurvy fellow ... Wonder not, nor admire not in thy mind why I do call thee so, for I will show thee no reason for't.[5]

Fabian comments: 'A good note, that keeps you from the blow of the law.' The challenge continues:

> I will waylay thee going home; where, if it be thy chance to kill me ... thou kill'st me like a rogue and a villain.

Fabian comments: 'still you keep o' the windy side of the law; good.' Although Fabian is encouraging Sir Andrew by praising the legality of his challenge, his advice is nonsense for nothing Sir Andrew says will protect him from legal action.

England in the age of Elizabeth was litigious and so the general public were to some extent familiar with legal terminology. The Shakespeare family were themselves involved in litigation. For instance, in the late 1580s Shakespeare's father John was involved in a number of actions relating to debt: in 1589 William joined with his parents in a complaint heard in the courts at Westminster against some relatives relating to a family debt.[6] These and other brushes his father had with the law are hardly a sufficient explanation for his wide-ranging knowledge of legal topics. His legal knowledge seems more extensive and detailed than one would expect in a layman. The missing years between his departure from Stratford at an unknown date, probably after 1585, and the publication of his poem *Venus and Adonis* in London in 1593 have led to endless speculation as to what he might have done in the interim. The first clear reference to him as an existing playwright is by Robert Greene in his *Groats-worthe of Witte* published in 1592. One suggestion has been that in the period up to that date he worked as a noverint – a clerk who drafted legal documents. This theory, most recently expounded by Eric Sams in *The Real Shakespeare*, depends in part on identifying Shakespeare as the author of an earlier version of *Hamlet*, the writer of which was referred to by Robert Greene in 1589 as a noverint. The accepted view is that Kyd was the author – indeed Greene himself refers to Kyd in the same passage, even if not directly as the author. Sams also points to the existence in the Folger Law Library of a copy of

Lambarde's *Archaeonomia* with the apparently genuine signature 'William Shakespeare' on the fly leaf. The book, as its name suggests, is a collection of ancient legal material which Lambarde published in 1568. Most of it is pre-Norman Conquest law and some of it relates to land tenure. It is unlikely it would have had much relevance to the work of a sixteenth-century law clerk. Shakespeare did write two plays set in early Britain, *Cymbeline* and *King Lear*, and so it is possible that he acquired the book not as a law student but as background reading for some work he was contemplating. Sams also points to a passage where Hamlet describes Claudius's commission sent in the hands of Rosencrantz and Guildenstern to England requesting Hamlet's execution on his arrival there. Hamlet rewrites it requesting the execution of his companions instead:

> I sat me down,
> Devised a new commission, wrote it fair.
> I once did hold it, as our statists do,
> A baseness to write fair, and laboured much
> How to forget that learning. But, sir, now
> It did me yeoman's service.[7]

This is a rather odd passage to invent, but that is hardly evidence to support the view that it is autobiographical. Even when all the evidence is assembled, the theory that Shakespeare was a noverint is speculative and in any event a noverint's experience would have been limited to that which could be obtained by drafting documents.

It remains the case, however, that Shakespeare plainly had closer contacts with lawyers than merely as a part of the audience in the Globe theatre. Apart from *The Comedy of Errors*, there is a case for *Troilus and Cressida* being performed in an Inn of Court. Other plays must have been performed in the Inns. It has already been noted that, the Globe being open to the elements, an indoor booking would have been very attractive in the winter months. There is a general perception that actors were regarded at this time by the upper classes as socially inferior, almost vagabonds. Indeed, Elizabethan proclamations declared that actors who were not under the patronage of the nobility were to be treated as vagabonds. It did not follow, however, that those who were so patronized were of a similar status; in fact it would indicate the contrary. The Queen's passion for plays must have given the actors some standing. Show business was certainly a way to fortune and so perhaps to respectability. The students of the Middle Temple certainly socialized with Jonson. There is evidence that some actors mixed with the students in the Inns of Court. The comedian Robert Armin, who is generally supposed to have created the part of Feste, had not been to university, but he had intellectual pretensions. In 1600 he wrote *Foole upon Foole*. It ran to a third edition in 1603 and in the preface to that edition he dedicated the work to the 'Gentlemen of Oxenford, Cambridge and the Innes of Court.' He went on to state that he has 'seen the stars at midnight in your societies'. He describes the Inns of Court men as 'nimble braind brands that burne without smoking' and speaks of drinking mutual toasts with them. He replaced Kemp as the chief comic actor in the Lord Chamberlain's Men about 1599. He was an excellent singer and (unlike Touchstone in *As You Like It*) was given the songs in *Twelfth Night*.

THOMAS GREENE

There was in any event a more intimate link between the playwright and the Middle Temple. Thomas Greene of Warwick, having been first educated in Staple's Inn, joined the Middle Temple in 1595 and was called to the bar in October 1602.[8] In 1603 he moved to Stratford upon Avon and probably from then on lived with the Shakespeares. In 1605 William bought some tithes (or the right to collect payments in relation to crops produced on land) at Wellcombe near Stratford. In 1609 Thomas Greene bought a share of the same tithes from Humphrey Colles, a fellow member of the Middle Temple. These were quite valuable, for when he left Stratford he sold them for £400. In due course a local landlord William Coombe tried to enclose some common land at Welcombe. The Corporation employed Greene to prevent the enclosure and eventually he succeeded at Warwick Assizes in persuading Lord Chief Justice Coke to forbid it. On 17th November 1614 Greene wrote of this dispute in his diary:

> As my Cosen Shakespeare was commyng to towne, I went to see him howe he did he told me that they assured him they ment to inclose noe further then to Gospell bushe and so upp straight (leaving out part of the dyngles to the ffield) to the gate in Clopton ... he and Mr. Hall say they think there will be nothing done at all.

He refers to Shakespeare a number of times as 'cosen', but he uses the same address for others. Thomas did play a considerable role in Stratford life. In 1603 he became Steward to the Court of Record in Stratford (trying cases involving property up to the value of £30). He also kept the minutes at the meetings of the Stratford Corporation. In 1610 he prepared the petition to James I which led to the grant of a Royal Charter creating Stratford a town. Thomas then became Town Clerk. In 1611 the borough gave him power to appoint a deputy, which perhaps reflected a growing legal practice in London. Thomas married Lettice Tutt from Hampshire. They had a daughter Ann in 1604 and a son William in 1608. When William was born, Thomas and his family were living with the Shakespeares in New Place. Ann and William were, of course, the first names of the Shakespeares;

THE SHAKESPEARES AND THE GREENES

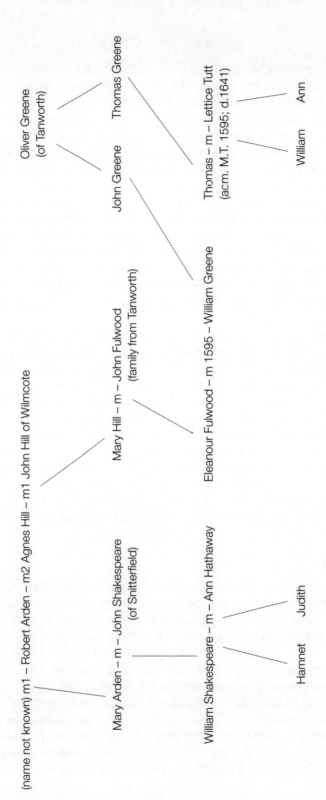

(name not known) m1 – Robert Arden – m2 Agnes Hill – m1 John Hill of Wilmcote

Oliver Greene
(of Tanworth)

Mary Arden – m – John Shakespeare
(of Snitterfield)

Mary Hill – m – John Fulwood
(family from Tanworth)

John Greene   Thomas Greene

William Shakespeare – m – Ann Hathaway

Eleanour Fulwood – m 1595 – William Greene

Thomas – m – Lettice Tutt
(acm. M.T. 1595; d.1641)

Hamnet   Judith

William   Ann

Thomas and Lettice and their children lived with the Shakespeares in New Place, Stratford in the same way the Shakespeares chose as the first names of their children the names of their close friends the Sadlers. Thomas bought a house in Stratford in 1608. This is the first reference in the Stratford records to him owning a house in the town, which suggests he had lived with the Shakespeares from his first arrival. His house was rented out for a year or two after 1608, while he continued to live with them. It was no doubt an arrangement that suited the two wives, as their husbands spent a lot of time in London. Many practising barristers seem to have been at pains to establish or maintain provincial roots, practising in London in term-time and living in the country in vacation or time of plague. Thomas gave up his job as Town Clerk in 1617, not long after the death of Shakespeare, and went to Bristol where he tried to obtain a similar post. Initially he failed to do so. He appears to have remained in Bristol for the rest of his life, though still attending term-time in the Middle Temple. Eventually in 1639 he did obtain the post of Steward to the Court of Record, but he died in 1640, his son succeeding him.

This historical sketch does suggest a close relationship between the two men and would be consistent with some family relationship. There are two possibilities: one a distant connection by marriage and the other that they were related by blood. Thomas Greene appears to have had a cousin by blood called William. William married a girl called Eleanor Fulwood in 1594. The Fulwoods were linked to the Shakespeares through William's mother, Mary Arden. Mary was stepsister to Eleanor's mother.

Since they were close in age and step-related, the two women would have been brought up together. The marriage of Eleanor and William took place at Aston Cantlow, a village close to Wilmcote, where the Ardens had their home, and Snitterfield, where the Shakespeares had theirs. Mary Arden and Thomas Greene are likely to have attended and maybe even the playwright or his wife. This connection, albeit distant, would explain why Thomas was welcomed in due course to live with the Shakespeare family in their splendid new house.

There is another more intriguing though less certain connection. Shakespeare had an uncle Henry who lived in Snitterfield and was buried there in 1595. There was also a Thomas Shakespeare whose name appears in the court manor records for Snitterfield on various occasions from 1563 to 1583, which would make him roughly contemporary with Henry. The baptism records for Snitterfield only commence in 1561. Thomas Shakespeare's name does not appear, but he may well have been born before that date. Some have conjectured he was another brother of John Shakespeare, Shakespeare's father, but there is no firm evidence to support this contention. In 1589/90 there was a burial recorded in Stratford of Thomas Green, alias Shakespeare. The alias could indicate either illegitimacy or a desire to perpetuate a mother's name. There are references to

Thomas Shakespeares in the Stratford records between 1572 and 1586, so he may have been one of these; again there are no birth records available. There is, however, a possibility that Thomas Greene of Snitterfield was the man buried under the alias.[9] The fact that the relevant parish records cease about the middle of the century, makes this an apparently insoluble puzzle. It is nevertheless a strange coincidence that someone of this name should have existed.

The Shakespeares might well have been keen to foster a relationship with the Greenes, who had grander antecedents. The Greenes claimed descent from a former Lord Chief Justice. During the Heraldic Visitation to Gloucestershire in 1621 Thomas Greene claimed the coat of arms of Sir Henry Greene, Chief Justice of the Court of King's Bench in 1369. In fact Thomas himself came from a cadet branch of the family who were farmers. His father, also Thomas, moved from the land into trade, becoming a mercer in Warwick. When Thomas junior entered the Middle Temple, he was named as son of Thomas Greene of Warwick, gentleman, deceased. Greene seems to have been held in reasonably high regard in the Inn, because in 1629 he became Treasurer.

There are two pieces of evidence which strongly indicate that Thomas Greene and William Shakespeare were associated prior to Thomas taking up his post in Stratford in 1603. Thomas Greene's brother John was admitted to Clement's Inn, but he seems never to have graduated to one of the major Inns. There was a lesser rank of lawyers called attorneys, who dealt with the practical steps leading up to a court action, but did not plead in court itself. In 1599 John acted as attorney for Hamnet Sadler in a legal action. Hamnet and his wife Judith were close friends of Ann and William Shakespeare. It was in 1585, when the Shakespeares had twins, that they named them Hamnet and Judith. When Shakespeare died, he left money to buy a memorial gold ring for Hamnet.

Another family that was close to the Shakespeares were the Quineys.[10] Adrian Quiney was a neighbour of William's father John and in 1552 the two of them were fined at the same time for making a dunghill in Henley Street. The two men rose in the world to play a prominent part together in Stratford local government. In 1598, Adrian's son Richard was involved in proceedings between the Lord of the Manor of Stratford, who had enclosed some common land, and the Town. He was sued with others by Sir Edward Greville for riot, they having allegedly flattened hedges that he had erected around land they claimed was common. Richard Quiney came to London and wrote a letter to Shakespeare requesting thirty pounds towards the cost of the action. As the letter was found in Quiney's papers he may never have sent it (or it may have been a copy). It reveals, however, that the Town used Thomas Greene as its solicitor to approach Sir Edward Coke, then Attorney General, for an opinion. The request was made early in 1601 and eventually the great advocate delivered an opinion favourable to the Town. Thomas Greene was not qualified as a barrister at this date and reference to him as a solicitor probably indicated no more than that he was a useful means to approach Coke. Richard Quiney's son, Thomas, eventually married Shakespeare's daughter Judith. Taken together, the connections with the Sadlers and the Quineys suggest that Shakespeare and Thomas Greene did know one another prior to February 1602.

If they were related and acquainted, it would be entirely natural for them to meet socially in London – for Thomas to attend plays and for William to be invited to dine in the Middle Temple. Thomas certainly had literary aspirations, though a small talent. He is credited with the authorship of a rather turgid poem, *The Poet's Vision and the Prince's Glory*, welcoming James I to London, and a sonnet to the poet Drayton. He is also said to have produced an edition of Chaucer in 1602. He is quoted by Manningham in his diary as saying that it is always better if there is a woman in the case.

HALES VERSUS PETTIT

There is more direct evidence that Shakespeare was familiar with the procedures in the Inns of Court. When students dined in the Middle Temple Hall, they did so in messes of four in order to facilitate discussion of legal problems. In the first part of *Henry VI*, Shakespeare sets the scene when the Yorkists and Lancastrians pluck their respective symbols of the white and red rose in the Temple garden. There are four noblemen present, plus a supporter of the Yorkists called Vernon and a lawyer. At the close of the scene Richard Plantaganet says: 'Come let us four to dinner.'[11] Shakespeare also refers to 'boltings' in *Troilus and Cressida*.[12] Boltings was the word that was used to refer to the less formal legal arguments in Hall – a Bencher presided over a moot and a member of Hall over a bolting. In context in the play, however, the word is used simply to mean sieving grain. It is possible, though by no means certain, that it bears a double meaning, the abilities of the law students being sieved by the mock argument. There is in any event better evidence of familiarity with mooting in *Hamlet*, which Shakespeare probably wrote close in time to *Twelfth Night*. When the First and Second Clowns come to dig Ophelia's grave, the First enquires why she is to have a Christian burial as she has committed suicide. The Second Clown replies that the Crowner (coroner), has decided she should have one. The dialogue continues:

> FIRST CLOWN: How can that be, unless she drowned herself in her own defence?

SECOND CLOWN: Why, 'tis found so.

FIRST CLOWN: It must be *se offendendo*. It cannot be else. For here lies the
point: if I drown myself wittingly it argues an act, and an act hath three
branches – it is to act, to do, and to perform. Argal she drowned herself
wittingly.

SECOND CLOWN: Nay, but hear you, Goodman Delver –

FIRST CLOWN: Give me leave. Here lies the water – good. Here stands the
man – good. If the man go to this water and drown himself, it is, will he
nill he, he goes, mark you that. But if the water come to him and drown
him, he drowns not himself. Argal, he that is not guilty of his own death
shortens not his own life.

SECOND CLOWN: But is this the law?

FIRST CLOWN: Ay, marry, 'ist Crowner's quest law.

SECOND CLOWN: Will you ha' the truth on't. If this had not been a
gentlewoman, she should have been buried out o' Christian burial.[13]

If Ophelia drowned herself wittingly, this would amount to a felony and
deprive her of the right to Christian burial. The humour at the expense of
the legal profession continues when Hamlet picks a skull from the ground
and imagines it is a lawyer's:

Where be his quiddities now, his quillets, his cases, his tenures, and his
tricks; why does he suffer this mad knave now to knock him about the
sconce with a dirty shovel, and will not tell him of his action of battery?
Hum! This fellow might be in's time a great buyer of land, with his statutes,
his recognizances, his fines, his double vouchers, his recoveries. Is this the
fine of his fines, and the recovery of his recoveries, to have his fine pate
full of fine dirt? Will his vouchers vouch him no more of his purchases,
and double ones too, than the length and breadth of a pair of indentures?
The very conveyances of his lands will hardly lie in this box and must th'
inheritor himself have no more, ha? [14]

The passage obviously involves some detailed knowledge of conveyancing
law.

Though the nice reasoning of the First Clown seems farcical, it closely
matches a reported case. In 1571 the case of Hales against Pettit was decided in the Court of King's Bench. Dame Margaret Hales brought an
action of trespass against Pettit.[15] As part of his defence he asserted that the
land upon which he was alleged to have trespassed was not hers. The argument turned on the fact that her husband Sir James Hales had committed
suicide by drowning himself. Suicide was a felony. When felons were executed, their goods were forfeit to the Crown. Lawyers for Pettit argued
that on his death the land in question was forfeit to the Crown. The two
Serjeants arguing for the plaintiff submitted that forfeiture could only occur
on the death of someone who had committed a felonious act. The act of

jumping into the water, although the cause of death, was not itself felonious and so forfeiture should not attach to it. Serjeant Walsh for the defendant sought to split the act into three branches just as the First Clown does:

> the Act consists of three Parts. The first is the imagination, which is Reflection or Meditation of the Mind, whether or not, it is convenient for him to destroy himself and what way it may be done. The second is the Resolution which is a Determination of the mind to destroy himself and do it in this or that particular way. The third is the Perfection which is the Execution of what the mind has resolved to do.

The absurdity of the Clown's division is that all his parts mean the same – to act, to do and to perform. The same criticism can be made of the lawyers. At any rate, the pattern of the legal submission is mirrored in the Clown's. Similarities are also to be found in the judgement of Lord Chief Justice Dyer:

> the Felony is attributed to the Act, which Act is always done by the living man; and in his lifetime ... Sir James Hale was dead and how came he by his death? It may be answered by drowning and who drowned him? Sir James Hale; and when did he drown him? In his Lifetime. So that Sir James Hales being alive caused the Death of the dead man. And then for this offence it is reasonable to punish the living Man who committed the offence and not the dead man.

The dialogue in the play has the same feel as this passage.

On this evidence there is a good case for supposing that Shakespeare was familiar with the case of Hales and Pettit. But how? The case had occurred much earlier when Shakespeare would have been too young to take note of it. In 1601 Plowden's reports were available only in Law French or Latin. Shakespeare could have read it, but it is more likely that he heard it being argued in a moot or bolting in Hall, or that Thomas Greene or some other Inn of Court friend was amused by it and drew it to his attention. The students in Plowden's own Inn would certainly have been familiar with his reports.

They would have laughed readily at jokes at the expense of lawyers. They would also have enjoyed jibes at those who sought to advance themselves socially, for the Inns were full of such people. This is the next subject for consideration and will reveal some apparent references in the text of the play to the family of the Treasurer of the Middle Temple.

CHAPTER FOUR

The Greasy Pole

_____

LADIES AND GENTLEMEN

In laughing at Malvolio's social pretensions, the Middle Templars would also have been laughing at themselves, for there were few better places than the Inns of Court to climb the greasy pole of social advancement. John Davies gives an example of the process in an epigram about Curio,[1] who has been an arch papist but 'nowe perceives that Romes ambition, is author of Romes superstition.' The powerful arguments of Basilius alone have caused this protestant conversion. Davies lists all the great Calvinist apologists who have left Curio unmoved:

> He saies their argumentes are sleight and weake,
> Basilius only doth to purpose speake.
> True Curio, true, Basilius on this theame
> Is able to saye more then all of them:
> For he has power to saye, recant thine error,
> And lo we shal be a privie counsellor.

Ben Jonson satirized the desire for social advancement in 1599 in *Every Man Out of His Humour*. Sordido has made money and sends his son Fungoso to an Inn of Court. 'He is a gentleman though his father be but a yeoman.'[2] Sogliardo, Sordido's brother, is 'so enamoured of the name of a gentleman that he will have it though he buys it.'[3] In due course he does buy his patent. Fungoso writes to his father that on Shrovetide 'we use always to have revels; which is indeed dancing: and makes an excellent show, in truth especially if we gentlemen be well attired, which our seniors note and think the better of our fathers the better we are maintained.'[4] With the money his father gives him, Fungoso buys a suit made in the style of a courtier. Sogliardo, having obtained his coat of arms, goes to court to woo a lady, with disastrous results.

Twelfth Night too is a play about class. When Olivia is first attracted to Cesario, she enquires: 'What is your parentage?' Viola/Cesario replies: 'Above my fortunes, yet my state is well. I am a *gentleman*.'[5] Olivia is obviously concerned that if Cesario is not a gentleman, he will not be a fit match for her. She repeats the line after Cesario's departure. The play is set in the noble courts of the Duke Orsino and the Countess Olivia. Orsino is consistently called a count during the play, but he is also described as the Duke of Illyria, which would make him socially superior to a countess. The contrast between the two households is accentuated by the use of poetry in Orsino's and prose in Olivia's. Olivia's uncle Sir Toby Belch brings Sir Andrew Aguecheek to woo Olivia. When Maria objects that Sir Andrew is a foolish knight, Sir Toby points out that he has an income of three thousand ducats a year.[6] For his part, Sir Andrew becomes downhearted because he feels he cannot compete with Orsino as a suitor. He says he will return home, but Sir Toby persuades him to change his mind:

> She'll none of the Count; she'll not match above her degree, neither in
> estate, years, nor wit. I have heard her swear't.[7]

The sub-plot involving Sir Toby and Maria is often played as if it were a below-stairs comedy. It is not. Maria is a waiting gentlewoman, not a servant. Although Sir Toby refers to her as 'my niece's chambermaid',[8] Sir Andrew refers to her as 'mistress' and a lady. Olivia herself describes her as her 'gentlewoman'[9] and she is described in the dramatis personae in the Folio edition of the plays as a 'waiting gentlewoman'. She is accepted as a match for Sir Toby.

In theory Elizabethan society was strictly hierarchical. Thomas Smith, Elizabeth's Secretary of State, described the English class structure in his *De Republica Anglorum* as comprising the nobility, the gentry, burgesses in the town, yeomen in the country and the lesser men who did not rule.[10] The good order of society was taken to depend on the strict maintenance of this class structure. In *Troilus and Cressida*, Ulysses famously describes how

> The heavens themselves, the planets, and this centre
> Observe degree, priority, and place ...
> O, when degree is shaked,
> Which is the ladder to all high designs,
> The enterprise is sick. How could communities,
> Degrees in schools, and brotherhoods in cities,
> Peaceful commerce from dividable shores,
> The primogenitive and due of birth,
> Prerogative of age, crowns, sceptres, laurels,
> But by degree stand in authentic place?
> Take but degree away, untune that string,
> And hark what discord follows![11]

The late sixteenth century, however, was a period of high inflation. Fortunes were quickly made. The theoretical social hierarchy was breached in practice by the social mobility of those with new money. There was a good deal of it in circulation by the 1590s. Some of it had been injected from the spoils of dissolving the monasteries, and some from privateering – Drakes's circumnavigation of the world made a profit of 4,700 per cent from the Spanish prizes he took on the way. Above all, however, English wool was a highly profitable export to Europe. The wool trade, which included farmers, spinners, weavers, mercers and drapers, boomed in the last two decades of the century.[12] There were something of the order of eleven million sheep in the kingdom (about three or four to every human).[13] The opportunity was there for the husbandman or craftsman to make sufficient money to rise to the status of yeoman and for the yeoman similarly to rise to the rank of gentleman. This prosperity bred a new confidence. Estimates of the population at this period can only be very approximate, but in the 1560s and 1570s the population rose at a rate of about five per cent per annum: a national population that stood at around 2,800,000 in the early 1540s had risen to over four million by 1600. London was a magnet for those who wished to increase their wealth or achieve their social aspirations. At a rough estimate the population of London stood at around 60,000 in 1520 and around 200,000 by the end of the century. Those with new money often chose to send their children to the Inns of Court where the status of gentleman at least might be achieved and patronage might possibly lead to greater things. As the sixteenth century progressed the Inns had grown more and more popular. In the first decade of the century there were about 90 men admitted to the Middle Temple. In the period 1551–60 about 250 were admitted, and in the last decade nearly 600.

To see yourself through the minimum seven years for qualification in an Inn of Court, you needed a measure of wealth behind you. In 1592 John Stow described the result:[14]

There is in and about this Citie a whole Universitie (as it were) of students, practisers or pleaders and Judges of the laws of this Realme, not living of common stipends (as in other Universities it is for the most part done), but of their own private maintenance as being altogether fedde by their place or practise, or otherwise by thier proper revenue, or exhibition of parents and friends: for that the young sort are either gentlemen, or the sonnes of gentlemen, or of other most wealthie persons.

In 1562 Gerard Leigh in his *Accidens of Armory* described the Temple in these terms (spelling modernized):

A place privileged by the most excellent Princess the High Governor of the whole island wherein are a store of gentlemen of the whole Realm, that repair thither to learn to rule and obey by Law to yield their fleece to their Prince and Common Weal; as to use all other exercises of body and mind where unto nature most aptly serveth to adorn by speaking, countenance, gesture and use of apparel, the person of a gentleman.

The rank of gentleman was not easy to define. It was not an ancient rank like knight or esquire, though those who held those ranks were undoubtedly gentlemen. An esquire (shortened in ordinary speech to squire) was a companion to a knight who carried his arms for him. The Latin name was 'armiger', which also became current English. A squire became entitled to a coat of arms and the address 'esquire'. The coats of arms in the Middle Temple Hall, of those who have been Treasurer or Reader, have the subtext 'miles' for knight or 'armiger' for esquire. Gradually during the Middle Ages the title esquire was applied more widely to those who were considered of equal social standing with esquires. A barrister's wig box still bears his name followed by 'esquire'; in the United States qualified lawyers of both sexes use the title. Being a gentleman denoted a certain level of substance, a certain level of education. Persons who held these in sufficient measure had their names prefixed with 'Master'. The Benchers of the Inns of Court are still called Masters of the Bench and addressed by members of Hall as 'Master'. Those who felt they had achieved the rank, simply signed themselves with the suffix 'gentleman'. The admission registers of the Middle Temple frequently use this description.

The rank of gentleman could be substantiated by the acquisition of a coat of arms. In *The Merry Wives of Windsor*, Justice Shallow complains about the treatment he has received from Sir John Falstaff:

SHALLOW: He shall not abuse Robert Shallow, Esquire.
SLENDER: In the county of Gloucester, justice of peace and Coram.
SHALLOW: Ay, cousin Slender and Custalorum.
SLENDER: Ay, and Ratolorum too. And a gentleman born, master parson, who writes himself Armigero – in any bill, warrant, quittance or obligation, Armigero.[15]

To be a justice of the peace he would sit in judgement in the magistrates court. 'Coram' simply means he sat on the bench – barristers still endorse their briefs 'Cor' short for coram with the name of the judge following. Custalorum and Ratolorum refer to the records of the court. He is described not only as 'Esquire', but also as 'Armigero', which means he has a coat of arms. Slender goes on to describe the Shallow family coat of arms as containing a dozen white luces. Sir Thomas Lucy, who lived at Charlcote Park near Stratford, had just such a coat of arms which contained twelve white luces or pikes and it has been suggested that he was the model for Shallow.[16] There is also a passage in *Hamlet*, in which Shakespeare equates the rank of gentleman with the possession of a coat of arms. It occurs in the grave-digging scene:[17]

FIRST CLOWN: There is no ancient gentlemen but gardeners, ditchers and grave makers; they hold up Adam's profession.

SECOND CLOWN: Was he a gentleman?

FIRST CLOWN: 'A was the first that ever bore arms.

SECOND CLOWN: Why, he had none.

FIRST CLOWN: What art a heathen? How dost thou understand the
Scripture? The Scripture says Adam digged. Could he dig without arms?

THE SHAKESPEARES ON THE MAKE

The history of Shakespeare's own family demonstrates social advancement culminating in the acquisition of a coat of arms.[18] Both Shakespeare's
grandfathers were small farmers near Stratford. When Richard Shakespeare
moved from North Warwickshire to Snitterfield in the 1520s, he rented
land from Robert Arden. In his will in 1556, Robert bequeathed sixty acres
of land to his daughter Mary, and in 1557 she married Richard's son John.
John had already moved by this time the few miles from Snitterfield to
Stratford. When he undertook the administration of his father's estate in
1560 he was recorded nevertheless as 'agricola', so that he still considered
himself then to be a farmer or husbandman.[19] He dealt from time to time as
a wholesaler in wool and other commodities. More particularly, he took up
the leather trade. Tradition has it that he was a butcher, but court records
state he was a 'glover' and a 'whittawer' – someone who cured and softened
leather skins. Shakespeare's plays show an intimate knowledge of the
leather trade.[20] In *Twelfth Night* Feste says – after a piece of word play – 'a
sentence is but a cheveril glove to a good wit; how quickly the wrong side
may be turned outward.'[21] 'Cheveril' is kid's leather. John Shakespeare had
moved from a life tied to the land into trade. His neighbours in Henley
Street were fellow tradesmen such as tailors and blacksmiths.[22] His prosperity grew to such an extent that by 1580 he was described in a court
record as a yeoman.[23]

John Shakespeare took part in local politics. Between 1561 and 1565 he
became successively burgess, alderman and finally High Bailiff, or mayor,
of Stratford upon Avon. From then on the borough records show his name
with the prefix Master.[24] In 1576 he made application for a coat of arms,
but either it was not granted or he did not persist with it, for another
successful application was made much later. Sometime around 1577 his
financial position seems to have taken a turn for the worse. His fellow
burgesses relieved him of liability for local taxes. He began selling off or
mortgaging family assets, including the land his wife had inherited from her
father. He failed to pay his debts and in 1582 he complained that he was in
fear of death and mutilation from four fellow townsmen. In 1586 he was
replaced as an alderman, because he had not attended Corporation meetings for a long time. The extent and reasons for his decline are the subject

of some controversy. They may be connected with a resumption by him of
the Catholic faith. In any event he retained the family home at Henley
Street throughout this period. William had been born there in 1564. He
married in 1582, and by 1585 Ann Hathaway and he had three children.
Although the precise date is not known, he probably left Stratford around
1587. Given the coincidence of time, it may be that the changes in his
father's status was one of the spurs that led William to seek his fortune in
the capital. If so, he had to start from scratch, seeking the status his father
had attained but then lost.

Surviving documents which John Shakespeare was required to sign, are
marked with two compasses, the emblem of a glover. This could have indicated that he was illiterate, although this is not definite, since literate people
did on occasion sign with the symbol of their occupation. In any event, as
a burgess he would have been entitled to claim free education at the local
grammar school for his son. Numerous grammar schools had been founded
after the dissolution of the Monasteries, particularly in the reign of Edward
VI. For many they proved the gateway to fortune. There is no record
that William actually attended Stratford grammar school. All the same,
his knowledge of the classics does indicate that he was schooled. In
Twelfth Night Sir Toby says to Sir Andrew after a night of revelling: 'Not
to be abed after midnight, is to be up betimes, and *diluculo surgere*, thou
knowest ...'[25] The full maxim 'diluculo surgere saluberrimum est' – to get
up at dawn is most healthy – appears in Lilly's Latin Grammar, which was
commonly used in schools. It is just the sort of tag a schoolboy would
retain.[26]

In the College of Arms there are preserved two rough drafts, both dated
20th October 1596, of a grant of arms to Shakespeare's father, John.[27] At
the end of one of these drafts is a note that John Shakespeare showed (presumably to the Heralds in 1596) a design for a coat of arms prepared by the
Clarenceux King of Arms twenty years earlier. Sir John Ferne in his *Glorie
of Generositie* (1586) stated that Bailiffs of towns were worthy of a coat of
arms, so it could well be that John had set about obtaining one as a result
of holding that office. There is no indication that this earlier design was
ever formally submitted or granted, and the later application would have
been unnecessary if it had been successful. The fact that John had been a
Bailiff of Stratford was noted on the 1596 application. The application is
prefaced with the assertion that King Henry VII had rewarded the family
for valiant service. This may have been a fiction. William Harrison in his
Description of England in 1577 stated that the Heralds in making grants
'do of custom pretend antiquity and service and many gay things.' John's
marriage to Mary Arden, daughter of Robert, is recited. Originally Robert's
name carried the suffix 'gent', but that is crossed out and esquire inserted
instead. The arms granted were 'Gold, on a bend sable a spear of the first,

the point steeled proper.' It would seem highly likely that the renewed application and its success were in large part due to the improved fortunes of William by this date.

The acquisition of the status of gentleman was followed by the acquisition of property to support it.[28] So in 1597 William purchased New Place – a fifteenth-century house in the centre of Stratford – and in 1602 a cottage and quarter-acre site nearby, presumably to house his servants. New Place, if not the best, was certainly one of the best houses in town. Also in 1602 Shakespeare paid £320 in cash (a sum probably equal to the annual income of a prosperous yeoman) for 107 acres of arable land in Old Stratford. In 1605 he purchased a lease of tithes of wool and lamb in Stratford and of corn, grain, blade and hay in Old Stratford, Bishopton and Welcombe. There are records of him lodging in London, but none of him owning property there before 1613, by which time he had retired to Stratford; this was probably, therefore, an investment. *Twelfth Night*, like other plays of his, was not published in his lifetime. In 1602 he was not looking for immortality, but did aspire to be a gentleman of property in a small country town.

MARRIAGE AND MANNINGHAM

Achieving an advantageous marriage played some part in the social advance of the Shakespeares. In Elizabethan times marriage was often an instrument to secure the family fortunes. It was not uncommon for girls to marry men considerably older than themselves and this, coupled with a high mortality rate, meant that many rich young widows were left on the marriage market. John Manningham in his diary gives examples of people furthering their position through marriage. On 11th January 1602 he records:

> Mr. Fr. Vane, a yong gent of great hope and forwardnes, verry well affected in the country already, in soe much that the last parliament the country gave him the place of knight before Sir H. Nevell; his possibilite of living by his wife verry much, shee being daughter and co-heire to Sir Antony Mildmay; and thought hir mother will give hir all hir inheritance; the father worth £3000 per annum, the mother's £1,200.[29]

On 16th October 1602 he quotes his friend Curle as saying:

> Mr. Bodly, the author promoter and perfecter of a goodly library in Oxford, wan a riche widdow by this meanes. Comming to the place where the widdowe was with one whoe is reported to have been sure of hir, as occasion happened the widdowe was absent; while he was in game, finding

his opportunity, entreated the surmised assured gent. to hold his cardes till he returned. In which tyme he found the widdowe in a garden, courted, and obtained his desyre; soe he played his game, while an other held his cardes. He was at first but the sonne of a merchant, untill he gave some intelligence of moment to the counsell, whereupon he was thought worthie employment, whereby he rose.[30]

Later he adds the information that the widow came from Devonshire or Cornwall and that her first husband had made his fortune trading in pilchards.[31]

John Manningham himself made a good marriage through contacts in the Middle Temple.[32] His father Robert lived and died at Fen Drayton in Cambridgeshire. He must have gained his livelihood from farming. John had a relative called Richard, whom he described in his diary as his cousin. In 1570 Richard left his home in St Albans and travelled to London to be apprenticed to a mercer in the City of London; he was admitted in 1578 to the Mercers' Livery Company.[33] He was nominated to be Rector Warden of the Company in 1594, but was not elected. He was plainly prospering because he purchased a substantial country house, Bradbourne Hall in East Malling, Kent.[34] But he had no children and seems to have adopted John as his heir, for John inherited the Hall in 1611. John's diary records frequent visits to Bradbourne. In his will Richard referred to John as his son in love, and John in his will refers to Richard as his father in love, although there was a forty-year age gap between the two men. There is still a substantial monument to Richard in East Malling church. Richard appears from entries in the diary to have been well educated, and to have been able to speak three languages and recite the first two books of *The Aeneid* by heart. John was admitted to the Middle Temple on 16th March 1597/8. Given John's background, the relationship between the two men and Richard's obvious wealth, it must have been the case that Richard stood the considerable expense of John's education. Richard's money was to enable John to achieve the status of gentleman, for in 1619, when there was an heraldic visitation to Kent, he recorded his coat of arms.

As a student John Manningham shared chambers with Edward Curle, and in about 1607 he married Edward's sister Ann. Curle's father William was a retainer of Sir Robert Cecil. He seems to have procured John a post of auditor at the Court of Wards: wards were minors (often heirs and heiresses) under the protection of the Crown. In his diary Manningham records that 'the Court of Wardes will send a prohibicion to anie other Court to cease from proceeding in anie suite, whereof themselves may have colour to hold plea in that Court.'[35]

In *Twelfth Night* Olivia, though not a widow, presumably inherited on the death of her father and brother. She was a woman of property. We have seen that Malvolio, to justify his aspirations to marry her, quotes the precedent of a lady marrying a yeoman.[36] A yeoman might be a man of substantial property, but he was not a gentleman. Sir Andrew's reaction to this precedent is to declare the lady a Jezebel.[37] Yet it is Malvolio's social pretensions which enable Maria to deceive him in the forged letter. 'Some are born great, some achieve greatness and some have greatness thrust upon 'em.'[38] He cannot have forgotten Sir Toby's cruel jibe when Malvolio interrupts the revellers: 'Art any more than a steward.'[39]

THE SHURLEYS

John Shurley, already noted as the Treasurer of the Inn in 1602, is a good example of how far social advancement could be achieved through membership of an Inn. John came from a reasonably prosperous family of Sussex gentry, which originated in Presteigne in the Welsh Marches. They arrived in Sussex in the fifteenth century.[40] One of John's forbears was Bailiff of Rye and this may have involved him in the delivery of fish to the royal kitchens and eventually to royal employment. The family monuments in the Shurley Chapel in Isfield in East Sussex chart their progress. John's grandfather, who died in 1527, is described as 'sumtime Chef Clerke of Kitchen to our Sov'ryn Lorde King Henry VII and Cofferer to our Sov'ryn Lorde Kyng Henry VIII'. John's father, Edward, is recorded as having succeeded his father as Cofferer to the King: the Cofferer dealt with the royal household accounts. The family built Isfield Place in about 1540. It remains a fine country house, though its size is now considerably reduced. The original great hall has been destroyed. The house was and is surrounded by a turreted wall on three sides, which was intended to be decorative and to impress. The main entrance is through a magnificent Renaissance carved-stone doorway bearing the family coat of arms. The same arms can be found in the east window of Middle Temple Hall.

To judge by their monuments, the family became considerably more affluent in the latter part of the century. The earlier family members are memorialized by an inscribed metal plate. The Treasurer's nephew, also John, who succeeded to the family seat, has an enormous marble tomb in the Shurley Chapel, with life-size effigies of himself and his two wives and his various children. In addition to his agricultural estate, he owned an iron furnace and forge. There was a good deal of iron mining on the Sussex Weald in the last quarter of the century, which supplied many needs including guns for the royal ships.[41] At what point John bought it is unclear, but he sold it in 1627 for £2,500.

Meanwhile his uncle John, who was to become Treasurer of the Inn, was making his fortune partly in the law and partly through marriage within the

Sussex gentry. He had joined the Middle Temple as a student in 1565. He married the daughter of a family called Kyme, who had bought up Grey-friars in Lewes when the monasteries were dissolved. Through his wife, John inherited the property and he eventually lived in it. Gradually he acquired other land in the vicinity.[42] His attempt to obtain the assistance of Sir Michael Hickes in acquiring appointment as Serjeant[43] was not immedi-ately successful. The Queen eventually granted writs of appointment to eleven Serjeants, returnable on the third day of the Easter term. Manning-ham in his diary states that the Queen refused to appoint twelve, 'saying she feared if there were twelve there would be one false brother amongst them.'[44] The Queen died before the return date and the writs had to be reissued in the name of James I. When that occurred, three more names were added, including those of John Shurley and George Snigge, his suc-cessor as Treasurer of the Middle Temple. John was knighted in 1603; his nephew John Shurley of Isfield was to buy a baronetcy from James I. His younger brother, George, also prospered in the law. He was a contem-porary of such students as John Davies and Richard Martin. He was later to succeed Martin as Reader in 1615 and in 1621 he became Chief Justice of Ireland. The Shurleys were now near the top of the social tree.

THE EXPEDITION TO THE SOPHY

Shakespeare appears to have paid a compliment to John Shurley, the Treasurer, by alluding to his family in *Twelfth Night*. There are two refer-ences in the text to some young men by the name of Sherley who went on an expedition to Persia. There were two families of similar name living in Sussex at this time. The crucial link between them is the marriage of the sister of the expeditionaries into the Treasurer's family. To understand the significance of this it is first necessary to trace in more detail the connec-tion between the Shurleys of Isfield and the Middle Temple. As there are two Johns from Isfield in this account the eventual Treasurer will be called John 1 and his nephew John 2. As already noted, John 1 was admitted to the Middle Temple in 1565. He was appointed Reader in 1587 and later in that year became a Bencher. John 2, the eldest son of the next generation, was admitted to the Inn in 1591. He never qualified, but he did sit as a Justice of the Peace in Sussex, where he ran the family estates he had in-herited. His younger brother, like his uncle before him, entered the law: George was admitted to the Middle Temple in 1588. All three of them would have been present at the feast at Candlemas, if they possibly could have been.

Crucially for our story, in 1595 John 2 married Jane Sherley of Wiston, also in Sussex. She lies beside him in their tomb at Isfield. Both families

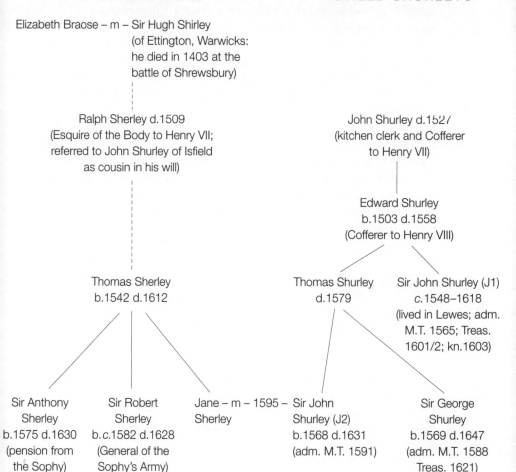

WISTON SHERLEYS

Elizabeth Braose – m – Sir Hugh Shirley
(of Ettington, Warwicks:
he died in 1403 at the
battle of Shrewsbury)

Ralph Sherley d.1509
(Esquire of the Body to Henry VII;
referred to John Shurley of Isfield
as cousin in his will)

Thomas Sherley
b.1542 d.1612

Sir Anthony
Sherley
b.1575 d.1630
(pension from
the Sophy)

Sir Robert
Sherley
b.c.1582 d.1628
(General of the
Sophy's Army)

Jane – m – 1595 –
Sherley

ISFIELD SHURLEYS

John Shurley d.1527
(kitchen clerk and Cofferer
to Henry VII)

Edward Shurley
b.1503 d.1558
(Cofferer to Henry VIII)

Thomas Shurley
d.1579

Sir John Shurley (J1)
c.1548–1618
(lived in Lewes; adm.
M.T. 1565; Treas.
1601/2; kn.1603)

Sir John
Shurley (J2)
b.1568 d.1631
(adm. M.T. 1591)

Sir George
Shurley
b.1569 d.1647
(adm. M.T. 1588
Treas. 1621)

varied the spelling of their name. It does not appear that they were related by blood, but they knew one another very well before the marriage and referred to each other as cousins. The seat of the main branch of the Wiston family, who spelt their name Shirley, was at Ettington close to Stratford upon Avon and had been let to Thomas Underhill, whose house at New Place in Stratford Shakespeare bought. In the fifteenth century a member of the family, Sir Hugh Shirley, fought for the King's party at the battle of Shrewsbury and was killed. In *Henry IV, Part I*, when Prince Hal in the course of this battle rescues his father from the Douglas, he proclaims that the spirits of valiant Shirley, Stafford and Blunt are in his arms.[45] Hugh had married into the Braose family who owned the Wiston estate in West Sussex. One of Hugh's successors, Thomas, built a substantial house at

Wiston, which was completed in 1573 (just as Middle Temple Hall was also completed) and included a hall with a double hammer-beam roof – very unusual in domestic architecture.

Of closer relevance to our story, Jane had two flamboyant brothers, Anthony and Robert, who also spelt their name Sherley. They were educated in the Inns of Court (though not the Middle Temple) and later became followers of the Earl of Essex. It was under his patronage that they travelled to visit the Shah of Persia, arriving in 1599. They were handsomely entertained. Robert Sherley eventually went as the Shah's emissary to the Court of Muscovy, and he later married the daughter of Ishmael Khan, Prince of Circassia. He never returned to England and died in Persia. Anthony returned via the north-east passage to Europe. He was persona non grata in England. The Queen was angry about the expedition (which Essex had sponsored without her permission), fearing it might spoil her relations with the Portuguese. So it was that Anthony, instead of returning to England travelled on to Rome where he met Will Kemp, the former comedian of the Lord Chamberlain's Men. Meanwhile two other members of the expedition returned to England. In September 1601 William Pay published *A new and large discourse of the Travels of Sir Anthony Sherley by Sea and over land to the Persian Empire*. Shakespeare, like most of his contemporaries, was undoubtedly fascinated by exploration. There are references in *Twelfth Night* to an expedition by the Dutchman William Barentz to the Arctic in 1597 ('you are now sailed into the north of my lady's opinion; where you will hang like an icicle on a Dutchman's beard')[46] and to Mollineux's new map of the East Indies published in 1599 ('He does smile his face into more lines than is in the new map with the augmentation of the Indies': Maria on Malvolio).[47] The Middle Temple owns two globes made by Mollineux.

There are two jokes in *Twelfth Night* about the Shah of Persia, who was also known as 'the Sophy'. Most commentators agree that these are allusions to the Sherley brothers' expedition (although the title of Sophie was also adopted by the Prince of Misrule in the Inner Temple – possibly a double joke). As Fabian watches Malvolio being gulled by the forged letter, he says: 'I will not give my part of this sport for a pension of thousands to be paid from the Sophy.'[48] Anthony Sherley claimed to have been given a pension of 30,000 crowns by the Shah. When Sir Toby wishes to terrify Sir Andrew with Cesario's reputation as a swordsman, he says Cesario has been fencer to the Sophy.[49] At Petworth House in West Sussex there is a portrait by Van Dyck of Robert in Turkish costume, sporting a large sword. It was painted in Rome in 1622 when Robert went as ambassador to the Pope on behalf of the Shah. Whilst it is true that Shakespeare could have inserted the reference to the expedition simply because of Pay's account, the joke is given particular prominence by being repeated. Given the notoriety of the expedition and the similarity of name, an audience in the small world of the Middle Temple would have been likely to make the connection between the Sherley brothers and the family of their Treasurer.

It has already been noted that the performance of *Twelfth Night* would have occurred as part of the 'post-revels'. The students in the Inns of Court were consummate revellers. Enter next, the Bright Prince of Burning Love.

CHAPTER FIVE

Revellers All

REBELLION

Christmas was a special time for revelling, although revelling took place at various festivals throughout the year. It was an important activity in medieval life which persisted well into the seventeenth century.[1] The word has its origin in the Latin 'rebellare' and the Old French 'reveler', both words meaning to rebel. Reversal of the natural order remained an important part of the concept of revelling, even if it was also to acquire the debased meaning of celebration and entertainment. Medieval society was hierarchical, with Pope and divine monarch standing at the head of church and state respectively. The ordinary man spent his days in arduous, repetitive toil. If he was not to rebel in the real sense, he needed an outlet for his passions. Revelling on holy days or feast days provided it. This is well illustrated by a case in the Star Chamber in 1611.[2] The constable of Rangeworthy near Bristol reported to the court that during a Whitsun revel he had found a disorderly, riotous assembly engaged in unlawful games and beastly and disorderly drinking. When he tried to arrest the perpetrators, he and his assistants were beaten. The villagers replied that they had held a Whitsun revel time out of memory, 'for the refreshing of the minds and spirits of the country people, being inured and tired with husbandry and continual labour.' They had been following their normal custom on such occasions of wrestling, running, leaping and dancing, which were accompanied by mild drinking. The constable's complaint was dismissed.

It was a popular device on feast days to reverse the natural order in church and state. In the Feast of Fools the lowly were exalted. In ecclesiastical houses an Abbot of Misrule would be appointed. There was a similar tradition of boy bishops. The appointment of Lords of Misrule extended down to town and village level. For instance in Marlborough in 1578 the chamberlain set aside 13s 8d for a gallon of wine and gunpowder against the Lord of Misrule's coming.[3] At Westbury in 1637, the minister reported that the young people were lured away from divine service by a revel organized by the Lord of the Summerhouse;[4] and at midsummer in Broadchalke there was a dancing match, following which in the darkness one of the young women was turned upside down and 'bishoped'.[5] Although it is not entirely clear what this ceremony involved, it was clearly vulgar and subverted the normal order by empowering a woman. Gender inversion and transvestism were common features of such festivities. Thus the tradition of the appointment of a Lord of Misrule in the great houses was part of a much broader pattern of traditional merrymaking.

STUDENT REVELRY

The students in the Inns of Court loved revelling. The Masters of the Bench also revelled, but their interpretation of the activity was rather more sober than that of the students. The office of Master of the Revels was established in the Royal Court on a part-time basis by Henry VII in 1494; it did not become permanent until 1545. By then it was also well established in the Inns of Court. Office-holding in the Inns could be expensive, and if someone refused to take a particular office he was fined. In 1509 there is a record of a fine imposed upon a member of the Middle Temple, who refused the office of Master of the Revels.[6] The Benchers' idea of celebrating Christmas was to hold solemn revels. These involved singing psalms and stately dancing. The minutes of the Middle Temple parliament frequently command that Christmas shall be celebrated solemnly and not grandly, which meant that the proceedings should be sober and not involve elaborate feasts and revelling. The students, however, had other ideas. Jonson acknowledged the role of the Prince of Misrule in his preface to *Every Man Out of His Humour*:

> when cap and gown is off and the lord of liberty reigns, then take it in your hands, perhaps may make some bencher, tincted with humanity read and not repent him.

Each Inn had its own name for its Prince of Misrule. In Lincoln's Inn he was the Prince of the Grange and in Gray's Inn the Prince of Purpoole. When in 1561 the Earl of Leicester was Prince of the Sophie in the Inner Temple, there is a contemporary description of the entertainment by Gerard Leigh (who lived near the Temple) in his *Accidens of Armory*.[7] The Prince, who adopted the name Paphilos, was

> served with tender meats, sweet fruits and dainty delicates confectioned with curious cookery, as it seemed wonder a world to observe the provision; and at every course the trumpets blew the courageous blast of deadly war, with noise of drum and fife, with sweet harmony of violins, sackbuts, recorders and cornets with other instruments of music as it seemed Apollo's harp had tuned their stroke.

The level of the entertainment may be gauged by the names given to some of the knights created by the Prince: Sir Bartholomew Baldbreech of Buttockebury in the County of Breakneck; Sir Randle Rockabite of Rascal Hall, County Rakehell; Sir Morgan Mumchance of Much Monkery in the County of Mad Mopery.

The full title of the Prince of Purpoole was Archduke of Stapulia and Bernardia,[8] Duke of the High and Nether Holborn, Marquis of St Giles and Tottenham, Count Palatine of Bloomsbury and Clerkenwell, Great Lord of the Cantons of Islington, Kentish Town, Paddington and Knightsbridge, and knight of the Most Heroical Order of the Helmet.[9] In the Middle Temple, the Prince D'Amour was elected by the students to rule over the Kingdom of Love. His full English title was the Bright Prince of Burning Love.

MASQUES

Masquing formed an important part of the entertainment. Like revelling in general, the masque seems first to have been introduced into the royal court, being later adopted in the Inns of Court. A masque was performed at Gray's Inn in 1526: it had a satirical element in it and Cardinal Wolsey took this to refer to him. An account appears in the chronicle of a member of Gray's Inn named Hall:

> This Christmas was a good disguisyng plaied at Greis inne ... The effect of the play was that lord governance was ruled by dissipacion and negligence: which caused Rumor Populi, Inward grudge and disdain of wanton sovereignetie, to rise with a greate multitude, to expell negligence and dissipacion and to restore Public welth again to her estate, which was done. This plaie was so set furth with riche and costly apparel, with strange divises of Maskes and it was highly praised of all menne.

The Cardinal, however, was not amused and sent for the author, Serjeant Roo. In a great fury the Cardinal tore his coif from him and sent him to the Fleet prison together with one of the actors. In due course, with the help of friends, they were released. The young Queen Elizabeth was entertained in 1565 with 'divers showes' by the gentlemen of Gray's Inn,[10] and in 1595 members of the same Inn performed a *Masque of Proteus* before her.[11] The principal characters were named Esquire, Proteus, Thamesis and Amphitrite, thus mixing the English and the classical, rather as Shakespeare mixes English and Italian names in *Twelfth Night*. The masque commenced with some blank-verse dialogue, ending in praise of the Queen. The set consisted of an adamantine rock which Proteus struck with a trident. The Christmas prince, chosen by the students, and pairs of his knights emerged from the opened rock, each pair accompanied by two pygmies. A newly devised measure was danced, followed by the knights, accompanied by their ladies, dancing galliards and corrantos. The pygmies presented the escutcheons of the knights to the Queen and the actors retired into the rock. The masque concluded with a song. The following night the Queen praised the gentlemen of Gray's Inn because they always studied 'sports' to present to her. The Christmas prince was presented with a jewel containing seventeen diamonds and four rubies, and promised he would be remembered with a better reward later.[12]

The disorderly nature of the period of misrule led the Benchers in the various Inns to discourage it in the 1580s and 1590s, with the result that revels did not occur every year. The Benchers would have agreed with the sentiments of Hamlet on the subject. When Horatio enquires about the meaning of a flourish of trumpets and ordnance, Hamlet responds:

> HAMLET: The King doth wake tonight and takes his rouse,
> Keeps wassail, and the swaggering upspring reels.
> And as he drains his draughts of Rhenish down,
> The kettle drum and trumpet thus bray out
> The triumph of his pledge.
> HORATIO: Is it a custom?
> HAMLET: Ay marry is't.
> But to my mind, though I am native here
> And to the manner born, it is a custom
> More honoured in the breach than the observance.
> This heavy-headed revel east and west
> Makes us traduced and taxed of other nations.
> They clepe us drunkards and with swinish phrase
> Soil our addition; and indeed it takes
> From our achievements, though performed at height
> The pith and marrow of our attribute.[13]

There is also a swing in the mood of the revelry in *Twelfth Night*. The text at first sides with the revellers, but eventually it is clear that Sir Toby and his friends have behaved appallingly; Malvolio was right to restrain their abuse of Olivia's hospitality. When revelry stoops to cruelty the revellers are rightly rebuked.

MIDDLE TEMPLE REVELS OF 1597/8

The students of the Middle Temple would have had none of such sentiments. There were revels in 1589/90 in the Middle Temple which ended in violent disorder. After that date there was an understandable gap until 1597/8, when the script stated:

It is not unknown how for these eight years past, the youthful, couragious, and victorious state of the Knight Templars hath been ruined; all men can speak of the infinite abuses, and lamentable desolations that have been made of Love and Armes, their ancient professions.[14]

This is obviously consistent with the dates mentioned above and attests that there were no intervening revels. The passage is corroborated by the fact that the records of the Inn parliament do not mention any revels in the same period. The revels of 1597/8 achieved renown. The young men who took part in them were specially talented. Several accounts of these revels exist. Benjamin Rudyerd, who appears to have participated in them, wrote a general description of the entertainment.[15] An incomplete script survives in the Harleian collection in the British Museum.[16] There is no obvious way to date it. In 1660 William Leake a printer near the Temple Gates was to publish a printed version of Rudyerd's account together with a large, though incomplete, part of the script used by the students. This is preserved in the Thomason Tracts.[17] That it was viable to publish such a full account over sixty years after the performance of the revels testifies to their fame.

Rudyerd describes the inception of the revels thus:

A brief Chronicle of the Darke Raign of the bright Prince of burning Love. Anno ab aula condita 27 the Lincolnians (the noble confederates with the Medio Templarians) to bring that ancient and general league to particular Feeling and Affection of the Gentlemen on both sides, invited the Templarians to their Solemnitys, entertained them with a variety of Musick and ended their friendly Revels and discourses with a sumptuous Banquet, that exceeded the plentifullest vein of description. The great number of their able company occasioned in us (that took our selves but beholders) an offer to create some one man, amongst so many worthy to be the Prince and head of all the rest. But our offer rebounded back upon us with more vehemency than it was made. Whereupon we were withdrawn into the Senate house to consult further, where matters were handled by way of comparison thus, and thus found that they were fitter for a multitude, we for a man and a Hall of capacity. One Stradilax, a Templarian (who was in great danger to have been Prince himself, if any man had thought him fit) ran down amongst them like Laocoon ardens, and with a most furious and turbulent action, uttered these two Proverbs, the one borrowed from a Smith, the other from a Clown, My Masters strike while the Iron is hot: Make hay while the Sun shineth. They presently with acclamations and sound of Trumpets, named Sir Martino Prince, promised him all their aid and furtherance, waited on him home to the Temple, and in making themselves believe he was Prince, thought to have made him believe so too. He, esteeming it rather a solemn leading to some fatal execution, fled from them. Then Stradilax stept up upon the stone Staires in the Porch of the Temple Hall, from whence nothing but Oysters ever opened their mouths with eloquence and spoke as followeth. Forasmuch as (most dear League Fellows) you are not only come down from your own house, but have also taken the pains to bring us home, like the Tile that doth not only slide from the Roof, but doth also fall to the ground, I am to tell you &c. But they went to bed so he did not tell them.

All that week was Seignior Martino continually importuned by his own Friends, pressed by a mighty expectation, and overborn with the stream of Rumor; all which he answered, more than for fashion sake, with these reasons, That other men heretofore, if they denied it, might hide their willingness under form of denial, for they for their years were unsettled for their life not so well known as they would be; for their experience untravelled; for their course unresolved; for his part he now rather desired to settle his name than to spread it, and thought it would be but a subject, to spend his former credit upon: only he could object to himself against all these Reasons, but again of a more inward love of that company which before time he had lived in, and now chosen for continuance, and that made him yield.

Then were Privy Seals directed to all within their Dominions towards the charge of this undertaking, but slowly returned. Yet notwithstanding did Stradilax make a great feast, and instead of Grace after it there was a libel set up against him in all the famous places of the City as Queen Hithe, Newgate, the Stocks, Pillory, Pissing Conduit, and (but that the Provost Marshall was his inward friend) it should not have missed Bridewell.

Now did many of Signor Martino's own Company forsake him; but some of them without excuse; for one said he would willingly stay but he must always have a care to the main chance. Another protested he would do him any service at any other time; but now he must needs go home to register his father's New-years-gifts into the Capon book, because the Clerk was newly put away for a Pre-contract with his mother's Chamber-maide. A third swore he would attend upon him, but his promise bound him to play the Prologue at Christmas before a Chine of Brawn at a great man's table. A fourth would needs be gone because he had no money, and his Wit was not come to his head, nor his land to his hands. There were many moe left their departure to construction.

This revolt and defection notwithstanding, the hope of the Lincolnian aid kept life in our resolution, until Palmerio de Oliva, the Prince's Perfumer carried a false scent in his cloathes, which had like utterly to have choaked the League and Amity between us, but did altogether lay flat our purposes. For Seignior Martino himself openly gave it over; Tailors were forbidden to proceed in their work and Stradilax had like to have lost the two shillings he delivered in earnest for a paire of Pantofles. Yet at the last did Signior Martino, at the earnestness of some honorable personages using reason of necessity, raise from the ground his own brethren upon his own shoulders against all these difficulties and was upheld by some of his own house, that were strangers to his love, rather for the true judgement of his parts, then for hope or desire of his acquaintance. Then went the Tailors forward and every one else had more work than a Tailor against Christmas; for these incertainties made both inventions and other provisions like the Tillage of Ireland, half mowed, half fallowed, half ploughed, half harrowed, half sowed, all rude.

The price of Feathers during the staggering did rise and fall ten groats a day.

Because the contributions, which the students required to stage their revels, were slow in coming in, the Prince was elected later than usual, on Christmas Eve. He was crowned with great ceremony on 26th December. The partying then continued almost unabated until Candlemas. In the course of it there were three elaborate masques, one performed at the Royal Court before the Queen, and also performances of two comedies. There was a battle between two knights, a mock trial, and there was dinner with the Lord Mayor of London.

The script reveals the reversal of authority which the Prince brings with him to the Inn:

Whereas before we were controulable at the nod of every doting Bencher, oppressed with the yoke of quarrelsome Cases, attired with a long doleful Robe and flat cap, and fed with thin liquor, and the hinder part of a rotten Sheep, we are now become subjects and servants to this famous Prince, that lives victorious in all Nations; we are prest soldiers under the sweet Banner of Love, where we receive every hour new encouragements in all our enterprises.

When a jury is called to try a discontented lover, the jurymen are told:

If any man do maintain, by word, writing, or overt Act, the Authority of Benchers or utter Barristers within his Excellencies Dominions, this is High Treason.

When the Prince appoints his Knights of the Quiver, he makes them swear to observe the rules of the order: one of these is that 'all knights of this Order be able to speak ill of Inns-a-Court Commons', meaning the food and drink provided in Hall.

As the Christmas Prince in the Middle Temple is the Prince of Love, his revels naturally centre on that topic. He is given a long list of titles relating to his abilities in love. His Champion complains that the chivalrous traditions of the Knights Templar have been ruined:

who of late hath taken the honorable course of Love, or so much as set foot in the pathway of Chivalry? Easie and low prized Venery hath been basely pursued, whilst desires illuminated by the Celestial flame of Beauty, have been accounted either Fictions or Frensies; none hath sighed, none hath indited, none hath publick Shews frequented, none in unsufferable cold a whole Winters night hath his Mistris door courted, or by the Chamber Windows entred to speak but one word, nay to have but one sight of her, whose Idea is the mover of his Motions. And as the vertuous, though laborious walks of Love have been thus unfrequented; so the wonted Feats of Arms now a long while have been unpractised ... The wiser sort of Templarians seeing these manifold corruptions, as well to repair their decayed State, as in doubtful adventures of Love to have one to whom, as to an Oracle, they may repair to be resolved for their controversies, have therefore assembled the general States of the Provinces, and with one consent ... have lifted to the seat of Government this Prince ...

Rudyerd describes the Prince himself as a perfect lover:

The Prince was of Face thin and lean, of a cheerful and gracious countenance; blackhaired; tall bodied, and well proportioned, of a sweet and fair conversation to every man that kept his distance ... He was very fortunate and discreet in the love of Women; a great lover and complainer of company.

The Prince's Secretary advises him that 'these lovely Ladies, who like bright stars have beautified your Court with their appearance, may with some delightful disports be entertained.' The sports, however, swiftly descend into bawdy: there is a sharp contrast between courtly aspiration and down-to-earth sex. The Prince's officers are lampooned in terms which are sexually explicit. The Lord President is to order the Council every two days to 'view the Subsidy book, and see what Ladies be deep in; and that those that are Light may have more laid upon them ... any Gentlewoman being taken in the Armes of any Gentleman, be presumed his Sister, or his Cousin at the least, and that she be presumed to be no better then swowning, and he striving to put life into her.' The Archflamen 'may allow Pluralities in Love to them which have extraordinary parts.' The Lord Marshall is to measure the length of all Weapons. The instructions to the Lord Admiral are particularly full of innuendo:

He shall take heed in sailing least he ... fall foul on some other Vessel, whereby he may break his Borsprit in the Poupe or some other part of her ... He shall suffer all such to pass quietly as Traffique into the Gulfe of Venus ... He shall see that all his Excellencies Ships have their Cape-stones in good order ... and that the Ship be well washt afore and after for fear of infection ... He shall sometimes look into Brest, and sometimes fall into Diepe.

The spirit of courtly love, however, does return in the person of the Master of the Revels, who is to see that 'no Gentleman's Voice drown the base Viol; and they shall dance in measure and love out of measure.'

The Revels show all the hallmarks of an end of term revue. Inevitably there are many legal jokes and cod law. At one stage a malcontented esquire is charged with treason to the Prince of Love. In the mock trial the jury are given silly Latin names, such as Simplicius Credulus of Hornsby and Vinius Bibulus of Maltsbury. This discontented lover is charged with various treasons including uttering

> prophane, beastly, odious, execrable, hellish, abominable, savage, heinous, horrible and traiterous speeches against the high and sacred Majesty of Love.

He is accused that:

> of thy wicked malice aforethought, and in great disdain of Love and all lovers, and to the great dishonor of his Excellencies Court, in the presence of his heroical person, having eaten of set purpose a certain contagious confection of Garlick and Assa fetida, [thou] did nevertheless presume to Court divers fair and beautiful Ladies, and didst excuse that thy ranke noisome, and pestiferous savour and exhalation by saying, Sweet Ladies, I have lately taken a new and excellent kinde of Tobacco late brought into his Excellencies Court from the North Indies.

In his trial it is asserted he claimed that none should be the Prince of Love but him, and that he 'requited his Mistris constancy and kindness with disdain and ingratitude,' wishing 'that he might shift her as often as he shifts his clothes.' His chambers having been searched under a warrant from the Chief Justice, his bad love poems were seized and recited to the court. The defendant is convicted and sentenced:

> Thou discontented Lover, because thou hast disdained to be true Prisoner to Love, whose imprisonment is the sweetest Liberty, The Court doth therefore award, that thou be delivered over to his Excellencies Captain of the Seraglia, who shall commit thee close prisoner to the most loathsome Dungeon in the Fort of Fancy, there to remaine fasting from Favours, and feeding on Melancholy till thou hast paid thy Fine and ransome, which shall be an Oration in praise of Love, and of his Excellency.

There is a good deal of mock oratory. The Orator makes a neat 'tuftaffeta' oration, which is answered by a handsome 'fustian' one. Tuftaffeta was a silk cloth and fustian a rough cloth – so there is an inverted joke since fustian would not have been handsome. Shakespeare uses the same comparison when Fabian comments on the riddle set by Maria in the forged

letter that it is a fustian riddle.[18] During one day there is a Sacrifice of Love
in which the students made confessions (no doubt exaggerated) of their
love lives. Stradilax's confessions are made in the style of a tailor's bill or
a memorandum with numbered items. Shakespeare uses a similar comic
device in *Twelfth Night* when Olivia itemizes her beauty.[19] There is also
a good deal of comedy of disorder, or misrule. Stradilax miscalls himself
a lord and carries a left-handed truncheon – a lord would carry his emblem
of rank in his right hand and in any event there is no such thing as a left-
handed truncheon. Other references in the more detailed script seem to
indicate that the truncheon represented the penis. Things past are foretold.
Women are to be praised for their inconstancy and dispraised in comparison to pork. A whale is found in London.

The scene is set against a bleak midwinter. The Thames is frozen and
the frosty ground unsafe for horses (there were particularly severe winters
in the 1590s). Stradilax makes a festival oration for a midwinter festival:
Twelfth Night is the high point. Rudyerd describes how two days before
Twelfth Night, the Lord Mayor of London's invitation to dinner was de-
ferred 'because of the preparation for Barriers and a Mask to the Court.'
That and the next day were spent preparing for the elaborate entertainment
that was provided:

> Upon Friday being Twelf-day at night there went to the Court 11 Knights
> and 11 Esquires, 9 Maskers, and 9 Torchbearers. Their setting forth was
> with a peal of Ordinance, a noise of Trumpets always sounding before
> them, the Herald next, and after two Esquires and two Knights. The
> Knights for their upper parts in bright armour, their hose of cloth of gold
> and silver; the Esquires in jerkins laced with gold and silver, and their hose
> as fair; all upon great horses, all richly furnished. Then came the Maskers
> by Couples upon Velvet Footclothes, their short cloaks, doublets and hose
> of cloth of gold and silver of nine several colours representing nine several
> passions; to every Masker a Torchbearer on a footcloth carrying his devise,
> besides a hundred torches born by servants. Never any Prince in this
> kingdom, or the like made so glorious and so rich a shew. When they came
> to the Court the Knights broke every man a lance and two swords; the nine
> Maskers like Passions issued out of a heart. All was fortunately performed,
> and received a great commendation.

The Prince's reign ended at Candlemas:

> Upon Candlemass night, the Prince wearied with the weight of Government,
> made a voluntary Resignation into the hands of the Optimates, intending a
> private life, wherein he required the advice of his Council. One advised him
> to follow the Sea; another to Land travel; a third to marry a rich widow;
> and a fourth to study the Common Law. He chose the last, and refused not

to the third if she stood in his way. He died of a common infectious disease, called Opinion, upon the sixth month of Candlemas day; and may be buried in Oblivion with his Ancestors if tongues dig him not up.

SHAKESPEARE'S REVELRY

Against this background it is not surprising that revels are a recurring theme in Shakespeare's plays. In *Much Ado About Nothing* they are a guise for romantic intrigue[20] and even if they are not described as such, they serve the same purpose in *Romeo and Juliet*.[21] In *The Merchant of Venice* it is 'Christian fools with varnished faces' who steal Shylock's daughter from him.[22] *A Midsummer Night's Dream* is built around a framework of revelling. Just as the Royal Court in England had its Master of the Revels, so did Duke Theseus in the person of Philostrate. He is ordered by his master to

> Stir up the Athenian youth to merriments;
> Awake the pert and nimble spirit of mirth.[23]

Theseus promises to wed Hypolita 'with pomp, with triumph, and with revelling.'[24] At the close of the play he demands entertainment:

> Come now; what masques, what dances shall we have,
> To wear away this long age of three hours
> Between our after-supper and bed-time?
> Where is our usual manager of mirth?
> What revels are in hand? Is there no play,
> To ease the anguish of a torturing hour.[25]

The play that is chosen is 'a tedious brief scene of young Pyramus and his love Thisbe very tragical mirth' devised by Peter Quince. Earlier in the play, when Puck first appears he informs a fairy that Oberon 'doth keep his revels here tonight.'[26] Titania, when she has confronted Oberon, gives him this invitation:

> If you will patiently dance in our round,
> And see our moonlight revels, go with us.[27]

In *The Tempest* the revels – in a speech mimicking the elaborate scenery of the masque – become a metaphor for the theatre and even life itself:

> Our revels now are ended. These our actors,
> As I foretold you, were all spirits and
> Are melted into air, into thin air:
> And like the baseless fabric of this vision,

The cloud-capp'd towers, the gorgeous palaces,
The solemn temples, the great globe itself,
Yea all which it inherit, shall dissolve
And like this insubstantial pageant faded,
Leave not a wrack behind.[28]

In *Twelfth Night* the theme of revelling appears early in the piece. Sir Andrew confesses that he has spent too much time in fencing, dancing and bear-baiting, adding 'I delight in masques and revels sometimes altogether.'[29] Sir Toby stimulates Sir Andrew into boasting of his dancing ability, and their first appearance closes when Sir Andrew asks: 'Shall we set about some revels.'[30] Sir Toby replies: 'What shall we do else? Were we not born under Taurus?' Their revelling is not the sophisticated entertainment of Duke Theseus, but the drunken brawling more often associated with revelling in the villages or even in the Inns of Court.

Today there are a number of wine bars where young barristers and bar students are to be found around the Temple, often to a late hour and particularly on a Friday. The Mermaid tavern near St Paul's seems to have supplied the same function in 1602. Some of the Middle Templars met there as part of a literary club and this provides another possible link between the Inns of Court men and Shakespeare. It also provides a link with Sir Walter Raleigh, who it seems attended the revels of 1597/8.

CHAPTER SIX

The Mermaid Club

BREAD STREET

In the Middle Temple Revels of 1597/8, the Prince of Misrule created Knights of the Order of the Quiver, who were required to swear an oath of loyalty to the articles of the Order. Article number 15 provided that any knight 'being asked where he dined, he must not say at the Tavern or the Ordinary, but at the Miter, the Mearmaid or the Kingshead in old Fish Street.' There is an area of London, just to the east of St Paul's Cathedral, which runs from what is now Queen Victoria Street to north of Cheapside, where the medieval street names relate to products, such as Bread Street, Milk Street and Wood Street. At the southern end of this area stood Old Fish Street (a small portion of which survives) and adjacent to it is Friday Street, so called because of the fish market held there on a Friday. References to meetings at both the Mitre and the Mermaid tell of them occurring on a Friday. Under the old religion only fish could be eaten on a Friday; after the Reformation the habit persisted, though it was followed less rigorously. Bread Street lies to the east of, and parallel to, Friday Street. The taverns round there were no doubt lively on a Friday night. A number of writers speak of a Mermaid tavern, which is sometimes referred to as being in Bread Street and sometimes in Friday Street, which suggests that there were entrances to it from both streets (there is today a public house, called the Serpent, at the southern end of those streets, which runs between them). There was also a Mitre tavern in Bread Street. The area would have been convenient for Blackfriars and the South Bank and close to the river. It was near to St Paul's where lawyers met their clients: it was part of the induction ceremony of Serjeants that they were allocated a pillar in St Paul's. St Paul's Cross was a centre of preaching and St Paul's Churchyard of bookselling. John Donne, who was a prominent member of the group of Friday-night revellers, was born in Bread Street.

There had been a Mermaid tavern in Bread Street as far back as the mid fifteenth century. The accounts of the steward to John Howard, Duke of Norfolk, make a number of references to this establishment.[1] Howard was slain with Richard III at Bosworth field and was Shakespeare's 'jockey of

Norfolk'.[2] The tavern appears to have been built on land belonging to the Fishmongers' Company. It was eventually destroyed in the Great Fire of London in 1666, after which the records of the Fishmongers establish that a lease was granted to Richard Fuller of the ground upon which the Mermaid tavern had stood. No map survives which shows its exact location. Friday Street, although now only a short street, at that time ran from its current position south-east of St Paul's to Cheapside, in parallel all the way with Bread Street. In fact the tavern was at the southern end of Bread Street. The Guildhall Hustings Rolls place it in the parish of St Mildred, as does a grant of the tenement; and St Mildred's lay at the southern end of Bread Street, south-west of Basinghall Street and near where the modern Friday Street is found.

There was a separate Mitre in Fleet Street (later a haunt of Dr Johnson) standing close to the Temple.[3] There is nothing to indicate that it was of good repute at this time, and it was sited next to the alleyways of Alsatia, which were the haunt of criminals. The Mitre in Bread Street seems to have been the one referred to in the Revels, given the geographical location of the other two hostelries named.

THE MERMAID TAVERN IN LITERATURE

The names of the Mitre and Mermaid taverns were associated more than once in contemporary literature. In 1608, in his play *Your Five Gallants*, Thomas Middleton (a student of Gray's Inn) wrote the following dialogue:

> GOLDSTONE: Where sup we gallants?
> PURSENET: At the Mermaid.
> GOLDSTONE: Sup there who list, I have forsworn the house.
> FULKE: For the truth is, this plot must take effect at Miter.
> GOLDSTONE: Why the Miter, in my mind for neat attendance,
>   diligent boys, and ... push excels it far.
> ALL: Agreed, the Miter then.[4]

Later Goldstone bids a courtesan remember that it is Mitre night.[5] She replies that it is indeed Friday. In 1598 Ben Jonson set two scenes in *Every Man Out of his Humour* in the Mitre, referring to it as the best house. In one scene a drawer called George enters and is addressed in these terms:

> O George, I could bite off thy nose for this now: Sweet Rogue, he has drawne nectar, the very soul of the Grape: I'le wash my temples with some on't presently and drink some half a score draughts; 'twill heat the Braine, kindle my Imagination, I shall talk nothing but Crackers and Fire-workes tonight.[6]

The scene is stated to take place on a Friday. The play must have been writ-ten shortly after the Middle Temple Revels of 1597/8, in which the Mitre is specifically commended. It was around 1597–8 that the young poets of the Middle Temple first started publishing their work. John Webster (a stu-dent in Middle Temple in 1602) in his later collaboration with Dekker, called *Westward Hoe*, also refers to a drawer called George at the Mitre.[7] This supports the view that there was a particular tavern of resort. Its where-abouts is not specified in the plays. In 1607, however, George Wilkins in his play *The Miseries of Enforced Marriage* refers to drinking in the Mitre in Bread Street; and in *Bartholomew Fair*, first performed in 1614, Jonson also associates the name of the Mitre with that of the Mermaid:

> I do feel conceits coming upon me more than I am able to turn tongue to. A pox of these pretenders to wit. Your Three Cranes, Mitre and Mermaid-men.[8]

He refers to the Mermaid as a source of inspiration in his Epigrams:

> But that which most doth take my Muse and me
> Is a pure cup of rich canary wine
> Which is the Mermaid's now, but shall be mine.[9]

That he is talking about the Mermaid in Bread Street is made clear:

> At Bread Street's Mermaid has dined and merry
> Proposed to go to Holborn in a wherry.[10]

A GROUP OF MIDDLE TEMPLARS

Jonson was a close friend of John Donne and both writers were clearly linked with a group of Middle Templars (already individually mentioned) – John Hoskins, Richard Martin, Benjamin Rudyerd, John Davies, Henry Wotton and a Bencher called Edward Phillips. Davies and Martin had arrived at the Middle Temple in 1587, Rudyerd in 1590, Hoskins in 1592 (the same year as John Marston, whose plays were performed by the same company as some of Jonson's) and Henry Wotton in 1595. Manningham mentions all of them at different points in his diary. John Donne had been admitted to Hart's Hall, Oxford, in 1584 at the age of twelve, and when he was nineteen joined Thavies Inn (on High Holborn). The next year he was admitted to Lincoln's Inn. He had become a friend of Wotton at Oxford and later wrote three verse letters to him. Jonson wrote two epigrams to Donne and three to Benjamin Rudyerd; and he dedicated his *Poetaster* to Martin. In 1660 Donne's son was to publish a volume of his father's poetry, together with poems by Davies, Hoskins and Rudyerd. This group was joined by two sons of lawyers – Thomas Overbury, whose father was a Bencher of the Middle Temple, and Francis Beaumont whose father was a Judge. Overbury was admitted to the Middle Temple in 1597 and Beaumont to the Inner Temple in 1600. He was only sixteen then and his fame as a playwright was to come later in James I's reign.

THOMAS CORYATE

Several of these men are connected by references in the writings of a young westcountryman called Thomas Coryate.[11] He appears to have cultivated the character of a buffoon in order to ingratiate himself with his fellows. Somewhere between 1608 and 1610 he wrote a collection of travel anecdotes, which was eventually entitled *Coryate's Crudities*. He had difficulty in securing its publication. It was, however, the custom amongst this group to write verses commending each other's new work to the public. Partly as a joke it seems, they decided to commend Coryate's work in either excessive or satiric terms. Fifteen poems resulted, which were published in 1611 with the book itself. The authors included Donne, Jonson, Martin, Hoskins, Edward Phillips and Inigo Jones, who was to become associated with the group. Another of the poems was written by Phillips' secretary, Laurence Whittaker; yet another by Lionel Cranfield, who became a successful businessman and later Treasurer to James I and Earl of Middlesex; in 1618 he obtained the office of Recorder of London for Richard Martin.

In 1615 Coryate travelled to India (a remarkable journey) and on the way there, and on his arrival, he sent five letters to his friends in England. One was addressed to Edward Phillips at his house in Chancery Lane, another to Laurence Whittaker, in which he asked the recipient to 'commend me also I pray to M. Martin though at a man's house in Wood Street he used me very perversely; but you may see my being in Jerusalem dooth make me forget my injuries.' This picture is consistent with Coryate being the butt of humour in the group and with Martin's reputation as a reveller and wit. The last of the letters is addressed from the 'Court of the Great Mogul resident at the town of Asmere to the High Seneschall of the Right Worshipful Fraternitie of Sirenaical Gentlemen, that meet the first Friday of every month at the signe of the Mere Maide in Bread Street in London.' The word 'sirenaical' may mean siren's (or mermaid's) men. The letter refers to such a meeting he had attended that had been presided over by the quondam Seneschall Laurence Whittaker. (If Whittaker were a former leader of the group, this indicates a measure of organization, as does the reference to meetings on a Friday night.) It concludes with greetings 'to all whose names I have expressed, being lovers of Vertue and Literature.' The names 'expressed' include Donne, Jonson, Martin and Hoskins. There is also a Latin poem, thought to have been written in 1611, that appeared under the pseudonym of Radulphus Colphabius and was entitled *Convivium Philosophum*:

Quilibet si sit contentus
Ut Statutus stet conventus
Sicut nos promisimus
Signum Mitrae erit locus
Erit Cibus, erit jus
Optimatissimus.

Roughly translated this means: Whoever is eager that the meeting should stand confirmed as we have promised, the place will be at the sign of the Mitre, there will be food and the very best wine. The list of those invited gives Latin pseudonyms and true names, the latter including Donne, Cranfield, Robert Phillips, Inigo Jones, Thomas Coryate and once again Richard Martin and John Hoskins. What occurred at these meetings may be gathered from a poem that was probably written about the same time, and is usually ascribed to Francis Beaumont. He wrote a number of plays with John Fletcher, amongst them one called *Wit Without Money*, in which one character asks another to

draw me a map from the Mermaid,
I mean a midnight map to scape the watches.[12]

In the preface to his poem he refers to the fact that he has been writing plays with Fletcher which made him defer their 'merry meetings at the Mermaid'. He continues in verse:

... in this warm shine
I lie and dream of your full Mermaid wine ...
 ... what things have we seen
Done at the Mermaid! Heard what words that have been
So nimble, and so full of subtile flame,
As if that every one, from whence they came,
Had meant to put his whole wit in a jest
And had resolv'd to live a fool the rest
Of his dull life.[13]

SHAKESPEARE AND THE MERMAID TAVERN

Shakespeare was about ten years older than most of this group of young men and none of the references to the Mermaid Club mentions him. He clearly knew Ben Jonson reasonably well, for he was named in the cast of

Jonson's *Every Man in his Humour* in 1598. The Lord Chamberlain's Men also performed *Every Man Out of His Humour* the following year. Jonson was to write of him in affectionate terms in his commendatory verses to the First Folio. Hugh Holland, who is also named as one of the company at the Mermaid, contributed a poem on the same occasion.

At a later date there is a specific connection between Shakespeare and the Mermaid tavern in Bread Street. In 1594 the records of the Fishmongers' Company indicate that an Edmond Williamson renewed a grant on the tavern for sixteen years.[14] The Company's subsidy rolls also speak of a William Williamson, and in 1598 a man of that name was prosecuted for having a hogshead of defective wine at the Mermaid in Bread Street. In 1600 a certain William Johnson is named in a complaint to the Star Chamber as a servant 'of William Williamson, a vintner of a common taverne situated in a street called Bread Street.'[15] Then in 1603 a schedule annexed to a will names a Mr Johnson, vintner, at the Mermaid in Bread Street, as a creditor. His name was to appear in a subsidy list of the Fishmongers in 1610 and in 1613 he witnessed William Williamson's will. Finally in Chancery records in 1616 Johnson is named as holding the tenure of the tavern. Now in 1613 Shakespeare purchased a house that had been built over the Great Gate in Blackfriars.[16] That purchase was made in the name of three people apart from Shakespeare – William Johnson vintner of London and John Jackson and John Hemming of London, gentlemen. Hemming was the well-known actor and co-editor of the First Folio. Their role appears to be akin to a trustee. The use of Johnson in this way indicates a reasonably close relationship, probably arising from Shakespeare frequenting the Mermaid tavern. If so, he must have had some familiarity with the literary members of the Middle Temple. This group deserves some further description.

THE MIDDLE TEMPLARS DESCRIBED

Richard Martin

In the Temple Church, apart from the tombs of the Knights Templar, there are only two monuments with effigies, one to the great Plowden and the other to Richard Martin. The latter's monument bears Latin verses written by his friend John Hoskins. In purely legal terms Martin does not seem to have achieved great distinction. He did become a Reader in the Inn, but he was not elevated to the rank of Serjeant like Hoskins and Rudyerd. However, the erection of such a monument to him must give some indication of his standing amongst his fellows. He seems to have misspent his youth. In 1590, together with a number of other students, he set up a Lord of Misrule in the Middle Temple without permission of the Benchers.[17] The revellers broke into chambers and forcibly extracted 'rent' for the Prince from the occupants. They were brought before the Benchers: one of them was expelled and the other seven fined £20, with a warning that a repetition of the behaviour would result in their expulsion too. Nevertheless on Candlemas night 1591 some of them, Martin included, entered the Temple disguised, broke open chambers doors and abused people within. Martin was expelled from the Inn, but he was later reinstated. If he was unpopular with the Benchers, he certainly appears to have been popular with his fellow students: hence his election to be Prince of Misrule in 1597. John Aubrey in his *Brief Lives* describes him as 'a very handsome man, a graceful speaker, facetious, and well-beloved.'[18] Despite these gifts he took a long time to qualify as a barrister: instead of the usual seven years he took fifteen, not being called until February 1602. When Jonson dedicated his *Poetaster* to him in 1606, he thanked Martin because for Jonson's 'innocence' he was 'once a noble and timely undertaker to the greatest justice of this kingdom.' Neither the nature of the 'innocence', nor the undertaking, nor the date is made clear, but the plea was probably made to Sir John Popham who was Chief Justice of the Queen's Bench from 1592 to 1607.

If Martin misspent his youth, he does seem to have become a reformed character. When James I came to London in May 1603, Martin was the chosen spokesman for the Sheriffs of London and Middlesex, and he delivered a flattering oration to the new king.[19] He then became a Member of Parliament from 1604 to 1611.[20] On St Valentine's day 1613, the King's daughter, Elizabeth, married the protestant Count Palatine of the Rhine; and the next day the Inns of Court celebrated this popular marriage by presenting two masques at court.[21] The Middle Temple and Lincoln's Inn combined to present one of them, the Inner Temple and Gray's Inn the other. Two members of the Middle Temple were appointed to arrange the first masque, and they were Richard Martin and Sir Edward Phillips. Phillips was admitted to the Middle Temple in 1572, called to the bar in 1578 and made a Bencher in 1596; he was elevated to Serjeant in 1603 (along with John Shurley), elected Speaker of the House of Commons in 1604 and appointed Master of the Rolls in 1611. The masque was an elaborate affair, the words for it being written by George Chapman (the playwright and translator of Homer), and the costumes designed by Inigo Jones. The mounted procession was headed by forty members of the two Inns involved, followed by eight masquers with torch-bearers and pages, and a dozen boys dressed as baboons for the anti-masque. Following them were three chariots full of musicians. Martin was by this time a member of the Council of the Virginia Company and this seems to have been the inspiration for the theme, since the masquers and their companions were dressed as Red Indians. The masque was very well received by the King. In 1615 Martin was appointed Reader in the Middle Temple, and in 1618 Recorder of London. Unfortunately his patron Lionel Cranfield demanded £1,500 as a sign of gratitude for the latter appointment and Martin apparently retired in disgust to his bed never to rise again.[22]

John Davies

In his early days as a student Martin's great friend had been John Davies, who was to have an equally colourful career.[23] He was christened at Tisbury in Wiltshire in 1569. His father was a wealthy tanner, who died when his son was young, but left enough money for John to be educated at Winchester School and the Middle Temple. Davies did not complete his degree at Oxford, but was admitted to the Middle Temple a few months after Martin in February 1588. He was involved with Martin and another friend called Fleetwood in the riots at Candlemas in 1591. In the autumn of that year the three of them travelled together to Holland. Davies seems to have been more assiduous in his studies than Martin, being called to the bar in 1595 after the minimum period for qualification. He was a poet of not inconsiderable quality and in 1596 published his poem entitled *Orchestra or a Poeme of Dauncing*. It was dedicated to Martin, who was described as Davies' dearest friend. Davies appears to have played a prominent part in the Revels of 1597/8, probably being the character Stradilax in the account written by Rudyerd. It is evident from that account that the students had some difficulty raising money to pay for the Revels. Amongst others they wrote to Gilbert Talbot, the Earl of Shrewsbury, asking him to send them money for their extraordinary designs. The Earl noted: 'This Privy Seale beynge brought unto me at X'temas 1597, in respect of the Prince d'Amore's kepinge his Revells in yt In of Courte, I sent him, by the hands of Mr. Davyes of that house £30.'[24] The description given by Rudyerd of Davies' part in the Revels is not altogether complimentary and shortly after they were over it is plain that Davies and Martin had fallen out in a serious way. On 9th February whilst the Benchers and members of Hall were dining, Davies entered the Hall armed with a dagger and accompanied by a servant and a stranger, both armed with swords. He approached Martin where he was dining, took a stick called a 'bastianado' from under his gown and struck Martin three or four times on the head with it until it broke. He then ran from the Hall and down the steps to a boat waiting on the Thames. As a result, the Benchers stripped him of his degree of utter barrister and expelled him from the Inn, ordering that he should never be restored. Davies thereafter applied much energy and skill in an attempt to regain favour with the Royal Court and the Middle Temple. Eventually, despite his original sentence, he succeeded and on 1st November 1601, at the feast for the Serjeants and Judges held on that day, he was formally re-admitted having publicly sought and obtained pardon from his victim.

The wounds from Davies' encounter with Martin in the Hall do not seem to have healed altogether. In Manningham's diary the entry immediately before the one recording the performance of *Twelfth Night* is headed 'Anagram': it reads 'Davis. Advis. Judas (Martin)'. There is a possibility that during the Revels of 1597/8 Davies tried to subvert Martin's role as Prince by stirring up jealousy against him. Davies appears to have been a physically unattractive man. An epigram attributed to Benjamin Rudyerd describes a character called Matho who has a pock-marked face and is so ugly that he does not need a vizard for a masque.[25] It is possible that Matho is Davies.[26] We are on more certain ground when Manningham in his diary describes Davies as 'wadling with his arse out behinde as though he were about to make every one that he meetes, a wall to pisse against ... he never walkes but he carries a clokebag behind him his arse sticks out soe farr.'[27] Manningham attributes this description to either Rudyerd or Overbury. He also recorded that after the accession of James I, Davies 'reports that he is sworne his [the King's] Man, that the K. shewed him greate favors Inepte (He slaunders while he prayses).'[28] When Queen Elizabeth died, Davies had attended, with Lord Hunsdon, upon King James in Scotland. The new king had strong literary interests and was already an admirer of Davies' poetry.[29] He was knighted in 1603 and appointed successively Solicitor-General for Ireland and then Attorney-General for that province. He was a considerable force in Irish politics and in 1626 was made Lord Chief Justice of Ireland, but he died before he could take up office.

John Hoskins

Hoskins, or Hoskyns, shared rooms in the Temple at different times with both Martin and Davies; and he stood surety for John Manningham when he was admitted to the Inn. Hoskins was called to the bar in 1600 and in the same year he married a rich widow. Hoskins was a link between Sir Philip Sidney and the later Elizabethan writers: he published an analysis of Sidney's prose style, and Ben Jonson transcribed a lengthy extract from this in his commonplace book. Between 1598 and 1603, he wrote a book on oratory called *Directions for Speech and Style*. In it he referred in passing to Davies' *Orchestra* and his assault on Martin. Hoskins also says that the reader will find an example of one form of rhetorical address in his speech as Clerk to the Council in the Revels 'alleging that tobacco does not bear responsibility for so many ill results as suggested.'[30] He later entered Parliament as the member for Hereford.[31] He became a hardy defender of the position that the King was subject to Parliament and the Law, and went on to deliver such an abusive attack on the Scottish influence in government that he was imprisoned in the Tower for a year. He was elected Reader in the Middle Temple in 1619 and elevated to Serjeant in 1623, so he must have succeeded in regaining royal favour. He had a high reputation amongst his contemporaries for his writing. According to Aubrey in his *Brief Lives*, Hoskins helped both Ben Jonson and Sir Walter Raleigh polish their work.[32]

John Marston

Marston's home was in Warwick, not far from Stratford upon Avon. John's father became a member of the Middle Temple in 1577 and was appointed Reader in 1592. As a barrister he acted on occasion for the town council of Stratford on Avon.[33] It has already been noted that the two Marstons acted as sureties for Thomas Greene when he was admitted to the Inn in 1595. John Marston junior is recorded as having been admitted to Brasenose College, Oxford, and the Middle Temple in the same year, 1592. As his father was Reader that year, he was specially admitted to the Inn and may well have continued to study at Oxford. Marston senior died in 1599, bequeathing to his son 'my furniture in my chambers in the Middle Temple my law books to my said son whom I hoped would have profited by them in the study of the law but man proposeth and God disposeth.'[34] It must have been clear to the old man that his son did not intend to follow in his footsteps, although Marston junior's writing does show some knowledge of the law. He appears to have continued to live in the Inn and to have been closely associated with it. He wrote some satires called *The Scourge of Villainy*, entered in the Stationers' Register in 1599, in which he satirized members of the Inn.[35]

Marston was a prolific playwright. The first play attributed to him, *Histriomastix*, is referred to by Jonson in *Every Man Out of his Humour* – which means that it must pre-date 1599. It has a cast of 150 which, if it were performed, would have required a large pool of amateur actors, even allowing for doubling. Finkelpearl (in *John Marston of the Middle Temple*) suggests that the play was performed in the Middle Temple, and that one of the characters is intended as a portrait of Jonson. After *Jack Drum's Entertainment*, the *Antonio* plays and *What You Will*, Marston went on to write *The Malcontent*, *Eastwood Hoe* (with Chapman and Jonson), *The Dutch Curtezan*, *The Parasitaster* or *The Fawne* (which Finkelpearl suggests drew on material in the Middle Temple Revels of 1597/8),[36] and *Sophonisba*. Marston's satire was to get him into serious trouble, for Archbishop Whitgift ordered that *The Scourge of Villainy* be burnt in 1601. He must have considered it prurient or corrupting, though Davenport[37] in his edition of Marston's poems and Finkelpearl[38] put forward a case that Marston's satires were written from a genuinely Calvinistic standpoint. His later plays seem to have caused offence to James I. On 29th June 1608 the king ordered the closure of all the theatres because he was incensed by two plays satirizing him. On 8th June 1608 Marston had been committed by the Privy Council to Newgate.[39] The two incidents are likely to have

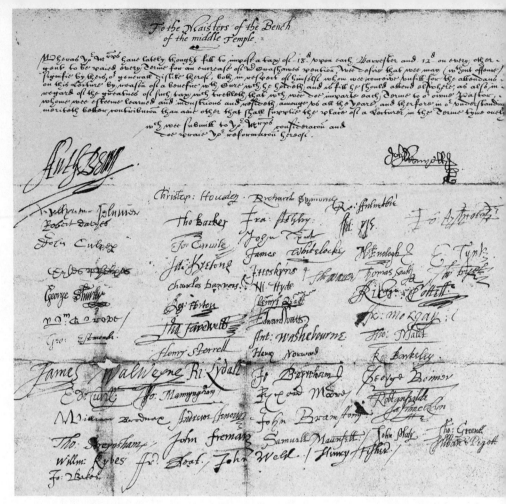

Petition sent by members of the Middle Temple to the Masters of the Bench in 1609 protesting about a tax imposed by the Bench to increase the pension of the Master of the Temple Church. The signatories include John Manningham, Thomas Greene, John Hoskins (Hoskyns), George Shurley and Edward Curle

been linked. The probable cause of royal displeasure is a portrait in *The Parasitaster* of Don Gonzago, Duke of Urbino, which was taken as a satire of the king.[40] After that, Marston seems to have given up the theatre and gone into the Church.[41] Whatever the authorities thought, Marston appears to have been highly regarded by his contemporaries.[42] An edict of the Prince d'Amour in the Revels of 1636 names Shakespeare and Marston in the same breath.

Henry Wotton, Thomas Bastard, Everard Gilpin

Three other personalities in this circle deserve a passing reference. Henry Wotton was a contemporary of Hoskins and Thomas Bastard at both Winchester and New College, Oxford.[43] Wotton was admitted to the Middle

Temple in 1595. By then he had already travelled widely on the continent of Europe, particularly in Italy, and he continued to do so. He became secretary to Essex in 1595 and went on various foreign embassies for the Earl. There is no evidence that he was involved in the Essex rebellion, but thereafter he found it prudent to go abroad. He was to gain royal favour when James ascended the throne, and in 1604 became Ambassador to Venice. He fell out of favour when the King learnt of his well-known jibe that an ambassador is an honest man sent abroad to lie for his country. Hoskins in his *Direcions for Speech and Style* described him as 'the noble studious Henry Wotton'. Wotton corresponded with John Donne with whom he was good friends from Oxford days.

Thomas Bastard was the one member of this circle not to join an Inn of Court. He went to Winchester in 1581 and to New College in 1586. He is chiefly important in that the satiric poems he wrote at Oxford feature some of the pseudonyms used by the Inns of Court wits, of which more in due course. Everard Gilpin, on the other hand, was a Cambridge man, who entered Emmanuel College in 1587, at virtually the same time as William Strachey. He was to join Gray's Inn in 1591. In 1592 his uncle married Marston's mother and in 1606 Gilpin himself married Marston's cousin.[44] The connection between the two men is reinforced by Gilpin's poem called *Skialetheia or A Shadowe of Truth*, published in 1598, for this work resembles Marston's *Scourge of Villainy* in its attacks on contemporaries under the cloak of pseudonyms. A contemporary writer, Sir John Harington, acknowledges that while these pseudonyms gave anonymity, 'who gat some of them may soone be guest.'[45] He also points out that the epigrams are pilfered from Martial.

Benjamin Rudyerd

Benjamin Rudyerd like Hoskins was called to the Bar in 1600. Much later these two also fell out and fought a duel. Rudyerd was knighted in 1618 and he was a Member of Parliament from 1620 to 1648, making a considerable contribution to debates in that crucial period of political history.[46] Jonson composed three epigrams about him.[47] In the first he wrote

Rudyerd, as lesser dames to great ones use,
My lighter comes to kiss thy learned muse.

Sir Walter Raleigh

Writing some sixty years after these events, John Aubrey spoke of a club of wits and heroes meeting at the Mermaid with Sir Walter Raleigh as one of that sodality. Aubrey has his critics, but at least he did have good second-hand sources. His grandfather had been a friend of Sir Carew Raleigh, the brother of Sir Walter, and Aubrey himself had met Raleigh's grand-children.[48] Aubrey was a member of the Middle Temple, and was close friends with the grandson of John Hoskins.[49] It has been objected that someone of Raleigh's standing would not have been found in a tavern. Jonson in *The Devil is an Ass*, however, wrote:

> ... eating
> Pheasant and godwit here in London, haunting
> The Globes and Mermaids, wedging in with lords
> Still at the table.[50]

suggesting that the aristocracy were to be found in taverns. A commonplace book dated to between 1621 and 1635[51] records the speech made by Hoskins as Clerk to the Council in the Revels of 1597/8, and an additional handwritten note states that it was Raleigh who challenged him to perform it ex tempore. The speech alludes more than once to tobacco. He quotes the soap-maker of Holborn Bridge as saying that he sees 'no reason why men should addict themselves to tobacco in Ramus method', and goes on to

> examine the comploots of Politicians from the beginning of the world to this day; What was the cause of the repentine mutiny in Scipio's camp? it is most evident it was not tabacco. What was the cause of the Aventine revolt and seditious deprecation for a Tribune? It is apparent it was not Tabacco. What was it moved me to address this Expostulation to your iniquity? It is plaine it is not Tabacco. So that to conclude, Tabacco is not guilty of so many faults as it is charged withal.

In the course of the speech the Orator (a separate character) proceeded to smoke tobacco, but then to deny that he had. Given Raleigh's connection with tobacco, this would be a suitable riposte to Raleigh's intervention. It looks as if Aubrey was right.

To date the only direct evidence of the meetings of the Mermaid Club has come from Coryate's writings. These placed the meetings around 1610. The reference to the Mermaid and Mitre taverns in the Revels of 1597/8, together with their description in literature in the early 1600s and now the connection with Raleigh at the time of those revels, all serve to put back the use of the Mermaid tavern as a place of literary resort by over ten years.

It has already been noted in passing, that in the poems they wrote these young men used classical nicknames for one another. The next chapter investigates the messages Shakespeare conveyed in the names used for the characters in *Twelfth Night* and reveals that the nicknames of two prominent students in the Middle Temple appear as names in the play.

Richard Martin (1570–1618), who was Prince of Love in the Revels of 1597/8: the memorial to him in the Temple Church. *Photograph by Christopher Christodoulou*

2 Edmund Plowden (1518–85),
Treasurer of the Middle Temple,
who was in charge of the
building of the Hall, 1562–73:
the memorial to him in the
Temple Church (*bottom*), and
a detail of the memorial (*top*).
*Photographs by Christopher
Christodoulou*

3 Robert Sherley (*c.*1582–1628), 'Fencer to the Sophy', painted in Rome by
Van Dyck, in 1622. *Petworth House, Sussex: reproduced by kind permission
of the National Trust Photographic Library/Roy Fox*

4 Isfield Place, Sussex, birthplace of John Shurley (*c.*1548–1618),
   Treasurer of the Middle Temple in 1602 (*top*).
   The Shurley family arms on Isfield Place (*bottom*).
   *Photographs by Christopher Christodoulou; reproduced by kind
   permission of Mr and Mrs Tillard*

5 Wiston House, Sussex, the home of Robert and Anthony Sherley,
   who both went on an expedition to the Shah of Persia in 1599 (*top*).
   The double hammer-beam roof at Wiston (*bottom*).
   *Photographs by Christopher Christodoulou; reproduced by kind
   permission of Harry Goring*

6 Staples Inn in High Holborn, London, which was attended by Thomas Greene
(d.1641) before his entry to the Middle Temple in 1592 (*top*).
Photograph by Christopher Christodoulou
The screen in Middle Temple Hall (*bottom*)

7 Middle Temple Hall (*top*).
Revellers in the Revels of 1597/8, as performed in 1998: (*bottom left*) the author
as the Lord Admiral; (*bottom right*) Paul Ansdell as the Prince of Love.
Photographs by Tracy Ayling

8 Coats of arms in Middle Temple Hall:
(*top left*) John Hoskins; (*top right*) Richard
Martin; (*bottom left*) John Shurley 1;
(*bottom right*) Thomas Greene.
Photographs by Christopher Christodoulou

CHAPTER SEVEN

What's in a Name?

THE NAMES IN THE PLAY

Illyria

Shakespeare is playing games with names from the beginning of *Twelfth Night*, teasing his audience with ambiguous references. We have seen that the title itself suggests Christmas festivities and yet is given to a play that does not refer to Christmas at all. At her first entrance Viola establishes the place of her shipwreck, and then puns upon it:

> What should I do in Illyria?
> My brother he is in Elysium.[1]

The lyrical sound of the name at once evokes a place where 'heaven walks on earth'.[2] The educated Elizabethan would have read another message into it. The Illyrians were originally a group of Indo-European tribes who occupied the Balkan Adriatic coast.[3] Their name was used to define a stretch of territory in what would now be part of Croatia and Bosnia. They were famous for drunken disorder; indeed the Italian slang for a drunkard was an 'Illyrian'.[4] They fought fiercely amongst themselves and against others and were particularly known for being pirates. Antonio, the sea-captain who rescues Sebastian, has fought in a sea-battle against Orsino's ships,[5] and Orsino describes him as a notable pirate and salt-water thief.[6] So Illyria is a perfect setting both for the drunken revels of Sir Toby and his friends and for the catastrophic arrival of Sebastian and Antonio.

The unnamed capital of Illyria, where the action occurs, is at once Dubrovnik, Urbino and London. Illyria is a Balkan name with, perhaps, a hint of the mysterious and the dangerous. The courtly manners and the Italian names of the characters suggest an Italian Renaissance court. The men's names are Italianized by the addition of an 'o' – Orsino, Antonio, Curio, Malvolio – and the women's by an 'a' – Olivia, Viola, Maria. A similar device was used in the Middle Temple Revels of 1597/8 when Richard Martin's name was changed to Sir Martino. In earlier plays Shakespeare had used Italy as the land of love.

Yet the play is just as clearly set in London's new West End. The Middle Temple Hall was situated outside the City walls on the edge of a rich suburb running along the dry 'strand' between Temple Bar and the royal courts at Whitehall. The Earl of Essex's house (formerly belonging to the Earl of Leicester) was immediately adjacent to the Inn. His name is commemorated in Essex Street, as other noble names are in Southampton and Bedford Rows, Somerset House and the Savoy. Those journeying from the City or Temple stairs to the royal court at Whitehall would travel by boat and the boatmen would call out 'westward ho!' to indicate their direction – Viola makes the same comment as she leaves Olivia's house for the Duke's court.[7] So the map of the Illyrian capital would have resembled this new western suburb. London's theatre district was then in the South End on the opposite side of the river, outside the City boundaries: a good place to lodge or work if you had enemies in the City. In that area there was a tavern called the Elephant. When Antonio and Sebastian arrive in the Illyrian capital, Antonio arranges that they should stay at the Elephant in the south suburbs.[8]

Anagrams

It is also clear that Shakespeare is playing games with near anagrams and riddles.[9] Olivia and Viola are near anagrams. Malvolio contains almost the same letters, and anagrammatic comparisons have been suggested in Orsino and Cesario too. When the gulling letter is left in Malvolio's path, it purports to identify Olivia's 'lover' by the initials 'M O A I'. Fabian describes this as a 'fustian' or rough riddle.[10] Malvolio is unable to solve the riddle, though the audience can see the tease. The similarity between the names Olivia and Viola reflects the similarity in their state. Each has been recently bereaved and is now alone in the world. Each loves one who is not available. Both of them are constant despite the hopelessness of their love. It has even been suggested that they are intended to be seen as one person, Viola being a symptom of Olivia's self-reflexive love.[11] Maybe this is simply part of the confusion which has been created deliberately at the heart of the play, whilst pointing to a unity, which will be achieved in the end.

Orsino

The play contains allusions to people whom the original audience would have recognized. Mention has already been made of William Strachey and Edward Kirkham, the Shurley brothers and William Barentz, the explorer. In the next chapter reference will be made to Mary Fitton, the Queen's gentlewoman, and to William Knollys. The importance of Orsino's name is stressed at the beginning of the play when the Captain informs Viola that he is a 'noble Duke in nature as in *name*'. The family of Orsini or Ursini were famous both as soldiers and as high clerics, and these occupations had enabled them to amass considerable wealth.[12] Their fine Gothic castle lies just to the north of Rome. In 1469 one of Virginio's forbears, Clarice Orsini, married a Medici called Lorenzo who was to become Lorenzo the Magnificent,[13] head of the Florentine government. Not only was he an adroit politician and soldier, but also a poet and patron of learning and the arts.[14] He patronized Botticelli and Leonardo Da Vinci and took the teen-age Michelangelo to live and sculpt in his palace. Clarice Orsini was a link to the zenith of the Renaissance.

In 1587 a later Medici became Ferdinando I, Duke of Florence. His sister Isabella had married Paolo Orsini; and their son was Don Virginio. Paolo soon fell in love with a young married noblewoman called Vittoria Accoramboni. In order that they could be together, they murdered their spouses. They then fled from Rome, but Paolo died soon afterwards and Vittoria was murdered in revenge. These events were notorious in Europe and inspired John Webster to write *The White Devil*. Duke Ferdinando took the young Virginio with him to Florence and brought him up as a son. Although by the sixteenth century the wealth and power of Florence had waned significantly, it still set European fashion.[15] Ferdinando spent large sums of money on the Pitti Palace, across the Arno, where the family now lived and also on the Boboli gardens which surround it. He bought rare manuscripts for the Medici library. He was also a great patron of the theatre and music, staging elaborate pageants and plays. Virginio would have arrived in London trailing clouds of Medici glory.

He was twenty-eight at the time of the visit.[16] His portrait, still in the possession of his family, shows him as a handsome dark-haired man. At the age of sixteen the Venetian Ambassador to Florence had described him thus:

> He has every grace, is ingenious, and discourses well on all subjects; apt to apply himself and succeed in any profession, especially in the military to which it would seem he is pointing himself; to the which there appears no other obstacle than a delicate constitution and a slender body which seem unfitted to support great fatigue ... yet he rides well.[17]

He had fought bravely against the Turks and had eventually been wounded in an unsuccessful expedition to capture the island of Chios.[18] An allusion to his name would immediately have produced a picture of the perfect Renaissance prince. The name Orsini is derived from the word for 'bear'. In the sixteenth century the bear was associated with melancholy,[19] which might reflect Duke Orsino's mood at the beginning of the play.

Viola, Olivia, Maria

What is more, the flower violet was considered to be a cure for melancholy.[20] The name 'Violet' was not, however, used in Elizabethan times as a girl's name. That tradition only started in the nineteenth century.[21] The name Viola (which is the Latin for the flower) seems to have been used as a name for the first time by Shakespeare – it appears in none of the sources and nowhere in contemporary literature. In his opening speech, when he suggests that music is the food of love, Orsino comments:

> That strain again! It had a dying fall.
> O, it came o'er my ear like the sweet sound
> That breathes upon a bank of *violets*,
> Stealing and giving odour.[22]

Shakespeare uses a similar image of the violet giving and taking in Sonnet 99. The name also has musical connotations. Viola suggests to the sea-captain a method of introducing her to Orsino's court:

> Thou shalt present me as an eunuch to him.
> It may be worth thy pains, for I can sing
> And speak to him in many sorts of music.[23]

It may be that Shakespeare originally intended her to be one of the singers, but later changed his mind.

Olivia was an Italian name.[24] The olive branch, of course, traditionally symbolizes peace. At the opening of the play Olivia has withdrawn from the world, and it is this peaceful image which prompts Viola to think that she would like to serve the lady.[25] When she first arrives at Olivia's on Orsino's embassy, Viola says:

> I bring no overture of war, no taxation of homage: I hold the *olive* in my hand; my words are as full of peace as matter.[26]

Olivia in fact does act as a peacemaker on occasion, for instance between Malvolio and Feste.

The remaining female name, Maria, was the Italian form of Mary. It is a basic, sensible-sounding name. Shakespeare had already used it for one of the Princess of France's waiting ladies in *Love's Labour's Lost*. Her character is not dissimilar to Maria in *Twelfth Night*, being quick-witted and humorous, but with her feet firmly on the ground.

The Comic Characters

The Italian tradition is continued with the name Feste. Apart from its connection with festivity, the name may also echo the Latin 'festinus' which connoted quick movement. Malvolio is a contraction of 'mala voglio' – Italian for 'I wish evil'. In the Folio edition it is actually spelt Malvoglio. This is not the first time that Shakespeare had indulged in such word play. Romeo's best friend is Benvolio – 'bene voglio', 'I wish good or well'; while the hero of *Much Ado About Nothing* is Benedick.

When it comes to low comedy in *Twelfth Night* the names are firmly English, in the same way that the very English constable Dogberry obtrudes into *Much Ado About Nothing*. There is nothing continental about Toby Belch and Andrew Aguecheek. The name Toby sounds full and rounded. The Toby jug depicts a fat man. Belch bespeaks the character's vulgarity and over-indulgence. It has been suggested that Andrew is a reference to the clown's name of Merry Andrew, but others have doubted whether this was in use at the time; the name can also convey courage, which would be ironic in view of the surname. For Aguecheek denotes cowardliness, which he constantly exhibits, and perhaps thinness. The two men represent a classic comic combination, the fat man and the thin man – Laurel and Hardy, Abbott and Costello, Little and Large. As is usually the case, the fat man is knowing and the thin man is the fool. It is important to note, however, that they are both knights. Sir Toby is the uncle of the Countess Olivia. Some of the young men in the Inns of Court would be knights themselves, and many the sons of knights. The Judges and some of the Serjeants would also hold that rank. The figure of the scion of a noble line fallen into over-indulgence or stupidity would be familiar and an obvious target for satire. These characters may also have had their origins in earlier Shakespearean characters. Sir Toby bears some resemblance to Sir John Falstaff and Aguecheek to Slender in *The Merry Wives of Windsor*.

Fabian and Curio

It remains to consider the names of the minor characters. That of Valentine is an obvious reference to the patron saint of love, an apt servant for Orsino who is so devoted to that cause. Cesario is probably a reference to Caesar, since Viola in her male guise conquers hearts, both Olivia's and Orsino's. Sebastian and Fabian are anglicized forms of Latin names. Sebastian was a soldier martyred by his fellows for his beliefs.[27] In Renaissance paintings he is generally portrayed as a handsome young man, which fits the dramatic effect he has on Olivia. Fabian is the English for Fabius. Quintus Fabius Maximus Verrucosus Cunctator was a Roman consul who fought against Hannibal.[28] After the Carthaginians had decisively defeated the Roman armies at the battles of Lake Trasimene (217 BC) and Cannae (216 BC), he was elected dictator. He took charge of the campaign, but his tactic was to avoid battles with Hannibal's armies and harass them, taking particular advantage of their extended supply lines. Hence his title of Cunctator or 'delayer' and the credit he is generally given for inventing guerrilla tactics. In *Twelfth Night* Fabian's part in the plot against Malvolio might make such a name apt. The name also meant roisterer. Yet on the face of it, there is something odd about the character. Fabian appears to have replaced Feste in the letter scene. Maria when planning to drop the forged letter in Malvolio's way says to Sir Toby and Sir Andrew: 'I will plant you two, and let the fool make a third, where he shall find the letter.'[29] When the scene occurs, Feste is absent and instead the new character, Fabian, arrives completely unannounced. All we learn about him is that he is called Signor Fabian and that Malvolio made trouble for him with Olivia about a bear-baiting. He is described in the dramatis personae as a member of Olivia's household. Even if Shakespeare had wanted for some reason to replace Feste in the letter scene, he could easily have used Maria. She drops the letter in Malvolio's way. Her only line thereafter is at the end of the scene, when she enquires what has happened. She must therefore have left and returned, but neither action is recorded. All this points to some last minute rewriting. It is also curious that he is called Signor Fabian. Fabian was an anglicization of either the Latin Fabius or the Italian Fabio. In the most obvious source document for the play, *Apolonius and Silla*, the heroine adopts the male pseudonym of Fabio, so that Shakespeare must have known of it. If Signor is used, why not Fabio?

At first sight the derivation of the name Curio is even more puzzling. If every other name has significance, what is the origin of this rather obscure name? There were in fact two well-known Curios in classical times.[30] They were father and son. The father lived from about 100 BC to 53 BC. His full name was Gaius Scribonius Curio. He was a lawyer, politician and soldier who opposed Caesar. His son, who bore the same name, died in battle in 49 BC, but his birth date is unknown. He followed the same professions as his father. Both men were supporters of Clodius. Curio junior's greatest claim to fame, however, was his friendship with Cicero, whom he loyally supported whilst Cicero was in exile. Cicero wrote letters to him, some of which are preserved in the collection of Cicero's letters to his friends (*Ad Familiares*). They demonstrate the closeness of their friendship, but reveal little of Curio's character. So why did Shakespeare use this name derived from a rather shadowy Roman?

STUDENT NICKNAMES

The Satires

The answer seems to lie in the epigrams and satires of the young men of the Inns of Court, where they frequently gave one another Latin nicknames, many of them uncomplimentary. In the 1580s and early 1590s Cambridge

University wits such as Nashe and Greene indulged in satiric attacks on their contemporaries; Greene in particular attacked Shakespeare in his *Groatesworth of Wit*. In the same period a group of students arrived in the Middle Temple who had passed through Winchester School and Oxford. John Davies, John Hoskins and Henry Wotton were all educated there, as we have seen, as were two other writers of epigrams who went to Oxford, Thomas Bastard and John Owen, the latter going on to the Inner Temple. The education at Winchester was rigorously classical.[31] One of the schoolmasters in the 1560s ordered that both at work and at play Latin should be used:

> When the boys comme to school and when they return home, when they play together, when they walk together, whenever they meet, let their speech be Latin or Greek. Let there be no place for lenience if anyone offends against this criminally.[32]

The boys wrote their own Latin prose and verse. Cicero was recommended as a model and the epigrams of Martial were used as the basis for exercises. At Oxford they entertained their contemporaries with epigrams and satires on the classical model, but written in English. They used Latin pseudonyms or nicknames for the objects of their attacks, but these were sufficiently obvious to get some of them into trouble. Hoskins' satires got him into such trouble with the University authorities that he had to leave the University before he had graduated and Bastard, though he obtained a Fellowship, had to resign it and retired to become a clergyman. Their style was followed by others who had not been at Winchester, such as Marston and Donne, both of whom went to Oxford, and Gilpin, who went to Cambridge. It is also found in the Parnassus Plays performed at Cambridge in 1598–1601. The same nicknames for those attacked recur in the writings of more than one author. Thus Davies and Marston both write of Philo and Rufus; Gilpin and Davies speak of Titus, Faustus and Paulus; Donne writes of Philo and Faustus. Rudyerd, Gilpin and Bastard all speak of Matho: Gilpin in his Epigram 20 describes Matho as the English Martial, and Rudyerd refers to him as if he had been called early to the bar. As Davies was probably the best of these writers and in fact was called to the bar earlier than his contemporaries, it has been suggested that he was Matho, as has been mentioned.[33] The identification of individuals is bound to be speculative, but, whatever the target aimed at, these Latin names were intended to poke fun at contemporaries in the Inns. In classical times, for instance, Matho had been described by Juvenal as a rich speculator who went bankrupt. Another name that appears is Tuscus, probably a reference to a Roman street called Tuscus Vicus, which was known as a haunt of prostitutes; and Luxurio also appeared bearing a similar innuendo.

In the script of the 1597/8 Revels there are frequent classical allusions. It has already been noted that at Candlemas the Prince gave his resignation to the *optimates*. The earlier Optimates were a self-perpetuating oligarchy of Romans who regarded themselves as morally and socially superior to their fellows and so more fit for government. They are encountered as far back as the second century BC, but Cicero tried to redefine their ideal of an elite in a morally acceptable way.[34] To describe the young men who surrounded the Prince of Love as *optimates* was obviously flattering.

Rudyerd's text also refers to Fabricius Spurtus. In Rome there had been a Fabricius Luscinus, who was a hero of the war with Pyrrhus in 280 BC. He was famous for his incorruptibility and was cited by Cicero as a model Roman citizen. It has been noted that one of the prominent characters in the revels is Stradilax of Milochius or Milorsius. The latter titles are probably a reference to Milo, the theme of Cicero's *Pro Milone*, and an opponent of Clodius. As we have seen, the real-life Curios were Clodians, and Clodius features as a nickname in many of the students' satires in the Inns of Court. Milochius might be the equivalent of Milochean, Milorsius or Milorsian, all of them meaning 'of Milo's party'. The satires reveal a good deal of jealousy between the students. Rudyerd's account of the Revels makes it clear that Stradilax practised against the Prince and stirred up enmity between him and the members of Lincoln's Inn. Throughout this account, Stradilax's contributions to the Revels are portrayed as a dismal failure. Such antagonism would be comparable to that between Milo and Clodius.

Curio

In the satires and epigrams written by the students, the nicknames which occur most frequently are Curio and Fabian. The former's obsession seems to have been with love and dancing. In his *Third Satire*, for instance, Marston writes:

> Shall Curio streake his lims on his days couch
> In Sommer bower? And with bare groping touch
> Incense his lust, consuming all the yeere
> In Cyrian dalliance, and in Belgick cheere.

Later, he has a whole satire to himself entitled *Curio Inamorato*. It is directed at both Curio and other young men who in the Marston's view make themselves ridiculous in love:

> Curio, aye mee! thy mistres Monkey's dead,
> Alas, alas, her pleasures buried.
> Goe womans slave, performe his exequies,
> Condole his death in mournfull Elegies ...
> Some puling Sonnet toles his passing knell,
> Some sighing Elegie must ring his knell.

In Marston's second book of satires there is one addressed *Ad Rithmum*, the rhythm of music, poetry and dancing. Curio is revealed as a skilful dancer:

> Come pretty pleasing symphonie of words
> Ye wel-matcht twins (whose like tun'd tongs affords
> Such musicall delight) come willingly
> And dance Levolties[35] in my poesie
> Come all as easie as spruce Curio will
> In some Courte hall to showe his capring skill.
> As willingly, come meete and jumpe together,
> As new joyn'd loves, when they do clip each other.
> As willingly, as wenches trip a round
> About the May-pole, after bagpipes sound.
> Come riming numbers, come and grace conceite,
> Adding a pleasing close, with your deceit
> Inticing years. Let not my ruder hand
> Seeme once to force you in my lines to stand,
> Be not so fearful (pretty soules) to meete,
> As Flaccus is the Sergeants face to greete.

The reference to the court hall and the Serjeant ties this passage to an Inn of Court. Marston treats the same theme in his *Tenth Satire* entitled *Humours*:

> Whoever heard spruce skipping Curio
> Ere prate of ought, but of the whirle on toe,
> The turne above ground, Robrus sprauling kicks,
> Fabius caper, Harries tossing tricks?
> Did ever any eare ere heare him speake
> Unless his tongue of cross poynts did intreat?
> His teeth doe caper, whilst he eates his meate,
> His heels doe caper whilst he takes his seate,
> His very soule, his intellectuall
> Is nothing but a mincing capreall.
> He dreams of toe turnes: each gallant hee dooth meete,
> He fronts him with a travers in the streete.
> Prayse but Orchestra, and the skipping art
> You shall command him, faith you have his hart
> Even capring in your fist. A hall, a hall
> Room for the Spheres, the Orbes celestiall
> Will daunce Kemps Jigge. They'll revel with neate jumps
> A worthy Poet hath put on their pumps.
> O wit's quick traverse, sance ceo's slow
> Good faith 'tis hard for nimble Curio.

This passage can be connected to the Middle Temple by (i) Marston's

94 WHAT'S IN A NAME?

membership of the Inn, (ii) the reference to a hall large enough to accommodate the spheres – the Middle Temple Hall was the largest in the Inns – and (iii) the specific reference to John Davies' poem *Orchestra*. 'Kemp's Jigge' is a reference to the dance composed by the chief comedian of the Lord Chamberlain's Men up to 1599, who was famous for his jigs.

John Davies also describes Curio in an epigram, showing him to be a man prepared to change his religion in order to secure social advancement;[36] and Gilpin attacks Curio in an epigram too:

> Curio threats my death in an Epigrame
> Yfayth hee'le eate his word, he's to blame
> And yet I think hee'le write; then ware of bleeding,
> Nay fear not, he writes nothing worth the reading.

Fabian

An even more popular target was a young man variously called Faber, Fabius and more particularly Fabian. We have seen Marston refer to him in passing in *Ad Rithmum*, as a good dancer. He also appears in Marston's *First Satire* as having a perpetuall golden coat and as someone who

> Hath been at feasts and led the measuring
> At Court.

In his *Fourth Satire* he puts one of the themes of the poem in his mouth:

> To morrow doth Luxurio promise me
> He will unline himselfe from bitcherie.
> Marry Alcides thirteenth act must lead
> A glorious period, and his lust-itch end.
> When once he hath foaming Aetna past
> At one and thirty being alwayes last.
> If not today (quoth that Nasonian)
> Much lesse to morrowe. Yes, saith Fabian,
> For ingrained Habites, died with often dips
> Are not so soone discoloured, young slips
> New set, are easily mov'd and pluck'd away
> But elder rootes, clip faster in the clay.

Gilpin makes even more frequent mention of him. Thus his *Sixth Epigram* reads:

> Since marriage, Faber's prouder than before
> Yfaith his wife must take him a hole lower.

The *Third Satire* is largely devoted to Fabian.

How like a musherom are thou quickly growne.
I knew thee when thou war'dst a thred-bare gowne
Siz'd eighteene pence a weeke, and so did I
As then thou wert faine my company,
Of mine acquaintance glad; how art thou alter'd?
Of wherein's thine estate so bettered.
Thou art growne a silken dancer and that
Turn'd to a caper, skipst from love to hate,
To daunce Ma pin, French galliard, or a measure,
Dost thou esteeme this cunning such a treasure?
Never be proud of that for dost thou know
That Laureat Batchelor Del Phriggio
He with a spade-beard can full mannerly
Leade the olde measures to a company
Of bare chinn'd boyes and with his nimble feete
Make our fore wearied Counseloures to sweat
For envie at his strange activities,
Because they cannot do't well as he.
But then a simple reveller thou art more ...
Thou hast had some doings with the Prince D'Amour
And play'd a noble man's part in a play.
Now out upon thee Fabian, I dare say,
If Florus should alledge that cause of pride
Hisse him thou wouldst to death for it and beside
Thou mightst have had som doings with that prince
Which wold have made thee less proude ever since.
Yet art thou stately, and so stately lo
That thou forget'st thy state and wilt not know
Them which knowe thee and it: so long thou has
True follower beene of fashions, that at last
Thou art growne thyself a fashion ...
These foolish toyes have quite disparaged
Philosophy thy mistris, and 'tis said
Thou art like to Damasippus for thy hayre
Precisely cut makes thee Philosopher
And nothing God wot else.

It is clear from these descriptions that Fabian and Curio were members of the Inns of Court and took part in Christmas Revels. Since the most recent Revels had been in the Middle Temple in 1597/8, and the poems were published in 1598 and 1599, it seems likely that it is these that are referred to. As Marston and Gilpin were related by marriage, they would have had friends in each other's Inns; and as Marston's family had been important in the Middle Temple before he joined it, Gilpin may have been drawn there.

Gilpin refers to his having known Fabian when he had a threadbare gown. Finkelpearl in *John Marston of the Middle Temple* takes this to mean that he was at Cambridge with Gilpin, where the latter indicates he was a relatively poor exhibitioner. The text does not say, however, that this was at Cambridge and members of the Inns of Court also wore gowns. What is more, reference to Davies' poem *Orchestra* seems to link these young men to the Middle Temple.

As Shakespeare picks his names with care in *Twelfth Night*, it would be an extraordinary coincidence if, in a play concerned with revelling, he had picked these two names at random. The most likely explanation is that he knew both the poems quoted and the people who were satirized in them, and he chose the names as a deliberate joke. The apparently late addition of Fabian to the plot, then makes better sense. It may also be noteworthy that the names of other minor characters such as Maria, Valentine, Sebastian and Antonio, appear elsewhere in the Shakespeare canon, whereas Fabian and Curio do not. It has already been noted that Fabian makes some legal jokes in the play.[37] Curio's character on the other hand is sketchy, but his first lines involve a pun on the heart:

> CURIO: Will you go hunt, my lord?
> ORSINO: What Curio?
> CURIO: The hart.[38]

If a 'Curio' in the Middle Temple had been known as an obsessive lover, as the satires indicate, this would have raised an easy laugh. Given the strong amateur acting tradition in the Inns, it could even have been that as a special compliment to the Middle Temple, these two young men were allowed to act in the performance of *Twelfth Night*. On 8th February 1602 Lord Chief Justice Popham wrote to Sir Robert Cecil about an entertainment that had been planned for the Queen:

> I have so dealt with some of the Benchers of the Middle Temple as I have brought that the House will be willing to bear 200 marks towards the charge of what is wished to be done, to Her Majesty's good liking and if the young gentlemen will be drawn into play what is their part, I hope it will be effected. Some of the young men have their humours, but I hope it will be overruled.[39]

The young men's part must have been as performers.

It remains to consider the direct sources for the play and some of the background to the character of Malvolio.

CHAPTER EIGHT

Sources

THE ITALIAN CONNECTION

Manningham names two sources for *Twelfth Night* as *The Menechmi* of
Plautus and *Inganni*, a near contemporary Italian play.[1] The second is
interesting inasmuch as it was not translated into English. A translation of
The Menechmi was published in London in 1595, though Shakespeare
appears to have known of it before that date when he wrote *The Comedy of
Errors*. The preface to the 1595 translation summarized the plot thus:

> Two twinborne sonnes, a Sicill marchant had,
> Menechmus one, and Sosciles the other.
> The first his Father lost a little had,
> The Grandsire namde the latter like his brother.
> This (growne a man) long travell tooke to seeke
> His brother, and to Epidamnum came
> Where th'other dwelt inricht, and him so like,
> That citizens ther take him for the same:
> Father, wife, neighbours each mistaking either,
> Much pleasant error, ere they meet togither.

The play is an accepted source for *The Comedy of Errors*, which was probably written in 1594, the plot turning on the confusion caused by twin
brothers and servants.

A number of Italian Renaissance plays developed drama from mis-
identification and gender inversion. *Gl'Inganni* ('the deceits') by Nicolo
Secchi was first performed in Milan in 1547. A merchant of Genoa takes his
son Fortunato and daughter Soria on a sea voyage, dressing the girl in male
attire for her protection. They are seized by pirates. Both mother and
daughter end up in Naples where the latter goes a step further and adopts
a male identity (Ruberto) to preserve her virginity. They are protected by a
gentleman of the city whose daughter Portia, sad to say, falls in love with
Ruberto/Soria. Meanwhile Fortunato also reaches Naples and is discovered
there by Soria. She substitutes Fortunato, who closely resembles her, for herself and he makes Portia pregnant. After further vicissitudes all is happily

resolved. There is no record of the play being translated into English or performed in England. In 1592 Curzio Gonzaga wrote a new version of it, in which the male soubriquet adopted by the heroine was Cesare, which is at least a curious coincidence.

There is another play of a similar name, which bears an even closer resemblance to the plot of *Twelfth Night*. *Gl'Ingannati* ('the deceived') was first performed in Siena in 1531 as part of the pre-Lenten carnival celebrations of a society of young men, who described themselves as thunderstruck with love. It was preceded by a sacrifice of love in which each member contributed a prized token from his mistress – note that the Middle Temple Revels of 1597/8 also included a sacrifice of love. The play has two references to Twelfth Night. The prologue states that 'the story is new and taken from nowhere but their own industrious heads from which your lots at Twelfth Night are taken.' It was the Italian custom at Epiphany to give presents, which were drawn in a lucky dip. Elsewhere in the text, one of the characters speaks of disturbing omens. Her master comments: 'What are you doing, talking like this to yourself. Twelfth Night is over.' These references are not significant enough to forge a connection with Shakespeare, but they do serve to identify the carnival elements in the play, which include disguise and cross-dressing. The play is set in Modena, in Lombardy. A rich man Virginio loses his son Fabrizio in the sack of Rome, which had occurred in 1527. He takes his daughter Lelia to Modena where she falls in love with Flamminio. At first he returns her affections, but he then transfers his love to Isabella. In order to pursue her love for him, Lelia disguises herself as a page (Fabio) and enters Flamminio's service. He employs her to carry messages of love to Isabella. Isabella, of course, immediately falls in love with Fabio. Fabrizio, who is still alive, then turns up unexpectedly in Modena and Isabella confuses him with Fabio/Lelia. Again all ends happily with Isabella marrying Fabrizio, and Lelia marrying Flamminio. There is a lengthy sub-plot in which an elderly suitor Gherardo tries to contract a marriage to Lelia and other characters conspire to stop him. There is also an eavesdropping scene in which two servants hear Isabella inviting Fabio/Lelia to come to her house when her father is out. The obvious resemblances between the texts of the romantic plot in this work and *Twelfth Night* do not prove that Shakespeare was definitely familiar with the work. As with *Gl'Inganni*, there is no record of an English translation of this play, nor of any performance of it in England, although a Latin version called *Lelia* was performed in Cambridge in 1595.

All the same there was an English prose work which clearly drew on this tradition and which Shakespeare almost certainly did know about. This is Barnabe Riche's *Farewell to Militarie Profession*, which was first published in 1581 and possibly reprinted in 1591, when it was entered in the Stationers' Register. He described his work as a collection of 'pleasaunt discourses fit for a peaceable tyme gathered together for the only delight of the courteous Gentlewomen bothe of England and Irelande.' One of the stories is that of Apolonius and Silla. A young duke called Apolonius lives in Constantinople. Returning from war against the Turks, he stops in Cyprus, where Silla, the daughter of the governor, falls in love with him. Unaware of this, he returns to Constantinople. She follows him by sea and is saved from rape at the hands of the vessel's captain when they suffer shipwreck; she loses her manservant in the wreck, but reaches land herself. She too adopts male attire and takes her brother's name, Silvio. She enters the service of Apolonius, who in the meantime has begun to court a rich widow called Julina (perhaps Manningham's error in describing Olivia as a widow sprang from his acquaintance with this work). He sends her 'faire woords sorrowful sighes and piteous countenances ... lovyng letters, chaines, bracelettes, brouches, rynges, tables, gemmes, jewels and presentes.' Silvio/Silla is employed as his go-between. 'Now gentilwomen, doe you thinke there could have been a greater torment devized wherewith to afflicte the hart of Silla, then her self to bee made the instrumente to woorke her own mishapp, and to plaie the attorney in a cause that made so much against her self? But Silla, altogether desirous to please her maister ... followed his businesse with so good a will as if it had been in her owne preferment.' Julina naturally falls in love with Silvio/Silla telling him: 'Silvio it is enough that you have saiede for your maister; from henceforth, either speake for yourself or saie nothyng at all.' Meanwhile the true Silvio has come to Constantinople in search of his sister. He meets Julina who, mistaking him for the page Silvio, takes him quickly to bed and becomes pregnant. She informs Apolonius she wishes to marry another, and when he discovers that this is his page Silvio, poor Silla is thrown into a dungeon. Confusion follows when Julina accuses Silvio/Silla of fathering her child. To Julina's consternation, the putative father is now revealed to be a woman. The true Silvio then appears and all is explained. Once more, everyone ends up marrying the right person.

Whilst Shakespeare was plainly acquainted with one or more of these texts, he also drew on his own earlier work. He had already devised a successful comic formula that was much more sophisticated than any of this possible source material. Julia in *Two Gentlemen of Verona* disguises herself as a man to pursue her love; Portia in *The Merchant of Venice* does likewise to appear as a lawyer. Much of the comedy of *As You Like It* arises from the masculine disguise of Rosalind, where it becomes a hindrance to true love. In *Much Ado About Nothing*, Benedick and Beatrice are persuaded they are in love as a result of overheard conversations; whilst each of them is too shy to declare true passion, each writes a love letter that is planted in the way of the other. Similarly, Sir Toby and Sir Andrew seem to bear respectively some resemblance to Falstaff and to Slender, as noted. In truth Shakespeare was more or less in the position of a modern writer of

situation comedy who is trying to find a new twist to a tried formula. His
new twist is the character of Malvolio.

His love for Olivia bears some similarities to the sub-plot of *Gl'-Ingannati*. Ridiculing an old man in love with a young woman was a
frequent comic device. It appears in the person of Gherardo when he seeks
the love of Lelia. He is encouraged in his folly by Lelia's nurse, Clemenzia,
even though she knows that her charge cannot stand him.

> CLEMENZIA: I'll tell you the truth – do you know, she'd like to see you go
> about dressed differently from this. Like this you look like a silly sheep.
> GHERARDO: Why a sheep? Have I offended her?
> CLEMENZIA: No but you always go about swathed in skins ...
> GHERARDO: I own the finest stuffs of any man in Modena. I'm grateful to
> you for telling me this. From now on you'll see me dressed differently.[2]

Although ridiculed by his servant Spela, he sets about changing his appearance:

> GHERARDO: I must go and adorn myself, I have decided to dress differently
> to please my bride.
> SPELA: All the worse for you.
> GHERARDO: Why?
> SPELA: Because you are already beginning to do things her way. She's going
> to wear the breeches.
> GHERARDO: Go to Marco's the perfumiers and buy me a box of civet for I
> mean henceforth to lead the amorous life.[3]

When Gherardo meets Fabrizio he wrongly supposes him to be Lelia in
male attire and scolds him on this account. Fabrizio, who is staying at the
Madman tavern, says 'I never saw anyone so mad as this old man who
has not been tied up or locked up.' The imprisonment of Malvolio may
similarly have been inspired by one of Riche's stories in which a scold is
imprisoned by her husband

> in a dark house that was on his back side; and then calling his neighbours
> about her, he would seem with great sorrow to lament his wife's distress,
> telling them she was suddenly become lunatic; whereas, by his gesture, he
> took so great grief as though he would likewise have run mad for company.
> But his wife (as he had attired her) seemed indeed not to be well in her wits
> but, seeing her husband's manners, showed herself in her conditions to be
> a right Bedlam. She used no other words but curses and bannings, crying for
> the plague and the pestilence, and that the devil would tear her husband to
> pieces. The company that were about her, they would exort her, 'Good
> neighbour, forget these speeches which doth so much distemper you, and
> call upon God, and he will surely help you.'

PURITANS

The comic invention in *Twelfth Night* plainly goes much further than these devices. The mainspring of the sub-plot is the opposition between the revellers – Sir Toby, Sir Andrew, Maria, Feste and Fabian – and the killjoy Malvolio. At the height of their confrontation Sir Toby berates Malvolio's puritanical zeal: 'Dost thou think, because thou art virtuous, there shall be no more cakes and ale.'[4] Maria, when she plans to leave the forged letter in his way, is asked by Sir Toby to tell him something about Malvolio:

> MARIA: Marry, sir, sometimes he is a kind of puritan –
> SIR ANDREW: O!, if I thought that I'd beat him like a dog.
> SIR TOBY: What, for being a puritan? Thy exquisite reason, dear knight?
> SIR ANDREW: I have no exquisite reason for't, but I have reason good
> enough.
> MARIA: The devil a puritan that he is, or anything constantly, but a time
> pleaser.[5]

Hypocrisy was a familiar jibe at puritans.

Those on the most radical wing of the Reformation were given the derogatory title of 'puritan'. It was a term which covered a multitude of non-sinners. In most of its various guises, however, it conveyed a rejection of traditional church government.[6] The Calvinist belief in the elect of God logically involved that no one could stand in authority over them. Likewise an insistence upon the authority of the scriptures meant that all could rely upon them, not just priests. The interpretation of these two basic ideas varied greatly: on the one hand there were the Presbyterians, who appointed pastors equal with their congregation; on the other there were extremists, such as the Quakers, who had no pastors at all. All were united in their dislike of the old order which they associated with the abuses they perceived in the Catholic Church. Parish feasts and processions were seen as no more than an extension of the rituals of the old church. Moreover, the division of society into the elect and the reprobates, left the former endless opportunity to censure the godlessness of the latter. In the latter part of the sixteenth century there was a continuing tradition of puritan opposition to popular festivals.[7] Thus in 1569 William Kethe, a puritan preacher in Dorset, denounced revelling as a threat to household order because it encouraged too great a freedom in servants. He also condemned those who entertained themselves on Sundays: 'Where God calleth it his holy sabbath, the multitude call it their revelling day, which day is spent in bull-baitings, bear-baitings, bowlings, dicing, carding, dancings, drunkeness and whoredom.'[8] This attitude spilled over into opposition to stage-plays. In 1579 John Northbrooke in his *Distraction of the Sabbath* observed: 'Are not unlawful games, plays interludes and the like everywhere frequented ... Was there ever seen less obedience in youth of all sorts, both mankind and womankind, towards their superiors, parents, masters and governors.'[9] Puritans called a playhouse a school of abuse or bawdy. In tragedies they saw only murders, treacheries and rebellions, and in comedies intrigue and wantonness.

In 1619, shortly after Shakespeare's death, a small oligarchy of puritans in Stratford upon Avon 'set all the town together by the ears, which is the true office of a puritan',[10] and during September that year there was a riot when town officers tried to take down a maypole.[11] There had long been a strong puritan presence in Warwickshire and a countervailing recusant faction.[12] In 1588 a Presbyterian synod in the county debated whether it might repudiate the government of bishops. The press printing the Marprelate satires on bishops was hidden in the county in 1589, and when the High Commission started to investigate the puritan movement and charged nine ministers in the Star Chamber, four of them came from Warwickshire. In 1592, when Commissioners were appointed in the county to suppress recusants, the name of Shakespeare's father appeared prominently among those suspected of Catholic sympathy.

The puritan influence was also strong in the City of London and the Mayor and Aldermen petitioned the Privy Council to restrain theatrical performances, stating that

> Neither in policye nor in religion they ar to be permitted in a Christian Commonwealth, specially being of that frame and making as usually they are conteyning nothing but profane fables, lascivious matter, cozonning devizes and other unseemly and scrurilous behaviour.[13]

It was no doubt to avoid their attentions that James Burbage built his first theatre outside the City's jurisdiction at Shoreditch. Later, he bought premises in Blackfriars, an area which, though within the City boundaries, constituted former ecclesiastical property under the jurisdiction of the Crown – one of the so-called 'liberties'. The inhabitants of Blackfriars were not amused and they petitioned the Privy Council to prevent the venture, pleading that he had bought rooms

> which romes the said Burbage is now altering and meaneth very shortly to convert and turne into a common playhouse, which will grow to be a very great annoyance ... to all the inhabitants of the same precinct, both by reason of the great resort and gathering together of all manner of vagrant and lewde persons ... and beside that the same playhouse is so neere the Church that the noyse of drummes and trumpetts will greatly disturbe and hinder bothe the ministers and parishioners in time of divine service and sermons.[14]

Burbage let the premises to the Children of the Chapel Royal.

Religion and the government of the Church were urgent topics for the students of the Inns of Court. John Manningham's diary is dominated by the thirty-five sermons he records. In Elizabeth's reign the debate about church government was carried on largely within the Church, for the puritan party hoped to reform it from within. A great public debate took place in the Temple Church. The Master, Richard Hooker, preached the established views of church government and published them in his *Five Books of Ecclesiasticall Polity*. He had become Master of the Temple in 1585. Walter Travers, who had been educated in Geneva and at Trinity College, Cambridge, was at this time the leader of the London conference of puritan clerics. Cambridge religious teaching was greatly influenced by Calvin; and the young men educated there, who formed Elizabeth's government, whilst supporting the authority of bishops, nevertheless had strong puritan sympathies. Lord Burghley had originally proposed that Travers should be appointed to the Mastership of the Temple Church, but he had refused to be ordained in the Anglican church and so Hooker had been preferred.[15] Travers in fact already had an afternoon lectureship in the Temple Church, which he had gained in 1581. When Hooker was appointed, he preached in the morning and Travers in the afternoon. There commenced a legendary confrontation to which the young men of the Temple flocked. It ended in 1586 when Archbishop Whitgift removed Travers from his post, fearing the effects of his preaching. Nevertheless, Travers continued to live in the Temple. In due course the leadership of the London puritans was taken over by Stephen Egerton who preached in a chapel in nearby Blackfriars called St Anne's.[16] Manningham records a sermon of Egerton's he heard in December 1602 in 'a little church or chappell up stayres, but a great congrecion, specially of women.'[17] Egerton was a signatory to the petition that was to bring about the removal of the Lord Chamberlain's Company from Blackfriars.

The character of Malvolio may have been a more specific response to *Cynthia's Revels*, written in the course of 1600 by Ben Jonson. It had as its alternative title *The Fountain of Self Love*, and it finished with a prayer against all 'self loving humours'. Malvolio's principal sin is self-love. Almost as soon as he enters the scene Olivia specifically accuses him of this. He disparages Feste's wit, and Olivia rebukes him: 'O, you are sick of self love, Malvolio.'[18] It is this weakness that Maria targets in order to exploit him. She says he is 'the best persuaded of himself, so crammed, as he thinks, with excellencies, that it is his grounds of faith that all that look on him love him – and on that vice in him will my revenge find notable cause to work.'[19] Malvolio soliloquizing conveniently demonstrates this humour.[20] Even before he has picked up the letter that Maria has forged to persuade him that Olivia loves him, he is imagining exactly such a picture. He believes that both Maria and Olivia find him sexually attractive; he imagines himself as Count Malvolio commanding seven of his servants to rush and fetch Sir Toby, so that Malvolio may rebuke him. He speaks of exercising the humour of state. It is Malvolio's self-regard which cruelly exposes him to the practical joke and forms the mainspring of the play's comedy.

SIR WILLIAM KNOLLYS

Hotson has suggested that Malvolio was directly modelled upon Sir William Knollys, the Comptroller of the Queen's Household.[21] He was the officer who controlled the Queen's domestic household. His father, Sir Francis Knollys, was appointed Treasurer of the Royal Household in 1572: he was a well-known puritan who opposed Archbishop Whitgift's assertion of the divine right of bishops and suppression of puritan preachers,[22] and he had also suggested the expulsion of all recusants. There is less evidence that his son was so extreme, but he probably reflected his puritan upbringing. Hotson points out that there are various textual references which could be consistent with his theory. In 1595 Sir Edward Fitton entrusted the care of his daughter Mary, aged seventeen, to Sir William Knollys. She was to become one of Elizabeth's Maids of Honour. In the course of 1600 she fell in love with William Lord Herbert, who later became the Earl of Pembroke, and the following year bore him a child. Queen Elizabeth seems to have got wind of the affair and to have publicly rebuked Mary in June 1600. When Sir Andrew Aguecheek describes his skills in dancing, Sir Toby Belch comments: 'Wherefore are these things hid? Wherefore have these gifts a curtain before 'em? Are they to take dust, like Mistress Mall's picture.'[23] This is generally supposed to be a reference to Mary Fitton's disgrace. Knollys was married to a widow older than himself and he also seems to have fallen in love with his protegée. He wrote letters, full of hyperbole, expressing his love. A popular lampoon was written, which appears to refer to the triangle of Knollys/ Fitton/Pembroke, so that Knollys' interest in Fitton must have been well known. If a fool in love is an obvious target of satire, the circumstances of Knolly's love is remote from Malvolio's calculated love for Olivia. There is another reference in the text which may throw some light on the question. Sir Toby Belch refers to Malvolio as a 'Peg a Ramsey'.[24] This is a reference to a popular ballad of that name which ran:

> When I was bachelor I led a merry life;
> But now I am a married man, and troubled with a wife …
> Give me my yellow hose again, give me my yellow hose.
> For now my wife she watcheth me: see yonder where she goes.[25]

The scenario for the song seems to bear a closer resemblance to Knollys' situation than Malvolio's. Yellow symbolized love.[26] It was also the symbol of jealousy. In the song it may have borne both meanings; Malvolio's yellow stockings simply symbolized love. Cross-garters consisted of a ribbon or tape placed around the leg below the knee, twisted crosswise at the back, brought forward above the knee and tied in a bow on the side. It was a fashion that became current in the 1560s but it was outmoded by 1600, cross-garters being worn chiefly by old men, puritans, pedants, footmen or rustic bridegrooms.[27] Hotson also points out that Malvolio, picturing himself as Count

Malvolio rebuking Sir Toby, says he will quench his familiar smile with an 'austere regard of control', which could well be a pun on Knollys' office.[28] He also quotes a passage from L'Estrange's *Jest Book* of about 1650:

> The Lord Knolls, in Queen Elizabeth's time, had his lodging at Court, where some of the Ladyes and Maydes of Honour us'd to frisk and hey about in the next roome, to hes extreame disquiete at nights, though he had often warned them of it; at last he getts one to bolt theire owne backe doore when they were all in one night at their revells, stripps off to his shirt, and so with a payre of spectacles on his nose and Aretine in his hand, comes marching in at a posterne doore of his owne chamber, reading very gravely, full upon the faces of them. Now let the reader judge what a sadd spectacle and pitiful sight these poor creatures endur'd, for he fac'd them and often traverst the roome in this posture above an houre.

This does bear some relationship to Malvolios's intervention in the revels of Sir Toby and his crew, but there is no known reference to the incident in immediately contemporary literature and nothing to indicate that it occurred before 1602.

SIR POSTUMUS HOBY

There is another piece of background evidence which may be relevant to the comic sub-plot. Around the time that Shakespeare was writing *Twelfth Night*, there was a case in the Star Chamber involving a puritan called Postumus Hoby. Shakespeare had reason to dislike the Hoby family, since the mother of Postumus, Elizabeth Countess Russell, had been the first signatory on the petition in 1596 from the local inhabitants protesting against the establishment of the theatre in Blackfriars.[29] On 16th November 1600, Sir Postumus Hoby brought a complaint of riot in the Star Chamber against Sir William Ewre.[30] Both parties were members of Gray's Inn and the suit must have been the subject of gossip in the Inns of Court, particularly as it had its funny side. The Hoby family were connected by marriage to the Burghleys, who were very influential in Gray's Inn. Lord Burghley admitted Postumus to membership of that Inn on 11th March 1588, only twelve days after the Earl of Southampton became a member.

When Postumus Hoby's mother had originally put his name down for entry to an Inn of Court, he had not wished to apply himself to the study of the law and had run away to the Isle of Sheppey. On his return, she gave up her plans to educate him as a lawyer and instead put him in the service of Lord Burghley. In 1596 Postumus was to marry Margaret, who was the widow first of Walter Devereux, brother of the Earl of Essex, and then of Thomas Sydney, brother of Sir Philip Sydney, the soldier and poet.[31] She had thus been twice widowed by the age of twenty-five. When Postumus had first begun to court her, she had not been receptive. He was apparently short of stature, and contemporary accounts give the impression that he did not have an attractive personality. His ardent puritanism, however, would have been in tune with Margaret, who had been brought up in the puritan household of the Countess of Huntingdon. His courtship of Margaret bears a curious resemblance to Orsino's courtship of Olivia. In September 1595 when Postumus visited her in Yorkshire he had found 'the layde complayninge of payne in her eyes and heade' from 'great lamentacion for the losse of the worthy gentleman her late husbande, for she could not speak of him without teares … The tender love she bare to him that was dead, made it grievous to her to hear of any newe.'[32] She was most unwilling to see Postumus and only allowed him a short audience. In November the same year, he visited her again with gifts of jewels and pearls. She still did not accept him, but was then put under great pressure from the Burghley family to agree to the match. Eventually she did and the marriage took place at her house in Blackfriars the following summer. Postumus invited his cousin, Anthony Bacon, telling him that there would be no music or dancing because neither he nor his mother wished it, only a sermon and dinner.[33] The diary that Lady Margaret later kept demonstrates the strict puritan nature of their household, for it is full of references to prayer, religious contemplation, bible reading and the religious instruction of servants.

She owned a house at Hackness near Whitby in Yorkshire, and the couple set up home there. Postumus became an assessor of taxes, a Justice of the Peace and also a Commissioner of Oyer and Terminer for the area, which effectively enabled him to sit as a Judge. He seems to have come quickly into conflict with the old Catholic families of the area, particularly the Cholmleys and the Ewres. In her diary for 26th August 1600, Lady Margaret recorded the visit of some strangers, including Lord Ewre; and on the 27th she wrote:

> After I was readie I spake with Mr Ewrie who so drunke that I sone made an end of that I had no reason to stay for.

The following day she wrote that she 'talked with Mr. Hoby about the abuse offered by Mr. Ewere.'

It was the events she alludes to that led Postumus to bring his complaint in the Star Chamber in November 1600. In it he recites how he had held his various offices in Yorkshire for some four years, and how his predecessor was William Lord Ewre. It suggests that Postumus had become unpopular because many people who had previously received favours and exemptions from Lord Ewre no longer did so and because of his attitude to Catholic recusants. He recounts in particular how he had secured the indictment and conviction of a Henry Cholmley of Whitby and his relatives, who numbered about eighty, for obstinate popish practices. Henry and his family had been compelled to attend divine service and take communion which they had not done for three years. All these activities, Postumus alleged, had caused his enemies in Yorkshire to conceive a deep malice against him. Their revenge took a bizarre form. On 26th August 1600, the day referred to by Lady Margaret, a party of about thirty men led by Ewre and including members of the Cholmley family arrived uninvited at Postumus's house at Hackness. Among them were some 'ruffenly serving-men and boys all weaponed with swords, rapiers and daggers.' They pre-tended they had been out hunting and were given hospitality. They had swiftly abused their welcome. They began to play at cards and dice. Then, when Postumus attended divine service in the hall of his house, and with his household began to sing a psalm, 'the said riotous persons being in the dyninge chamber which is over the hall in your subjects house did trample and stampe with their feete and did besides singe a blacke santis, as they term it, or some such other songe makeinge wilde and strainge noyses in disturbance and derision of prayer and the service of Almighty God.' The following day, Postumus told them that if 'they were pleased to use his howse in gentlemanly and kindly manner and leave of their disorderous courses they should be welcome to him.' They reacted by reviling him. His wife was sick at the time and some of the rioters tried to break into her chamber. Eventually they did leave, breaking windows as they went. The Star Chamber enquired into the matter at various hearings, which with adjournments extended throughout 1601. The rioters were eventually convicted and ordered to pay a substantial fine on 26th February 1602.

There are some resemblances between the account given in the complaint made by Postumus and the relationship between Malvolio and Sir Toby and his friends. In each case the lady of the house is in the background, one of them sick, the other bereaved. There is riotous behaviour abusing hospitality. Postumus's intervention bears some resemblance to Malvolio's, although Postumus is in his own house. Both are unpopular because of their puritanical behaviour. Both offer the rioters a reprieve if they mend their behaviour. Thus Malvolio says: 'If you can separate yourself and your misdemeanours, you are welcome to the house.'[34] The hearings, which were to be spread over two years, must have caused a good deal of amuse-ment within the Temple and Shakespeare may well have heard of the case. Even if it is not an immediate source, it gives an insight into the background to *Twelfth Night*.

The various pieces of evidence that point to *Twelfth Night* having been first performed in the Middle Temple, are given more force by the fact that another of his plays also seems to have been first performed in an Inn of Court.

CHAPTER NINE

Postscript: 'Troilus and Cressida'

The story of Troilus and Cressida is referred to in *Twelfth Night*. At the beginning of Act III, when visiting Olivia's house, Viola gives Feste a coin as a tip. He asks for a second:

> FESTE: Would not a pair of these have bred, sir?
> VIOLA: Yes, being kept together and put to use.
> FESTE: I would play Lord Pandarus of Phrygia, sir, to bring a Cressida to this Troilus.[1]

The suggestion that *Troilus and Cressida* was written for an Inns of Court audience, was first made by Peter Alexander in the 1920s.[2] Most recently, it has been expounded by W.R. Elton in *Troilus and Cressida, and the Inns of Court Revels*.[3] It is a view which has had its detractors.[4] There is a strong case that it was written for private performance and, in that event, an Inn of Court would be the most likely candidate. Elton was given access to an early version of the manuscript of this book; the theories in relation to the two plays are mutually supportive. The argument with regard to *Troilus and Cressida* depends partly upon the circumstances of its publication and partly upon the content of the play. It is beyond the scope of this book to re-hearse all the arguments in detail, but certain elements may be highlighted here.

The play was entered in the Stationers' Register on 7th February 1603,[5] and the Prologue contains what is generally accepted to be a reference to Ben Jonson's *Poetaster* which was played in 1601. Dekker and Chettle had written an earlier version of the story of Troilus in 1599, but their play had been performed by the Lord Admiral's Men. The play registered in 1603 was stated to have been acted by the Lord Chamberlain's Men, so that it must have been Shakespeare's version. These two dates indicate it was written close in time to *Twelfth Night*. *Troilus and Cressida* was registered by Mr Roberts 'for his copie to print ... when he hath gotten sufficient auchtority for yt.' It is not clear what further authority he needed, but it could have been from the owners of the script. In any event, there is no evidence that he did print it. There was a later registration in January 1609 by Richard Bonion and Henry Walleys (an associate of John Marston). This time it was published and the original title page stated that it had been performed at the Globe. That, however, was replaced by a fresh page which omitted the reference to the Globe. To this first Quarto edition was attached an introductory epistle addressed from 'a Never Writer, to an Ever Reader. News. Eternal Reader, you have here a new play, never staled with the stage, never clapper-clawed with the palms of the vulgar.'

It does seem odd, even if it had been written for private performance, that it should not have entered the public repertory. There are two possible explanations. One that has been put forward is that the size of the cast suggests that the regular company must have been supplemented by extras.[6] These would have been readily available in an Inn of Court. In *Troilus and Cressida* there are twenty-seven speaking parts, together with soldiers in both the Greek and Trojan armies and servants. The number of speaking parts, however, is not noticeably greater than, say, that in *Julius Caesar* or *Hamlet*. Even if the number of nobles in *Troilus and Cressida* made doubling particularly difficult, the problem would not be so great as to prevent performance in a public theatre. The other explanation might be that those who originally commissioned the piece owned it, or in any event had to give permission for further performance. For the Epistle to the Quarto edition urges the reader not to 'like this the less for not being sullied with the smoky breath of the multitude; but thank fortune for the scape it hath made amongst you, since by the great possessors' wills I believe you should have prayed for them rather than been prayed.' The reference to the reader praying to 'the great possessors' (in the plural) because they had kept the text private, might be consistent with ownership or possession by some institution. Whatever the reason, the evidence does seem to establish that the first performance must have been before 7th February 1603 in private and that it did not pass into the repertory at the Globe thereafter.

Shakespeare had been familiar with the story of Helen of Troy and the Greek and Trojan heroes at least a decade earlier, because he refers to them in *The Rape of Lucrece*.[7] Anyone with the most basic classical education would have heard the story. He would certainly have read Chaucer's dramatic poem *Troilus and Criseyde*. Thomas Speght had produced an edition of this work in 1598. In the same year George Chapman brought out his translation of *The Seven Books of the Iliad of Homer*. These two events seemed to have generated a special interest in the story of Troilus, since in 1599 Dekker and Chettle produced their version. Just as Shakespeare wrote his own version of *Hamlet*, following an earlier play of the same name, so he produced his own *Troilus*.

The classical subject matter of Troilus and Cressida would have been popular with an Inns of Court audience. The debate on the importance of the natural order by the Greek generals, and their doomed folly, which has been likened to the fall of Essex, are both developed in high style. The love story, which is treated both lyrically and comically, would have pleased the students. So too would the lascivious commentaries of Thersites and

Pandarus. These very much fit in with the tone of contemporary student poetry. As in *Twelfth Night*, distant action is related to contemporary London. At the end of the play, Troilus dismisses Pandarus to a life of ignominy and shame. Pandarus closes the piece by lamenting the hypocrisy of those who are prepared to use his services, and yet despise him. He speaks both of a hall and of the fact that the audience may include some people who have caught syphilis in the brothels of Southwark:

> As many as be here of Pandar's hall,
> Your eyes, half out, weep out at Pandar's fall;
> Or if you cannot weep, yet give some groans,
> Though not for me, yet for your aching bones.
> Brethren and sisters of the hold-door trade,
> Some two months hence my will shall here be made.
> It should be now, but that my fear is this,
> Some galled goose of Winchester would hiss.
> Till then I'll sweat and seek about for eases,
> And at that time bequeath you my diseases.[8]

The brothels in Southwark are frequently referred to in the poems written by the students of the Inns of Court. Southwark lay in the jurisdiction of the Bishop of Winchester. In addition to the reference to a will in this passage, there are a number of other legal allusions in the play. For instance, Pandarus describes the lovers' first kiss as given in fee farm or perpetuity.[9] When he sees them kissing again he quotes 'in witness whereof the parties interchangeably.'[10] And there are a number of references to natural law.

Beyond these, it is possible to identify in the play various themes which would have appealed to an audience in an Inn of Court. The play may be linked to the notion of misrule, albeit less obviously than in *Twelfth Night*. Thus, whilst Ulysses praises the advantages of order, the Greek army demonstrates all the elements of disorder. Indeed, the Trojan war itself is the height of folly, even to the point of madness. If Malvolio's 'love' for Olivia strikes at the social order, so the love of Troilus and Cressida undermines the rationale of the conflict. Of course, to the audience that love makes more sense than the warring armies.

The text also makes use of rhetorical devices. It demonstrates not only how it should be done, but how it should not be done. As John Hoskins' work *Directions for Speech and Style* demonstrates, the students of the Inns of Court were acutely interested in rhetoric. This was no doubt because of the Renaissance spirit, but also because their future livelihoods might depend on it. Parts of the text of the play could be viewed as falling within the tradition of revelry which prevailed so strongly in the Inns. In the nineteenth century it was regarded as a problem play. This may have arisen in part from an apparent inability to marry the formal elements outlined above with a more immediate 'love interest'. Be that as it may, this kind of internal evidence that the play was written for an Inns of Court audience is at best persuasive, since the Inns of Court men attended the public theatres.

Nevertheless, at the commencement of the play, Shakespeare appears once again to be in the mood to make in-jokes. The stage direction for the entry of the Prologue describes him as entering in armour and also states specifically that he is armed. This is taken to be an allusion to the armed prologue in Jonson's *Poetaster*. Moreover, for a play about valour, the text has an unusual opening, with Troilus casting off his armour and refusing to fight. Pandarus urges patience using the analogy of baking a cake (i.e. bread), which has to be taken through several stages. The baker must tarry the grinding, the bolting, the leavening, the kneading, the heating of the oven, the baking and the cooling. The literal meaning of bolting was the sieving of flour after the wheat had been ground. Students in the Inns, however, were also sifted by 'bolting'. After dinner they had to take part in mock legal arguments. Those presided over by a Bencher were called 'moots' and those by a member of Hall were named 'boltings', as noted. Students would have to tarry after dinner, as unwillingly as Troilus, to undergo their bolting.

If the play was first performed in an Inn of Court, could the Middle Temple be a candidate? The Prologue announces the story of the siege of Troy which is about to be told. His audience would hardly have needed much introduction to that story. He makes the point, however, that the action does not start with the rape of Helen or even with the beginning of the siege:

> our play
> Leaps o'er the vaunt and firstlings of those broils,
> Beginning in the middle.[11]

Could it be that this too is a pun? Modern lawyers refer to Inner and Middle without the addition of Temple. As with all possible puns, who is to know exactly what double meaning was intended? A registration date on 7th February 1603 could be consistent with a performance at Candlemas. John Manningham has no entry in his diary for that feast in 1603, although there must have been one. He does, however, record that about that date the Treasurer George Snigge was rumoured to have paid £800 to be made a Serjeant, so he would have wanted to equal any entertainment offered to the Serjeants by John Shurley. The evidence regarding the publication of *Troilus and Cressida* does suggest that it was written for private performance. This in turn strengthens the argument that internal evidence indicates an Inns of Court audience. Whatever the reality behind the lines in the prologue, the suggestion that *Twelfth Night* was commissioned for performance in the Middle Temple is strengthened by the probability that *Troilus and Cressida* was written for a similar audience.

The time has come to highlight those parts of this text which reveal fresh information about *Twelfth Night* and to pull together the various arguments that point to 2nd February 1602 being a first night.

CHAPTER TEN

Skeleton Argument

NEW MATERIAL

A work of this sort inevitably relies heavily on the work of others. They are acknowledged in the end notes, and particular mention has already been made of C. L. Barber who revealed the social background to the play, L. Hotson, who investigated some of the people mentioned in the text, and P. J. Finkelpearl, who wrote vividly about the life of the students in the Inns. Approaching existing material from a new standpoint, however, may well give a valuable fresh perspective. Here the anatomy of an individual performance helps to demonstrate how Shakespeare put together a play for a particular audience. Moreover, detection often resembles the assembly of a jig-saw puzzle: the whole picture is not clear until the last vital pieces are in place. It may, therefore, be helpful to highlight some of the material which, it is suggested, is novel.

The identification, for the first time, of Kirkham as the Yeoman of the Wardrobe underlines the nature of an in-joke that Shakespeare was making in *Twelfth Night* and ties it (together with evidence from *Hamlet*) to contemporary competition in the theatre. It is also interesting to note how he inserts this reference to contemporary characters into a dramatic scene which is quite unconnected with them. Bard though he was, Shakespeare was ready for the easy laugh. Analysis of the script of the Revels of 1597/8 in the Middle Temple produces a vivid picture of the life of students in the Inn, which formed the backdrop to the original performance. Beyond that, it brings into relief the misrule which reigned at Christmas in the Inn – the spirit around which the play revolves. Others have noted the similarity between Feste's description of Olivia's house and Middle Temple Hall. Reference in the Revels script to the windows in the Hall demonstrates the pride of the Inn in them, thus increasing the likelihood that Feste's very specific description of a hall to the imprisoned Malvolio is in fact a description of the Middle Temple Hall. The description of the Mermaid Club is mostly gathered from existing sources, though it is not collected so comprehensively elsewhere. The references to the Mitre and Mermaid taverns in the Revels script indicate that the people who made up the club were meeting in those taverns much earlier than hitherto thought. The speech of the Clerk to the Council firmly connects Sir Walter Raleigh with the group and thus increases its prestige. The identification of the immense literary talent in the Middle Temple helps to explain why the performance took place there.

The treble connection between the date of performance of *Twelfth Night*, the end of misrule and the Serjeants' feast appears to be new. The discovery of the letter from the Treasurer of the Inn seeking preferment to the rank of Serjeant is at least consistent with a commission from him to entertain the existing Serjeants. The connection between the Sherley brothers, who are mentioned in the text, and the Treasurer of the same name is completely new, as is the suggestion that the play is linked to the venue by the use of the nicknames of two well-known students. The existence of Thomas Greene and his membership of the Inn have been noted elsewhere. However, the research of Christopher Whitfield, proving a link by marriage between Greene and Shakespeare, has not hitherto received the publicity it deserves. Greene's presence in the Inn has not been linked to the performance of *Twelfth Night*, nor has he been proposed as a possible source for some of Shakespeare's legal knowledge.

It has been suggested before that the performance of *Twelfth Night* was a first night, but without hard evidence to support the contention. Others have rejected it. Now the support is provided and in particular evidence indicating a commission by the Treasurer of the Inn.

A FIRST NIGHT

In deciding whether the performance of *Twelfth Night* in the Middle Temple was indeed a first night, all material old and new is relevant. Since there are no records of entertainments in the Middle Temple that are contemporary with 1602, the case that the performance was a first night must rest upon circumstantial evidence. It is a legal truism that circumstantial evidence may be stronger than direct evidence. The Scottish Judge, David Hume, wrote[1] that 'the aptitude and coherence of the several circumstances often as fully confirm the truth of the story, as if all the witnesses were deponing to the same facts.' Oscar Wilde expressed the same argument more colourfully when Lady Bracknell said: 'To lose one parent, Mr Worthing, may be regarded as a misfortune; to lose both looks like carelessness.' At the same time, it is necessary to bear in mind that before an inference can be drawn safely from primary facts, all other reasonable possibilities must be excluded. If Mr Worthing's parents had died in the same train crash (the line being immaterial), then Lady Bracknell's inference would have been invalidated. In the current context, it is necessary to consider whether the text might have been written for performance elsewhere, and then adapted when it was performed in the Inn. There is evidence that the text of other plays by Shakespeare were altered between successive performances. Textual connections in themselves could, therefore, be consistent either with a commissioned piece or with the adaptation of an existing text to a particular venue. The answer will lie in considering how integral any references in the text that are relied upon are to the structure of the play. It should be borne in mind that any commission there may have been would have been given to the Lord Chamberlain's Men, rather than to Shakespeare himself. In the scheme of things, the Company seems to have been more important than the playwright. Shakespeare appears to have made his money from his share in the Company, rather than from fees for plays; his share in the Company may have been his return for the plays he supplied. Nevertheless, his reputation must have been considerable by the early 1600s, and his authorship would have given added kudos to the occasion. The evidence will now be summarised under various heads.

Motive

Motive is unnecessary for proof, but it may provide the logical confirmation of independent evidence. John Shurley, the Treasurer in 1602, had a strong motive to stage a prestigious entertainment at the Serjeants' feast since he hoped to become a Serjeant himself, and the existing Serjeants and the Judges might influence the appointments. Early in 1601 the Lord Chamberlain's Men had fallen out of favour with the Government because of their apparent support of the Essex rebellion through their performance of the abdication of Richard II. Internal evidence in the Players' scene in *Hamlet* strengthens this view. The Earl of Southampton had been disgraced as a result of the rebellion. His and the Government's connection had been with Gray's Inn. A commission from the Middle Temple could have been welcome.

Other commissions

Harold Brooks, in his introduction to the Arden edition of *A Midsummer Night's Dream*, contends that the play was written to grace a noble wedding, although always intended for performance on the public stage. He suggests that a likely occasion would have been the marriage of the granddaughter of the Lord Chamberlain, Lord Hunsdon, the patron of Shakespeare's Company.[2] This theory is not universally accepted. Hunsdon was, however, a member of Gray's Inn and could well have been responsible for the Company performing *The Comedy of Errors* there. There is also a possible theory that *The Merry Wives of Windsor* was written for the Garter Feast in 1597.[3] A commission to the Lord Chamberlain's Men to perform a new play is credible.

Thomas Greene

Thomas is an obvious point of contact between the Inn and the playwright. The text of the Gravediggers' scene in *Hamlet* indicates that Shakespeare was familiar with a case reported in Plowden's *Reports* in Latin or Law French. Maybe he had been Greene's guest at dinner in the Inn and had heard argument about the case in a moot or bolting. Since the Shakespeares had a coat of arms by 1597, William would have been socially acceptable in an Inn, particularly one with a strong Warwickshire connection. As a final-year student Thomas would have been involved in the organization of the light-hearted post revels.

Date of composition

Reference in *Twelfth Night* to a play by Dekker that was first performed in the spring of 1601 points to its composition being after that date. John Shurley became Treasurer of the Middle Temple in May 1601. The play also bears evidence of hurried writing and failure to check its continuity. Such evidence has to be approached with circumspection since that is true of much of Shakespeare's work. It may nevertheless be of particular significance here. Thus Viola is built up as a singer of songs, but then that role is assigned to Feste. Feste is originally assigned the role in the letter scene, but then Fabian replaces him. There is no compelling reason in the text for these substitutions. The change of singer was probably because of the singing ability of Robert Armin, who played Feste. The coincidence that a student in the Middle Temple had Fabian as nickname, strongly suggests that this latter change was incorporated to make a joke about the real Fabian, or even to allow him to act in the play. This substitution alters the structure of the play at this stage and so is unlikely to have been a later change to accommodate a fresh venue.

Recent performance unlikely

Manningham was uncertain of the title, starting to write Mid and then crossing it out. This might have been because he was not a theatre buff; but if *Twelfth Night* had had a recent successful run, he would have been likely to have heard of it. If the Lord Chamberlain's Men had simply been invited to perform a play of their choice, one that had been in the autumn repertoire would have been an unlikely selection, since a large part of the Middle Temple audience would already have seen it.

Theme is apt for date and venue

The thematic organization of the play around misrule at Christmas would have been particularly appropriate on the day that marked the end of the period of misrule. A play about love would have been well suited to performance in the Kingdom of Love, ruled over by the student Prince D'Amour.

In-jokes

The text refers to a number of people who would have been known to the audience. The most obvious is Orsino. Malvolio's reliance on the precedent of the Lady of the Strachy marrying the Yeoman of the Wardrobe, has been revealed as a reference to a member of Gray's Inn, well known to the Middle Templars, and his partner in the theatrical company of the Children of the Chapel Royal. If this is an in-joke, there are likely to be others.

Double title

Manningham's diary demonstrates that the play had a double title from the time of its inception. This is almost the only play in the canon with such a device. John Marston, who was a member of the Middle Temple and a Warwickshire man, had written a play called *What You Will*. The most likely explanation of the double title is that Shakespeare was making a jibe at Marston.

Description of the hall

The Middle Templars were justly proud of their new Hall. A compliment to it would be apt recompense for the commission of a new play. The description of Olivia's house by Feste when he is baiting Malvolio describes the geographical position of the walls, suggesting a real building is being referred to. The description exactly matches Middle Temple Hall. The joke is about a light building and the Hall was one of the first to use new glass technology to produce a large light room.

The Shurleys

If John Shurley had commissioned the play, a compliment to his family would also have been apt. The two references to the visit of the Sherley brothers to the Shah of Persia suggests yet another in-joke. Since the Treasurer's family had been connected to their close friends and namesakes by a recent marriage, the suggestion gains further credibility.

Fabian and Curio

The names of the characters in *Twelfth Night* appear almost without exception to carry a message for the audience. The message in relation to Fabian and Curio is opaque until it is realized that these were the nicknames of two prominent students and revellers in the Inn.

Conclusion

Even if some of the individual arguments set out above can be attacked, they are sufficiently relevant and cohere closely enough to make a substantial case that this was a commission and a first night. The play might have been performed at the Royal Court shortly before 2nd February; the references to the expedition to Persia, however, would not have been welcome there, since the Queen was very annoyed about it.

Is there, then, any evidence as to how it was performed?

CHAPTER ELEVEN

The Original Performance

Although the fact of the performance of *Twelfth Night* is certain, precisely how it was performed is far from clear. There was a tradition of theatrical performance in the halls of noblemen and in the Royal Court that goes back to early in the century. The obvious place to erect a stage would have been in front of the hall screen, which in the case of a hall like that at Middle Temple would have provided a sumptuous backdrop. There is a drawing by Inigo Jones of a stage erected for a performance of a play called *Florimene* in a royal hall in 1635: it shows a raked stage in front of the hall screen.[1]

Our visual picture of a commercial theatre in Elizabethan times derives in particular from a drawing of the Swan Theatre by a visiting Dutchman called De Witt.[2] The back of the stage area bears a close resemblance to a hall screen. There is a trestled stage with a back wall containing two double doors, with a gallery above. R. Hosley in *Shakespeare 400* compared the form of this backdrop to the screens in the Middle Temple and Hampton Court and found a remarkable coincidence between them. He concluded that the backdrop and tiring house in contemporary theatres was derived from such hall screens, with which the travelling players would have been very familiar. The Swan drawing does not show any inner area at the back of the stage for use in the course of the play, although presumably the space at the back of the doors could have been used. Many Elizabethan plays do require such an area.[3] Some of them also require an area above the stage. De Witt's drawing shows a gallery which could serve such a purpose, but this is apparently full of wealthy spectators. That may simply have been because the particular play he saw did not require an upper area. T. J. King in *Shakespearean Staging 1599–1642* has analysed the stage directions in *Twelfth Night*, demonstrating how they would fit a simple stage with two rear entrances. Thus Act II, Scene 2, commences with the direction: 'Enter Viola and Malvolio at severall doors'. When Malvolio is imprisoned the directions say he is 'within'. He could merely have been behind a curtain hung over one of the entrances. Caution is necessary since these directions could have been added to the prompt book for later performances in a theatre. Nevertheless, King's theory that the play was performed in front of the screen is at first sight beguiling.

There are, however, some technical objections to it. Since the Middle Temple has a convenient gallery, it would seem strange not to have taken advantage of it, yet none of the action is directed to take place 'above'. There would, in fact, have been obvious opportunities to use it, for instance when Malvolio first obtrudes into the late night revels of Sir Toby and Sir Andrew,[4] or when the revellers spy on Malvolio picking up the forged letter.[5] In the latter scene, a box tree is set for them to hide in, a property which the use of the gallery could have avoided. More practically a stage set against the screen would have prevented access to the body of the Hall in the usual manner. As the feast at Candlemas was a very important occasion, the Judges and Serjeants were received with great formality and their procession into the Hall ought not to have been impeded. The problem could have been obviated if the stage had been erected after dinner and shortly before the performance. Most particularly, however, the Benchers and their distinguished guests would have dined at the opposite end of the Hall on High Table. This would have placed them a long way from the action and in a position where audibility would also have been a problem. Moreover, this was February and the fire in the middle of the Hall would have been lit. The smoke drifting up to the lantern in the roof would have given them a poor view. It is possible that the Benchers and their guests left after the solemn revels and before the more light-hearted entertainment; but, given the prestige of the Lord Chamberlain's Men, this would seem unlikely. They could have moved their seats, but this would not have been consonant with the importance of their position. In modern times, when entertainments take place in the presence of the Benchers, the most natural place for them is in the space between the High and students' tables.

Leslie Hotson in *The First Night of Twelfth Night* postulates that the play was performed in the round.[6] As we have seen, his theory was that the play was first performed at the royal palace at Whitehall on Twelfth Night 1600/1. Even if this theory is discredited,[7] the descriptions of a play on that occasion that survive may give some guidance to how a hall was adapted for stage performance. Don Virginio Orsino, who attended, described the scene in the Great Hall as 'gradi con dame atorno' – galleries with ladies all around. It is apparent from accounts of the provision made for other plays that such galleries would have been erected on scaffolding. Don Virginio is at this point describing the scene immediately before the dancing starts, but the play itself commences after the ball is finished. In any event, the Lord Chamberlain, in his description of the scene, does relate it to the performance of the play: 'In the Hall, which was richly hanged and degrees placed rownd about it, was the play after supper.'[8] Performances in the Hall of the royal palace presented the same problem as those in the Middle Temple Hall. The action must surely have taken place reasonably close to the Queen; if she had sat at one end of the Hall, the stage should at least have been in the middle. All this evidence is perhaps inconclusive, but the records of the Revels Office throw further light on how plays were staged in the royal halls.

In 1588 there is a record of the necessary preparations for the performance of a play in the Great Chamber at Richmond:

> Framing posts and railes for plaies, setting up degrees in the great chamber, nailinge on Brackettes and boordes for the people to sett on, making newe Halpaces for the Quenes Majesties use, and a new stage xiii foot square for the Plaiors to plaie on, and Halpaces for the Lordes and Ladies to sett on, and iiij other Halpaces for the people to stand on.[9]

Accounts for the Whitehall palace for the year 1601–2 provide for

> making readye the Haull with degres, with bounds on them and footpaces under the State[10] ... framing and setting up a broad stage in the middle of the Haull ... framing and setting a roome with a Flower[11] in it in the round window in the Haull for musitions.[12]

Similarly on Shrove Sunday 1604 there are preparations for a performance by Shakespeare's Company, now the King's Men:

> Charge for making readye the haull with degres ... with a Stage in the myddle ... altering of a Stage in the haull to bring it nearer the King.[13]

This last reference faces up to the problem, adumbrated earlier, about the play being accessible to the most distinguished persons in the room. Taken together, these passages seem to support the view that the plays were performed either in the round or at any rate surrounded by trestles in a horseshoe shape. It is most unlikely that scaffolding would have been erected in the Middle Temple Hall. The audience would in any event have been seated on benches.

A performance in the round, however, would have presented another problem: where would Malvolio's prison have been? How could he have been 'within' on a round stage? As we noted earlier, the stage direction could have been a later addition for a theatre performance. Hotson's solution to this problem was to have him in a small tented house. He points out that the records of the Revels Office provide for scenery including 'small frame and canvas mansions or houses'. He suggests that the Elizabethan stage directors used properties more than is generally acknowledged. The evidence to support this view is scant. Nevertheless, the joke about Malvolio being in darkness in a light room would have been particularly funny if he had been inside a canvas prison house in the middle of the room. If a box tree could be set, so could a light tented house. Hotson suggests that with the two noble houses of Orsino and Olivia playing such a prominent part in the play, there could have been two frame and canvas mansions permanently on stage, with the parties issuing alternately from them. There is insufficient evidence to establish this, but his basic theory that the play was performed in the round is tenable. Another possibility would have been to clear away some of the dining tables and place the remaining seating in a horse-shoe shape, allowing the screen to be used as a backdrop.

Uncertainty about the location of the stage in the original production, at least leaves a modern director free to choose his own, a flexibility of which the bard would surely have approved.

𝕸𝖎𝖉𝖉𝖑𝖊 𝕿𝖊𝖒𝖕𝖑𝖊 𝕳𝖆𝖑𝖑.

◆

SIDE ROW No. ....   SEAT No. 570

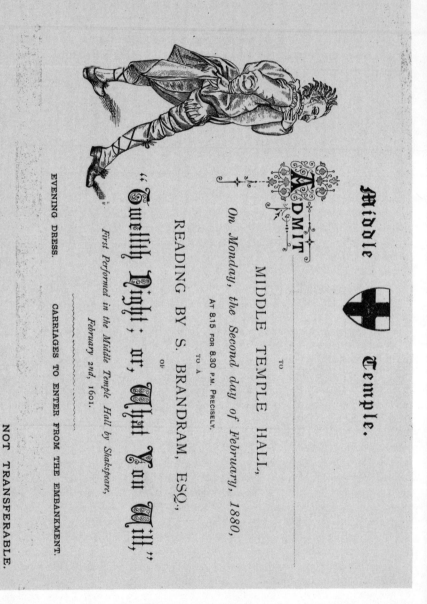

𝕸𝖎𝖉𝖉𝖑𝖊 𝕿𝖊𝖒𝖕𝖑𝖊.

ADMIT

TO

MIDDLE TEMPLE HALL,

On Monday, the Second day of February, 1880,

AT 8.15 FOR 8.30 P.M. PRECISELY.

TO A

READING BY S. BRANDRAM, ESQ.

OF

"𝕿𝖜𝖊𝖑𝖋𝖙𝖍 𝕹𝖎𝖌𝖍𝖙; 𝖔𝖗, 𝕬𝖍𝖆𝖙 𝖄𝖔𝖚 𝕬𝖎𝖑𝖑,"

First Performed in the Middle Temple Hall by Shakspeare,
February 2nd, 1601.

CARRIAGES TO ENTER FROM THE EMBANKMENT.

EVENING DRESS.

NOT TRANSFERABLE.

Ticket for the reading of *Twelfth Night* by S. Brandram Esq in Middle Temple Hall
on 2nd February 1880

Later Performances

Later performances of *Twelfth Night* in the Middle Temple Hall are obviously not as important as the original, but they form an amusing tailpiece. They have used a variety of stagings. It was not in fact known until the nineteenth century that the play had been performed in the Hall in Elizabethan times. John Manningham's original diary was to become part of the Harleian collection of manuscripts and was first published in *The Annals of the Theatre* by John Payne Collier in 1831. The first occasion when this information was put to use was on 2nd February 1880. Mr Brandram presented a one-man reading of the play, which was praised in the minutes of the next Inn parliament as brilliant, varied and dramatic. He performed on a platform erected at the west end of the Hall. The Masters of the Bench were each allowed to bring two guests, of whom ladies formed a large proportion. There were other visitors of exalted or representative rank. Members of Hall were also admitted so that the total audience was 615 with a further fifty students in the gallery. This is far more than the Hall is allowed to accommodate now. Miss de Fontblanque performed songs incidental to the play and the choir of the Temple Church sang glees from Shakespeare's plays. Supper was provided for all and the total cost was £250.

A later attempt to produce a full performance of the play was less successful. In 1892 two expatriate American actresses, Elizabeth Robins and Marion Lea, had failed in their attempt to present *Twelfth Night* in Middle Temple Hall. Also in the 1890s the famous actor/director, William Poel, formed the Elizabethan Stage Society, the company being at that time largely amateur, although he was a pro-fessional: its aim was to reproduce authentic Elizabethan staging. In 1895 they tried to reproduce the original performance of *The Comedy of Errors* in Gray's Inn Hall. Next in 1896 *Two Gentlemen of Verona* was performed in Merchant Taylors' Hall. Then on 12th February 1897 they came to the Middle Temple Hall and played *Twelfth Night*.[1] Rather curiously, Poel erected a stage with a proscenium arch formed from carved columns and an architrave. There was a gallery at the back, which was not in fact used in the performance and a traverse curtain which when drawn, as it was some dozen times in the course of the performance, provided a front area where exterior scenes were enacted. Shaded lanterns hanging from the roof lit the stage. It all appears to have been modelled upon Poel's idea of an Elizabethan stage. The Society sold some of its costumes in 1895 and the catalogue contained a number of them that seem to have come from this production. Poel had costumed the whole of Olivia's household in black, since he insisted that this was the custom in Elizabethan times. Orsino's court, on the other hand, was modelled on the court of Elizabeth, most of the costumes being in two shades of crimson. There were beefeaters, halberdiers and court ladies in farthingales made of figured silk damask and lined with old gold damask. Poel also tried to orchestrate the voices of the cast, choosing performers with the following voices: Viola (mezzo soprano), Olivia (contralto), Sebastian (alto), Antonio (basso profundo), Sir Toby (bass), Sir Andrew (falsetto), Malvolio (baritone), Maria (high soprano), Orsino (tenor), Clown (tenor). The music was performed by the Dolmetsch Trio. Arnold Dolmetsch had written it in the Elizabethan style and he and his wife and daughter performed it on instruments contemporaneous with the original performance. They used an Italian virginals made in 1550 and a Venetian lute from 1560 together with a treble and bass viol. The performance drew a distinguished audience, headed by the Prince of Wales, who was a Bencher, Princess Louise and the Duke of Teck, Lord Halsbury (the Lord Chancellor) and Lord Poynter (President of the Royal Academy). The production was heavily oversubscribed and received reasonably favourable reviews.

In 1913 Mrs Alfred Lyttleton wrote on behalf of Mrs Granville Barker requesting that the latter's secretary should be allowed to examine the Middle Temple records for any account of the performance in 1602. She added that the Granville Barkers cherished a dream of giving a performance of the play in the Hall. The letter was forwarded to the Treasurer via Sir Robert Finlay, a former Attorney-General. The Benchers were at first favourable to the idea of such a performance. Miss Ponsonby, the secretary, mooted the question of the King and Queen attending and enquired if tickets might be sold. Edward Atkinson, the Treasurer, refused this commercial request. When Miss Ponsonby asked if they might be sold privately, Atkinson endorsed the letter 'dates unsuitable, we cannot allow a charge'. For the moment the project foundered. Mrs Granville Barker, whose stage name was Lillah McCarthy, did not give up, and eventually in 1916 she succeeded in promoting a fête in honour of the Red Cross. By this time Sir Robert Finlay was Lord Finlay, the Lord Chancellor. Perhaps his influence, coupled with the war effort and charitable objects, had caused a change of heart. Excerpts were presented from both *Twelfth Night* and *Much Ado About Nothing*, in which Ellen Terry played Beatrice to Sir George Alexander's Benedick and Lillah McCarthy played Viola. Sir Andrew Aguecheek was played by Leon Quatermain. Arnold Dolmetsch and a consort of recorders, violin, viols and virginals performed Elizabethan music, and the Temple choir performed Elizabethan songs. An 'incident of Elizabethan England' was also enacted in which a bride and groom were welcomed by the lord and lady of the manor, impersonated by Ellen Terry and her husband, Dennis Neilson Terry. Among the Elizabethan guests were Sir Frank and Lady Benson and Robert Atkin. Mrs Patrick Campbell presided in the tea-tent in which amongst others Miss Gladys Cooper personified the tea-rose and Marie Lohr the sweet pea. The tea-waitresses and programme-sellers were made up of society ladies, including Miss Elizabeth Asquith, Miss Nancy Cunard, Miss Evelyn Curzon, Miss Lloyd George, Lady Diana Manners (Cooper) and Mrs Gerald (Daphne) du Maurier. Shakespeare's will and Kitchener's call to arms were exhibited.

In 1934 an amateur company called the Holywell Players presented the play between 28th and 30th June. It was performed at the dais end of the Hall, rather inappropriately against the background of the portraits of the Stuart monarchs. This was part of an endeavour by the then Treasurer, Mr Micklethwait KC, to revive the social life of the Inn. There was plainly a family connection with the company because Orsino was played by Eric Micklethwait. *The Times* waxed lyrical about the performances of Viola and Maria and above all about Christopher Warner's Malvolio, which it likened to that of Beerbohm Tree. Judges in the audience included Sir John Simon and Sir Boyd Merriman. It seems likely that some of the great advocates of the day who belonged to the Inn also attended, amongst them Sir Patrick Hastings, Sir Henry Curtis Bennet and Theobald Mathew.

The first attempt to celebrate an anniversary of the original performance came in 1951. It was only an attempt because the Benchers failed to take account of the change in the calendar in 1752 and celebrated the 350th anniversary a year too early. When a reporter from the *Evening Standard* pointed out this error, a spokesman for the Inn said: 'We have made no effort to check the question of whether this is a mistake. It is a niggling point.' The reporter found this surprising, expressing the view that 'surely barristers live by niggling over points of law.' According to the *Daily Express* the Benchers' first idea had been to perform the play themselves, under professional direction. They had engaged the flamboyant actor-manager Donald Wolfit, who had not been impressed by their thespian abilities and had insisted that his own company should perform it. Three performances of the play were given, but only Benchers and their families were able to buy tickets.[2] The proceeds went to legal and theatrical charities. The play was once again acted at the dais end of the Hall on a narrow raised stage. A large 'book' stood at the back, the pages of which were turned to provide a backdrop to the action. Wolfit himself played Malvolio and his wife, Rosalind Iden, played Viola. On 2nd February itself, the Queen and Princess Margaret attended and the cast were introduced to them after the performance. The Queen apparently expressed sorrow that the show was over. The critics were less kind and criticized the production, particularly because the actors were largely inaudible.

The New Shakespeare Company presented the play in the Hall in July 1964. This young professional company included Annette Crosbie as Viola, Michael Blakemore as Sir Toby, Michael Crawford as Feste and Stephen Moore as Sir Andrew. Not surprisingly with a cast of this quality, the play was well reviewed. They were described as surrendering themselves to romance, the masquerade and extravagance. The music on this occasion was written by Johnny Dankworth and the songs were described as instantly singable.

When the Hall itself was 400 years old in 1970, Jonathan Miller brought an amateur company, the Oxford and Cambridge Shakespeare Company, to put on the play. Miller treated the twins, Viola and Sebastian, as 'emblematic Gemini mystical twins, whose divine androgyny retunes the jangled keyboard.' The former Queen, now the Queen Mother, again attended. The production subsequently toured the United States and Canada. Clive Barnes, the critic of *The New York Times*, commented that it should never have been set before a serious critic. I hope that this modest work will not suffer a similar fate.

APPENDIX II

The Revels of 1597/8

There follows a transcription of the script of these revels published by William Leake of Fleet Street in 1660.

The Epistle Dedicatory

Welcome. You will not be backward in giving him an *Honourable Reception*, when you understand he is *your Prince*, one that owes to you his very *Creation*, and has no other *Historiographer* than an eminent person of your own Society. His *Raign* was short, but prosperous; the *Genius* of the *Nation* being then heightened by all the accesses of *peace, plenty, Wit, and Beauty* in their exact perfection. They who have been borne as it were out of time, and under the sullen influence of this latter ill-natured Age, who look on the past innocent and ingenious pleasures and divertisements wherewith your *Honourable Society* used to entertain itself and the whole glory and *grandeur* of *England* as *Romance* and *Fabulous*, may here reade that exaltation of *Wit*, wherewith all ears were charmed, and wish for the return of those blessed days, wherein you who come not short of your *Predecessors* in any Ornaments of soul or body, may have the like opportunities of giving yourselves and the *Age* you live in, the same excellent entertainments. But that it had been injurious to *you* who gave this *Prince* life to have it conceal'd to whom he owes his being, I had not used anything like a *Dedication*, his own *Native lustre*, and powerful charms being so attractive, that it will be a hard matter for any ingenious person to see, and not buy such variety of *Wit* in a volume of no greater *bulk* nor *price*. The *attendant Poems* were the offspring of divers eminent *Wits* of the same age, and never yet appeared in publick, having confined themselves to the fortune of so *Illustrious a Prince*; whose *person* being waited on, and *Court adorned* with the choicest and noblest beauties of *England during his Monarchy*, it cannot be improper to have the *Muses* now appear to do honor, and pay a just duty to his *History*. In the whole *Collection* there is not anything of the gall and venome which has mixed itself with the Ink of these last twenty years, but *wit* born long before our unhappy *intestine divisions*, and has that mark of eternity, that is not like to grow old, but is still new, florid and innocent, and shall continue in *reputation*, during the lives of *Time*, and your *Honourable and Learned Society*, two *joint-tenants*, whereof there can be no *Survivor*.

Your humblest and most Devoted Servant

W.L.

[This is followed by a list of books printed or sold by William Leake at the sign of the Crowns in Fleet Street between the two Temple Gates.]

Le Prince d'Amour:
or
The Prince of Love

The stile of the Prince D'Amours, *and the Blazon of his Arms.*

The high and mighty Prince, *Lucius, Elius, Pulcher, Eratosthenes, Aphroditemanes, Potharcus, Erotopegniopolimarchus, Lypothumyacrantor, Pomphilopelinices,* Prince *d'Amours,* Palsgrave of *Hartsbroken,* Duke of *Suspircia,* Marquess of *Braineswound,* Governor of *Florida* and *Exultantia,* Great Commander of all the Seas from the Streights of *Genoa* to the Bay of *Porto Desiderato,* and chief General of all *Venus* forces, from *Iapan* to *Quevera* by the West; and from *Rio des Amazones* to *Lapland* by the North; in all people and Nations that understand the language of Seeing and Feeling.

He beareth *Or,* three Marmozites Scutimotant proper.

On a Wreath of his colours, out of a Chaperoon Maladvisee, Pali Gules and Vert, of doubled Ermine tasseled Ore, a Mound declining proper, supported by two Hydraes pullulant, bezanted, proper, mantles Gules, and doubled Ermine.
His word, *Plena sunt omnia.*

The reasons why he hath these Titles, and how he came by the dignities, and why he beareth these Arms, and this crest, are these.

He is called *Lucius,* because he was born under the best Constellation (*oriente Luce*) when *Mercury* and *Venus* were predominant; the influence of which Planets wrought in him two effects, Beauty and Eloquence.

Elius is the name of his Family, and hath seconded the name of *Lucius* in the first Prince of the Imperial Blood ever since the *239 Olympiad.* This name was made famous by *Lucius Elius Commodus,* Emperor of *Rome,* but especially by *Lucius Elius Antoninus,* who in the 1045 year after *Rome* was built, came over into this Isle, where amongst the *Damotriges* in the West, he gave first root to the noble race from whence this Prince is descended by twenty-seven degrees.

Pulcher was a nick-name first imposed on him by the ancient enemies of his house; the *Turpiliones* and the *Carlones,* in derision of the black hair of this Princes stock; but by continuance of time, the same is now used as an ornament of his stile, derived from the Greek word *Poluchier,* that is many hands, whence it was asked, *An nescis malias Regibus esse manus?* that is, subordinate Officers and States to govern under him his several Provinces.

He is called *Eratosthenes* of devotion and valour; of his devotion to the sacred Muse of Love, *Erato,* Recordress of all heroical actions; and he is called valourous by reason of the famous and worthy Grecian *Sienelenes,* that was in the *Trojan*

Horse, from whom this Prince is lineally descended by the great Grandmother.

His other names he received from *Venus*; as *Aphroditomanes* of his Extasie, and more than humane spirit in Love.

Potharcus, for his chief Regency in that Affection.

Erotopegniopolymarchus, for his excellency in Love-devices.

Lypothuniacrantor, for the managing of his Passions: And,

Pomphilopolinices, for that he generally prevails in all his Attempts.

He is Palsgrave of *Hartsbroken*, an ancient, but now decayed Castle in *Gelderland*.

Duke of *Suspircia*, an Honor of large endowments in *Italy*, neer to Cape *Vechio*, which Seignior *Zelotypo* now holdeth of this Prince by Cornage.

He is Marquess of *Brainswound*, which is a City in *Swetherland*, where the people wanting an head, by free election, chose this Prince for their Marquess.

Governor of *Florida* and *Exultantia*, in which Countries he served young under *Cupid*, and from him had first the charge of a Company, after of a Regiment.

Commander of all the Seas from the Streights of *Genoa* to the Bay of *Porto desiderato*; he got this honor by battering the Forts of *Genoa*, and entering the Streights some seventeen yeers since; and so then pursued the Victory through the maine, till he attained the desired Bay.

Chief General of all *Venus* forces from *Japan* to *Quivera* by the West, *etc. Japan* is an Island in the furthest part of the Longitude of the earth by the East, where his Excellency first began his exploites, and so marched up continually till he came to the uttermost point Westward, where he ended in *Quivera*.

Rio des Amazones is in the South, where he undertook mighty adversaries in single Combat, and so strengthened and increased Northwards, till he vanquished *Lapland* by Composition, as *Jupiter* vanquished *Danae*.

In all people and Nations, *etc*. The *Chynois* understand other Nations by Characters; the *Troglodites* by whispering; the vulgar sort of people understand one another by words; but the Subjects of this worthy Prince express their mindes by looks and touches, the most significant utterance of amorous Passions.

The Blazon of his Armes declare their own meaning.

First he beareth Or, known to be the most resplendent, pure, and richest metal.

Three Marmosites scutimotant proper, whose framing of themselves to imitation of entertainment, declares courtesies in this Court.

On a Wreath of his colours, *etc.* The *Chaperon male advisee*, signifies nothing but the conceipt of mirth that over-reacheth the limits of the World.

The superscription of his Crest, *Hodie mihi, cras tibi*, declares most lively the Equity and Justice of this Prince, giving to every man his due; notwithstanding the cause should concern himself.

Supported by two Hydra's pullulant, *etc.* The two Hydra's signifie, that the multi-tude of the Supporters and Fortifiers of his estate are impossible to be suppressed.

The Word is *Plena sunt omnia*, signifying the fullness of this Prince's perfections.

But for that, all these Titles, Stiles, Honors, Dignities, and Armes, are contained in this one most worthy Title of all, The Prince *d'Amours*; therefore long live and reign the most invincible and glorious Prince *d'Amours*.

Sound Trumpets

An Herald having thus proclaimed the Princes Title, and blazoned his Armes, a Champion spake in justification of his Election, Enthronization and Title, and in commendation of his person, concluding with a Challenge to any man that should oppose it, or say the contrary, as followeth.

The first Champions speech

Though it seem superfluous at the Coronation of a Prince, to dispute the lawfulness of his Title, for that at such time Competitors are either clean rooted out, or so curbed through fear of the general applause and conspiration of mens minds, as they expect rather opportunities of after Innovation, than at that time to declare themselves; yet lest we might seem carried away with the stream of Faction, the ordinary enemy that prejudiceth right; I whose Oratory consisteth rather in my Sword than my Pen, will, for the satisfaction of the World, in few words lay open the evident right the high and mighty Prince *d'Amours* hath to his Title and Empire.

It is not unknown how for these eight years past, the youthful, couragious, and victorious state of the Knights Templars hath been ruined; all men can speak of infinite abuses, and lamentable desolations that have been made of Love and Armes, their ancient profession. For who of late hath taken the honorable course of Love, or so much as set foot in the pathway of Chivalry? Easie and low-prized Venery hath been basely pursued, whilst desires illuminated by the Celestial flame of Beauty, have been accounted either Fictions or Frensies; none hath sighed, none hath indited, none hath publick Shews frequented, none in unsufferable cold a whole Winters night hath his Mistris door courted, or by the Chamber Windows entred to speak but one word, nay to have but one sight of her, whose Idea is the mover of his Motions. And as the vertuous, though laborious walks of Love have been thus unfrequented; so the wonted Feats of Arms now a long while have been unpractised. There's not one that is now swarty with the heat and dust of the School, by managing his Weapons from morning to night. But who, in matter of difference, relieth more on his Manly courage, than on witty evasions to shift off a quarrel, he is now esteemed unexpert and Fool-hardy; Nay, so far hath proceeded this making War by Wit and writing, as men wretchedly abandoning the ancient and unassaultable Fort of the Buckler (I think because the expence of Swords was too great) that the merciless troops of Catchpoles dare now make Inrodes to the very Gates of our Cities, where the *Aqueduct in Platea fletensi* had wont to be the uttermost border of their approach.

The wiser sort of Templarians seeing these manifold corruptions, as well to repair their decayed State, as in doubtful adventures of Love to have one to whom, as to an Oracle, they may repair to be resolved for their controversies, have therefore assembled the general States of their Provinces, and with one consent (a matter rare in voluntary elections) have lifted to the seat of Government this Prince, for his lineaments and presence Prince-like, of years flourishing, and fittest for the Travailes and Assaults of Love, of expence in his private estate bountiful, and therefore now to be hoped magnificent, of tried courage and all-approved valour; copious and facete in discourse, sweet in conversation, ripe of judgement, and (which is chiefest of all) deeply experienced in all honorable Foreign and home Loves.

These praises being not to be put on and taken off at pleasure, but even native, and rising out of the very root of his generous and Princely disposition; though the tenor of his Government will declare them to be such as I have said; yet that it might appear our Assembly of the States to have been expedient, nay highly necessary, our consultation mature, and election most fit; I have as sparing as I may, given a slight view of the unmatchable eminency of them.

And lest flattery might be imputed to me, for having uttered much, I have spoken no more than by Combat I am ready in my person to maintain.

Wherefore I aver, that this our Monarch hath been most wisely chosen, most worthily enthronized, and most rightly entituled, *The high and mighty Prince d'Amours*.

Now, if any dare say the contrary to this which I have spoken, let him take up my Gantlet, the pledge of my Assertion.

And so he threw his Gantlet on the ground.

Which a strange Knight taking up, with an undaunted courage, spake to this effect.

And the pledge of thy Assertion, behold I take it up! Do you wonder at my words? be you appaled at my demeanor? and could you not be astonished to see a Throne invaded, and an unknown Usurper laying violent hands on the Title of another? I had thought the Beauty of each particular Lady here present, had so entirely possessed their amorous servants, as I feared my self should be put off from accepting this Challenge through the throng of Knights, whereof each one would have maintained his Lady and Mistris to have been the Prince of Love. But I see where the Object is not excellent, the desire is but ordinary; and therefore no marvail if none here undertake this Combat, the cause being wanting that should incite them thereunto. Pardon me (Ladies) that I extenuate your Merits; your

Beauties and Vertues in several deserve superlative praises. Comparison maketh wretches; and to be thus matched with the unmatchable, is the onely way that blemisheth your lustre. You may marvail what creature should be of such perfection, as so many rare Beauties as be here summed up together, yea and being so curiously adorned for the honoring of themselves, their Lovers, and this Assembly should notwithstanding be found defective to paragon one Lady. But cease your wondering: And yet why say I so? The whole face of the Earth is struck with admiration of her; the Lady whom I would name (had I a name of force to express the life of her demerits) is so prodigally adorned with the excellencies of Nature, as in the generality of things there being nothing that may be wished to be added unto her, she remains the onely Divine Pattern of all creatures to imitate. It may be some of you having took counsel of your Beauty-multiplying-Glasses, or being puffed up with the praises of your passionate servants, will envy my words; but let me tell you thus much; the sincerity and the immortal Graces of this Lady of whom I speak of, have Conquered Envy, yea Death itself; so that now the pains of all clear discerning spirits are invoking the Assistance of the Celestial Powers, that they may worthily write of the Trophees of these her Conquests.

Now, for you, Sir Champion, Have you never heard of the Lady of that fortunate Island? 'Tis in vain to say no: Her Kingdom seated in the midst of the Waters, gives the Windes free liberty to spread her glorious fame every where. How darest thou then boulster out the Usurper of her Rights. Will the world nere leave off to quarrel her Titles? She, who in the tempestuous Garboiles of other Nations, sits peaceably in her own Throne, must the Ornaments of her Scepter be assaulted by violence? and the Name which she holds dearest; by an Intruder be wrested from her? I tell thee, Sir Knight, that the truely Regal Title of Prince d'Amours, wherewith thou guildest thy Tyrannical Lord, is the essential Cognizance of my dread Soveraign. She it is, who though the Beams of her Majesty infuse Awe and Reverence, yet tempers the dazeling Raies thereof with the gracious aspect of Bounty. Other Princes accounting Regal Power chiefly to consist in the enlarging of their Territories; She, by uniting mens hearts unto her, hath made herself a minde subduing Conqueror; Hath it ever been seen that the Laws of Friendship should be observed between two zealous adorers of one Celestial Beauty? The very power she hath over Love himself is so great, as with friendship he can now comfort himself to sue for her graces. The world counts it fabulous that the daughter of Phebus could change men into Beasts; but posterity shall wonder to hear that thing which we see, and long may see, that the daughter or the eternal Son hath turned us Beasts into Men. I ne list, ne can; or if I could, time will not permit me to number each particular rarity whereby this great Empress of Mens hearts leads their affections into admiration. But can Majesty endure to be vailed for the poorest to approach unto it? Can it prize the Conquest of Mens Loves before the acquisition of other Kingdoms? Can it bear such sway over Friends, Lovers as they shall preserve Friendship, and yet affect an Unity? Can it make such strange Metamorphoses of Beasts into Men, without proposing this as the most glorious end; namely, the Love of her Subjects? If she then, by these sweet Victories have gained herself the Soveraignty over Mens hearts, how comes thy Lord to be Prince d'Amours? Have the beams of his Mercy, Fortitude and Truth, drawn the oppressed stranger to seek the comfort of his protection? Hath his Regal power served to ballance the corners of the Earth, that they oversway not one another, in the mean while nothing approaching to himself, though just cause, fit occasion, sufficient means have not been wanting for the performance? These great actions of Piety, and none but such as these may challenge the never dying title of Prince *d'Amours*. But if no such divine qualities thou canst ascribe to thy Lord & Master, this name will not fit him, it is too heavy for his shoulders. If thou givest him this title for being a perfect Lover, why there are numbers in her Court who in this point would scorn to yeild thy Master the Prerogative. But let him herein be as absolute as he can be; yet know, all Lovers are servants; 'tis the beloved hath the Soveraignty; Let him account then his glory to consist in obeying. A servant of Love is so great a title for him, that I fear me he will never worthily deserve it; fi[f]th then, in her high and supreme estate, her sweet and more than debonaire conditions, her choosing to win rather mens minds than foraign Empires, her attempering her favors in so just a proportion, as although they be fought by all, yet concord is preserved; her civilizing her subjects, whom time past accounted barbarous; her succcouring of the afflicted stranger, and her infinite moderation in counterpoising the uneven parts of the World, be manifest tokens that she proposed, as the scope of her actions, not onely the goodwill of her subjects, but even the universal Love of mankinde. I therefore say, and say, and say a third time, That thy Master is an Usurper, and none but my Lady and Mistris is the true Princess *d'Amours*.

But what need these disputations; Come, our swords must decide the right of this Title.

Now the two Champions being to try the Combat; the form observed therein was as followeth.

The challenger first presented himself within the Lists; whereupon an Herald made a Proclamation, saying:

Behold here Chavalliero de Belta *Challenger in this combat, who is entered into these Lists Royal to do his devoire against* Chivalliero de Luna *Defendant.*

And then again the said Herald by way of Summons to the Defendant.

1. Summons.

Chivalliero de Luna, *Defendant in this Combat, appear now, and come into these Lists; for this night thou hast undertaken to acquit thy Pledges, and defend thy person against the Champion of the famous Prince d'Amours, who challenged thee to maintain the cause of this Combat.*

2. Summons.

The time passeth, therefore come without delay.

3. Summons

Appear in, and save thine honor; for the time is almost spent wherein thou didst promise to perform thine enterprise.

Then appeared the Defendant and shewed himself within the Lists; whereupon the Herald said,

Behold here Chivalier de Luna *Defendant in this Combat, who is entered in this List Royal to do his devoire against* Chavalliero de Belta *Challenger.*

Then were their Oaths given them severally; and first to the Challenger.

1. Oath

You shall swear by the Sacred Scepter of Love, with as great a Zeal and Religion as ever impatient and hungry Lover did swear to his Mistris, That whatever is contained in your Challenge is true; and that you will maintain it upon the person of your Adversary: So help thee Cupid *and his gentle mother,* Venus.

Then to the Defendant.

You shall swear by the Sacred Scepter of Love, with as great a Zeal and Religion as every impatient and hungry Lover did swear to his Mistris, That your Assertion is true, and that you will defend your person against your Adversary: So help you Cupid *and his gentle mother* Venus.

The Second Oath.

To the Challenger

You shall swear that you have brought no other Armor or Weapons, than these wherewith you do now appear to be armed (such Weapons excepted wherewith Nature did furnish you at your Nativity) And that you have neither Engin, nor counterfeit Instrument, but such as may be lawfully used in the Encounters of Love; and that you have no Charm or Inchantment, Hearb, Root or Leaf, Mandrage, Hypomanes, Potatoes, Eringoes, Cantharides, or any other potent Conjuration to raise the spirit of Love; and that you put your trust in Love and Nature, your Cause, and your own Valour: So help you Cupid, *and his gentle mother* Venus.

The like to the Defendant.

Then was given them a third Oath, *viz.*

You shall swear one to another to do your uttermost endeavor and force to prove your affirmations, either by death or denyal of each other before ye depart these Lists, and before the bright star of Venus *go down this night: So help you* Cupid *and his gentle mother* Venus.

Then was a Proclamation made to this effect.

We charge and command, in the name of the famous Prince d'Amours, *that no man of what estate, title or degree soever, shall approach within four foot of these Lists, nor shall utter any speech, word, voice or countenance whereby the Challenger or Defendant may take advantage, upon pain to lose Life, Living and Goods, to be taken at the Prince's pleasure.* With this conclusion, *Long live the famous Prince d'Amours.*

The Prince seeing both the Champions resolute, and ready to encounter each other, gave order to stay them, putting off the Tryal by Combat to another time.

And in the mean space advised with his counsel, whether he should expose the tryal of his Title to the hazard of a single combat.

Herein three of his Councel delivered their opinions.

And first his Secretary spake to this effect.

Seeing your Excellency hath resolved to be advised by your Councel, silence were now a sin unsufferable, which I have always taken to be near allied to Vertue, because it imposeth a moderation, and therefore commendable. But my minde being now fully repleat, and possessed wholly with admiration, compelleth my tongue to testifie outwardly my inward sence of joy, and my hearts exultation for that which I have always desired to see, that which I have longed to see, and yet have ever failed to see, is now lively presented before me. And what is it? (for I hold you long in expectation). It is in one man an exact Union of all Excellencies, and of all heroical vertues a perfect composition, for we see the height of a Princely courage submitted to councel and consideration; his magnanimity and magnificence joyned with Prudence and Temperance; and his vigor of youth for execution, mixed with the Maturity and stayedness of deliberation. But I must not spend the time in praises, though never so justly occasioned, because your Highness requireth counsels. And what is it that is called into consultation; namely, whether a Prince that is puissant in Power, of large and ample Territory and Dominion, shall expose his Diadem and Dignity to the uncertain event of a doubtful combat? Why, if his Legions had been mustered, and all his Army Royal drawn into the Field, to confront the daring Forces of an equal enemy opposed; and the question were then made, whether so great a State and Empire were at one battail to be hazarded; which without the death of millions of men could not be ended; yet should I hardly be induced to be of that opinion, that a wise Prince (such as I worthily esteem his Excellency) were to set all upon the fortune of a day, no more then a wary Gamster will venture all at a cast. But rather would I advise how these Force[s] should be seconded; and the second being overthrown, how they should be again re-inforced: yea some places of Retreat I would have always reserved, where we might from all showers of former misfortunes be sheltered and succoured, where new Breath, new Vigor, new Alacrity might be recovered. This is not spoken to that end that I would have the noble Prince *D'Amours* (who hath been always victorious) either basely to turn his back, or cowardly to creep into corners, no more then I would have the bright Beams of the Sun to be obscured with a cloud, or with darksome night to be overshadowed. But if, by some disastrous Fortune of the field, his unmatchable Forces should at some incounter, by devise or strategem, happen to be overmatched; or if by slie intelligence, or secret Ambuscadoes any part of them should be intrapped and intercepted, they might yet again and again be reunited, and his Excellency shine

brighter then before in the midst of his Troopes, to the terror of the enemy, like the
Sun when it hath newly been eclipsed.

Then, if a Royal Dignity and State Imperial be not to be committed to the doubtful
Chance and Fortune of a day, when whole Regiments of Infantry, with infinite of
Cornets of Cavallery stand ready to defend it; where the weak and wearied may be
refreshed and seconded by the strong; and where many Cowards by a few men of
courage may be enheartened; were it wisdom to commit a matter of so great
moment to be decided by two Champions in a single combat! where, if the valour of
the one be never so assured, yet by the Agility, Slight, or Policy of the other it may
be overmatched; yea, oftentimes when all these parts are between them indifferent,
or that the ballance weigheth heaviest on that side we would have it, there
happeneth some unexpected accident which utterly overthroweth our hope, and
deludeth our expectation. How often have whole Armies been discomfeited by some
Prodigy unaccustomed, even when the Victory was almost assured! yea many times
by matters of very slender consequence, and ridiculous importance? As by a false
Alarum given by Friends mistaken for Enemies, by a shout or cry suddainly raised,
by the flight of a Bird, by the neighing of an Horse, by the Winde, by the Rain, by
the shining of the Sun; and by signs seen in the Firmament. If these things have been
of power to give Victory to the vanquished; and to take it from the Victorious; If
they have been able to sway whole Armies and mighty Nations, shall they be of less
Force to prevail with two single Combatants? Shall any duellist or Champions
be exempted? Amongst the Histories of Antiquity, which are stored with these
Examples; the Folly of the *Sabines* and the *Romanes* about the beginning of the
Romane Empire, is fit to be remembred, that the like by us might be avoided. These
Nations striving for Dominion, the one to defend their ancient liberty, and the other
to bring them in subjection; agreed to end their controversies by three Champions
on each side elected. The *Romanes* made choice of three whom they called the
Horatians; the *Sabines* of three other named the *Curiatians*. It happened whiles they
fought in view of both Armies, that two of the *Horatians* were slain by their several
Adversaries; and yet the Victory, which the *Sabines*, upon so good saccels, with
great likelihood expected, fell afterwards to the *Romanes*, beyond all expectation;
for the third *Horatian* which survived, finding himself overmatched, flying from his
enemies the *Curiatians*, which were three to one, and they still pressing him, he
singled each of them as he followed, and dispatched all of them; by which means
the *Sabines* became subject to the *Romanes*, who would hardly otherwise have
conquered them. Now they that like it, may follow the example of the *Sabines*, and
commit the like Folly to lose their Liberty and Dominion which they might have
preserved. But the noble Prince *d'Amours*, by me shall never be advised to yield to
be overcome, before he be overcome, and before he feeleth himself to be overcome;
that is, before he see his innumerable Armies defeated, millions of men in his
defence slain and sacrificed, all his strong Towns and Garrison spoiled, burned,
or dismantled; all his succours from his confederates intercepted, and in a word,
himself utterly discomfeited. For what? shall he therefore be deposed from his
Dignity because a stranger claimeth it to be the free-hold of another, and the ancient
inheritance of his Mistris? And when all other Allegations fail him, because he
cannot prove any late seizen, or possession, will have recourse to his Writ of Right,
and desire to have it tried by *Duellum vadiatum*, a tryal sometimes used in the
fortunate Island; but that Trial hath even there been long out of use, and must not

by us be revived in a matter of so great moment. The liberty of a million of men is no way to be adventured on the worth of one man, be he never so worthy. Therefore if I may advise your Excellency, let this strange Knight be dismissed, and let him shew better Cards for the Conquest of a Kingdom then the single Force of one Champion, if he mean to have it. In the mean time, by your Governors of Provinces, by your Lieutenants, Colonels, and great Commanders, let your men be mustered; let your Infantry and Cavallery be prepared, Magazins of munition and Store-houses of provision furnished; let your Frontiers be well fortified, and your Garrisons re-inforced; let your Navy Royal be new rigged for the Seas, equipped and ordered. Then, if intelligence be brought that the confines of your Territories are like to be invaded, let your valorous person in Golden Armor be inclosed, and upon a cuoragious horse gallantly mounted, that the brightness of your glorious aspect may be like the shining of the Sun in his triumphant Chariot, whereby the enemy may be daunted; till then, let the name of War and Fight be banished, and your wonted Courtly recreations be recontinued, that these lovely Ladies, who like bright stars have beautified your Court with their appearance, may with some delightful disports be entertained.

The tryal by Combat being upon this occasion put off, the Prince began to settle his Estate in a peaceable form of Government; and to that end caused all his Officers to assemble themselves together, and caused to be read unto each of them respectively by the Clerk of the Councel his several charge and duty in form following.

The Charge and duty of the Officers of the Prince d'Amours.

And first to the Lord President.

The President of the Councel is to give order for the Aged, that they may not be long standing; and if they urge any reason unto their Ladies, they follow it not effectually or to the point; to give the Prince notice that if any of the Councel have more Reason then Love, he may be put from the Counsel Board. If any deal in Love-matters without personal view, the sufficiency of his Judgement may be doubted of. That once in two dayes they view the Subsidy book, and see what Ladies be deep in; and that those that are Light may have more laid upon them. That Proclamation be made, that any Gentlewoman being taken in the Armes of any Gentleman, be presumed to be his Sister, or his Cousin at the least, and that she be presumed to be no better then swowning, and he striving to put life into her. That they have Spies abroad that shall signifie all such men as Traitors which Love for the Common-wealths sake, and not for their own; and that most of their deliberations be about the Seige of *Sluce*, the Battery of Brest, or the sacking of Maidenhead.

The Archflamen.

The *Archflamen* is to dispense and Canonize; having taken the confession of any Lovers, he is not to discover it but to the parties whom it concerneth; he is to give absolution or dissolution for false Protestations, affectionate Oathes, etc. To enjoyn Penance to Lovers impotent in performance, that they fast upon dry Alegant, cold

Lobsters, Oysters, and Hartichokes, and such like tamers of the flesh. To dispense with all them that have unhandsome Mistresses, that it shall be lawful for them, with the Favors and Gifts which they receive from Ill-favoured, to purchase fair Mistresses; and that they may allow Pluralities in Love to them which have extraordinary parts. To Canonize such as do works of supererogation, as to give Gifts before they have received any Favors; such as kiss the stool whereon their Mistris sate, or do go to the Tailors to kiss the sheers wherewith their Mistris Gown was made.

The Lord Chancellor.

He is to take care and see that all Evidences having the Privy Seal may be fair in-rolled; to award a *Subpena* upon the Plaints in Love that have no remedy in Law, and by decree to award Covenant to be held upon promise without witness; to bear special compassion to the Petitioners, to command his Master of the Rolls to keep all Ladyes above fourscore for ancient Records.

The Lord Marshall.

The Lord Marshall is to order and marshall all Combats and single fights; to appoint fit time and place; time, between shutting in of the Evening and opening of the Morning; the Place, under certain Lists between Canopies barred in with staves; to measure the length of all Weapons, and specially to appoint the Truncheon for the fight; to exempt the maimed in the Princes service, and the disabled by Age or sickness; and to adjudge all Combats worthy of Imprisonment which are not fought within the lists aforesaid.

The Lord Treasurer.

The Lord Treasurer is to receive all the Revenews of the Crown; as Sighs, Sonnets, Tears, Vows, Protestations, *etc.* and to give allowance and Pensions out of them to all such as desire them, by keeping several likings of several Mistresses together; and shall be specially beneficial to Poets, Musicians, Players, French conceited Cooks, and Loves Harbingers.

Lord Chamberlaine.

The Lord Chamberlain to keep all Roomes voide of Spies, sweetly perfumed, the Couches made all for advantage, that the Windows admit but twilight, to cover Blemishes, and discover perfections, to accommodate Ladies in chambers to their content.

Master of the Horse.

The Master of the Horse to convey the Princes Mistris secretly in Coach or Litter; to stay Horses for suddain and secret journeys, as well to appoint places of meeting upon the way, or if necessity require it, in the Coach it self; for which purpose he may take up at his pleasure Beasts for his Highness Saddle, *Irish* Hobbies, *English* Hackneys, Low-country Mares, *Spanish* Jennets, *Barbary* and *Neapolitan* Coursers, or other sort for variety of pacing wherewith his Highness is delighted.

Lord President of the Province of New-Inne.

That he be always able to send an Army out of his Province to the Temple of Love, trained and exercised in many encou[n]ters, that they have good knowledge in matters of Justice, in Arraignment of Offenders that have not used secrecy, but have been too open in their dealings, or have burnt or spoiled the Princes loving Subjects.

Lord Admiral.

He shall see all his Excellencies Ships well rigged and tite and sound.

He shall take heed for bearing too much sail least he spring his Mast, or perish his Main Yard.

He shall take heed in sailing lest he come athwart the haulse, or fall foul on some other Vessel, whereby he may break his Borsprit in the Poupe, or some other part of her.

He shall be sure always to have some Pinnaces abroad to the Southward, there to surprize some Carvel of Advise, whereby his Excellency may be informed when any Vessels of worth comes into those parts.

He shall suffer none of his Excellencies Navy to sail lower than the *Mediterranean* Seas and yet no further to venter into the Streights then he may bring them safe and sound out again.

He shall suffer no Ship to come near him, but he shall make her strike and come under his Lee.

He shall, in passing the narrow Seas, be continually sounding least he run his Ship aground so that he cannot soundly get it off again; neither shall he come to an Anchor in foul ground.

He shall never pass by our Associates in the Low Countries, but he shall bestow on them a Fire of his great Ordnance.

He shall suffer all such to pass quietly as Traffique into the Gulfe of *Venus.*

He shall see that all his Excellencies Ships have their Cape-stones in good order, that they may be always able to weigh their Anchor, and to hoise their main-Yard, cool his Ordnance for fear of firing by still going, and that the Ship be well washt afore and after for fear of infection.

He shall see, that after any tedious and tempestuous Voyage, every Ship be brought into a dry Dock, there to be new graved and trimmed for another adventure, and look well to the stopping of all Leaks.

He shall not in any case board any with his Excellencies ships, but at the encounter to fight off and on for fear of firing, and yet for his honor he shall rather fire then yield.

He shall give direction that the Ordnance in every ship be well mounted, and upon good Carriages, and so levelled that upon any encounter they may shoot the adverse party between Wind and Water.

Item. It is his Excellencies pleasure that his good ship called the *Garrick*, for her old tried service, shall carry the Flagge in the high main Tuppe by day, and the light in her Poupe by night.

He shall scoure the narrow Seas between the *Sound* and the *Sleeve*. He shall sometimes look into *Brest*, and sometimes sail into *Diepe*; and he shall have an especial care to keep his Excellencies Subjects from being spoiled by the *Dunkirks* commonly called *Crosbiters*.

He shall be sure so to keep the Winde of any ship he meeteth, that he may safely (discharging his Ordnance) come off and on at his pleasure.

He shall press no men into his Excellencies ships, but such as known every point in their Compass, so as they may be able to steer directly upon any of them; and such as can readily prick their Card, whereby upon any suddain occasion they may bring their ship into a safe harbor.

Lord Privy Seal.

It is his Excellencies pleasure that his Lordship put the Seal onely to matters of Privity.

Lord Saint George.

Lord Saint *George* and Commander of *Lambeth Marsh* not to part any that go into the Feilds without intent to hurt one another; and that he see that such as have Warrant to keep open house from the Captain of the *Seraglia*, return not hidden fire over water to the endangering of the Princes household.

Comptroller.

The Comptroller of the houshold to Control all course and rough behaviours in Love, as ruffling of Ruffs, breaking of Perewigs, and renting of Ante-praedicaments.

Secretary.

To keep close matters of Estate, as paintings, boulstings, powderings, surflings & suffumigations; To maintain Intelligences in the Dominions; especially between them of *Sweveland* and the Prince, to open all letters which begin with, *After my hearty commendations* or end with, *Yours in the way of honesty.*

Lord Chief Baron.

To take order that when any Knight hath his *Quietus est*, his Lady accomptant hath her *Exoneretur*; that he shall *tot* many and *nichil* few.

Captain of the Guard.

That his Soldiers follow the order of Launce Knight, that is, to be furnished with a [blank] kinde Companion; that they be able men by their drinking to prove *Copernicus* Assertion to be true, *viz.* that the earth goes round, and the heavens stand still.

Lieutenant of the Tower.

To keep *Cupids* Captives close Prisoners, that their Diet be no daintyer than upon hope, and their Walks no further than their Mistris Windows; to set all unruly Lovers in the Stocks, and Recusant Ladyes on the Rack; and that it is Treason in him to suffer any Lady to escape that he hath under Arrest.

Captain of the Seraglia.

The Captains of the *Seraglia* of ancient time were Eunuches, for which this man is dispensed withall, and thereof is able to shew his sufficient evidences, *Et Iscopletes testes*; to provide good Physitians for the Ladies that are sick of the Mother, and see that they be humble, and submit themselves to his Highness pleasure; to license houses of Entertainment.

Master of the Revels.

To see that none Court with Apothegmes, the news of *France*, the lack of lights, mislike of Musick, or of the Room; that no Gentlemans Voice drown the base Viol; that they dance in measure, and Love beyond measure.

The Herald.

That he take no painted Face for a Scutcheon and say she beareth Gules: To derive no Pettigree from an hundred years before the Creation, without warrant out of *Amadis de Gaule*, or *Bevis of Hampton*; to draw no mans Progeny from *Virgils* Gnat, unless he be a friendly Gentleman, nor from *Bucephalus Alexanders* Horse, unless he be valiant, nor from the Capitol Goose, unless he be vigilant.

The Prognostication.

Seeing it hath pleased your Excellency to grace me with the Dignities of the Lord-Lieutenant of the middle Region of the Air, Master of the Thunder-bolts and Hailestones, Surveyor of all Crinite Comets, blazing and falling Stars, fiery Exhalations, and of all sorts of Vapors and *Ignes fatui* in the lower Region; and for that there are none of these but that they do effectually work upon this Climate of Love; to satisfie your Excellencies expectation, I have observed certain conjectures of things likely to be done this year; which here I submit to your Highness deepest censure.

All Astronomers, till this night of the world have stood gazing upwards for a heaven, which they could never be well acquainted with, they dwelt so far asunder. My self (either by skill or chance) have fallen upon a new heaven nearer hand, more sensible, though of equal incertainty, which is a woman. And lest any should esteem this learning as an idle devised Fancy, let them compare it with the heaven above us, and they shall perceive in what due proportion this heaven under us respecteth it, as well in the several points and Circles, as in the workings upon mens bodies.

The points for the two Poles are the two leggs, the Supporters and Movers of the whole fair frame; and he that knoweth not the *Zenith*, I would he might never come near the *Nadir*.

For the Circles, I will speak onely of the Zodiack and Equinoctial; and of those but partly; for I doubt not but part of this Astronomy will sufficiently instruct a man for the whole, it is so pleasant and easie.

The Zodiack, being a flaunt Circle, reacheth from the corner of the left heel to the top of the right shoulder.

This Zodiack hath twelve signs; I will name but three; the rest I will leave to the handling of those that write after this kinde.

Pisces is placed beneath in the Leg, as the ancient Astromomer *Horace* hath well noted, [?] *formosa superne, Destruit in Piscini.*

Capricorne, under the Arme, as *Martial* saith, – *Namque putatur Valle sub alarum trux habitare Caper.*

Virgo, above *Pisces*, in a rough place, according to the Poet, *De virgine fecimus ursam.*

The Equinoctial maketh even the day and the night at the girdle, the upper Hemi-spheres hath day, and the lower night.

Some whose travails and experience have searched far into Countries, have found a burning Zone, and report it to be inhabitable.

For the working, they are by motion, by light, and by influence, motion of their bodies, light of their eyes, and influence of their powerful love. And seeing man is called a little world, why should not a woman be said to be a great world? for it is the greater thing that contains the less, and not the less the greater.

By the divers Aspects and Conjunctions of Planets in the Heaven, I foretel these ensuing Events.

First, That if this Prince Reign not long, he is much the more like himself, Prince of Love, because not much Love wrongs by this Globe can endure long.

There will be great complaints made of the Princes Scepter, the Rectifier of Beauty, and Doorkeeper of Virginity, which the Vulgar call a Busk, or Gag-thigh; it will stand in the way of many young men, who will discourse upon the points of his Scepter: Politicians will find holes in it; but the Lawyers will put it aside with a nice difference, and argue the case most profoundly.

Much of the Princes Ordnance is likely to miscarry; some spoiled with over-heating, some rusted for want of scowring, some cast away for lack of pruning the Tuch-holes; many of the Ordnance will requoil at the very discharge.

Much of the Princes press money shall be light and crack't within the Ring, yet it may go currant if it be handsomely slip't in.

The distressed Ladies may (if they will) obtain such relief and bounty in the Court from the Prince and his Knights, that although they come hither empty, they may go out full of content.

Many women shall receive great thrusts at the first entrance, and many men will be forced to stand for want of a good room.

Some women will lose their Gloves, Scarves and Fans; but they may find better things if they will vouchsafe the taking up.

Many Ladies may be lodged in the Princes Court, more to their ease and pleasure, than to adventure a dark journey home-ward.

Many men shall be given to live Monastically within their Cloyster, and will not come out for fear the vanities of the world take hold of them.

It will prove a very dangerous thing for a man to write his own name.

For the Officers.

The *Arch-flamen's* Cap shall be subject to interpretation, but the lining of it shall make good sport.

The *Earl-Marshals* Truncheon will be the worse for ordering of single Combats, and the greatness of his place will distract his Carriage many ways.

The *Lord Chamberlains* Staffe may chance to be tip't with red.

The *Captain* of the Pentioners shall ere he be thirty years old turn into a woman.

The *Clerk* of the Councils note of the duty of the Officers shall help furnish some that are out of discourse.

The *Orator* shall be made Master of the *Apothegms*; Emperours, Kings and Princes shall not escape his comparisons; Pedlers, Cooks and Tinkers shall not avoid his similitudes: he may chance to scowre up old *Euphues* unto brightness and wear off the Cotton of the figure *Agnominatio*.

Some Revellers shall receive great down-falls, for presuming to imitate the heavens in their circular motions.

My self cannot prevent, though fore-see my own misfortune. The Orator will miserably flout me with an *Apothegme*, telling me that while I stare at a Star, I fall into a Ditch; but I know when he finds me in, he will willingly help me out to have my place; he will call me *Thomas Buckminster* the Prognosticator, and salute me by the name of his very good friend, when he slily means *Friend* the Almanack-maker; but if any be so childish to call me Dade, whose years cannot allow me to be their father, let them take heed to be not verified upon their posterity.

For the weather.

You shall have such great Whirle-winds, that many men shall be blown up, and not seen in the year after.

Many nights about Midnight there will be great Inundation of Waters, and Eruption of Springs out of the sides of Hills.

The diseases that will happen to men this year are stiffness in the Limbs and the Stone; Ache in the back, pains in the head; many Revellers shall be suddenly stricken with such a Lethargy that they will forget where to find the Prince or their *Pantofles*. Diseases incident to women this year are the Falling sickness, Stoppings and Obstructions, Tumors and Swellings.

The Prince shall have power from the Heavens to cure the Princes Evil, commonly called the Green Sickness.

Thus hath your Excellency heard my judgement of the two fore quarters of the year; the two hinder-quarters, which I hope will be more acceptable, shall be put in with the next fit opportunity.

The Princes Orator having made a ridiculous and senseless speech unto his Excellency, the Clerk of the Council was requested to make an Answer thereunto at *ex tempore*, which at the first he refused; but being importuned, he began and said:

The *Fustian* Answer made to a *Tufftaffata* Speech:

Then (Mr Orator) I am sorry that for your Tufftaffata *Speech, you shall receive but a* Fustian *Answer. For alas! what am I (whose ears have been pasted with the Tenacity of your Speeches, and whose nose hath been perfumed with the Aromaticity of your sentences) that I should answer your Oration, both Voluminous and Topical, with a Replication concise and curtal? For you are able in Troops of* Tropes, *and Centuries of Sentences to muster your meaning: Nay, you have such Wood-piles of words, that unto you* Cooper *is but a Carpenter, and* Rid *himself deserves not a Reader. I am therefore driven to say to you, as* Heliogabalus *said to his dear and honourable servant* Reniger Fogaffa, *If thou dost ill* (quoth he) *then much good do thee; if well, then snuffe the candle. For even as the Snow advanced upon the points vertical of cacuminous Mountains, dissolveth and discoagulateth it self into humorous liquidity; even so by the frothy volubility of your words, the Prince is perswaded to depose himself from his Royal Seat and Dignity, and to follow your counsel with all contradiction and reluctation; wherefore I take you to be fitter to speak unto stones, like* Amphion, *or trees, like* Orpheus, *than to declaim to men like a Cryer, or to exclaim to boyes like a Sexton: For what said* Silas Titus, *the Sope-maker of Holbornbridge? For* (quoth he) *since the States of* Europe *have so many momentary inclinations, and the Anarchical confusion of their Dominions is like to ruinate their Subversions, I see no reason why men should so addict themselves to take* Tabacco *in* Ramus Method; *For let us examine the Complots of Polititians from the beginning of the world to this day; what was the cause of the repentine mutiny in* Scipio's *Camp? it is most evident it was not* Tabacco. *What was the cause of the Aventine revolts, and seditious deprecation for a Tribune? it is apparent it was not* Tabacco. *What moved me to address this Expostulation to your iniquity? it is plain it is not* Tabacco. *So that to conclude,* Tabacco *is not guilty of so many faults as it is charged withal; it disuniteth not the reconciled, nor reconcileth the disunited; it builds no new Cities, nor mends no old Breeches; yet the one, the other, and both are not immortal without reparations: Therefore wisely said the merry conceited Poet* Heraclitus, *Honourable misfortunes shall have ever an Historical compensation. You listen unto my speeches, I must needs confess it; you hearken to my words, I cannot deny it; you look for some meaning, I partly believe it; but you find none, I do not greatly respect it: For even as a Mill-horse is not a Horse-mill; nor Drink ere you go, is not Go ere you drink; even so Orator Best, is not the best Orator. The sum of all is this, I am an humble Suitor to your Excellency, not only to free him from the danger of the Tower, which he by his demerits cannot avoid; but also to increase dignity upon his head, and multiply honour upon his shoulders, as well for his Eloquence, as for his Nobility. For I understand by your Herald that he is descended from an Ancient house of the* Romans, *even from* Calphurnius Bestia, *and so the generation continued from beast to beast, to this present beast. And your Astronomer hath told me that he hath Kindred in the* Zodiack; *therefore in all humility I do beseech your Excellency to grant your Royal Warrant to the Lo. Marshal, and charge him to send to the Captain of the Pentioners, that he might send to the Captain of the Guard to dispatch a Messenger to the Lieutenant of the Tower, to command one of his Guard to go to one of the Grooms of the Stable, to fetch the Beadle of the Beggars, ut gignant stultum, to get him a stool; ut sit foris Eloquentiae, that he may sit for his Eloquence. I think I have most eratoriously insinuated unto your apprehension, and with evident obscurity intimated unto your good consideration, that the Prince hath heard your Oration, yea marry hath he; and thinketh very well of it, yea marry doth he.*

The Prince is now resolved to create for the great honour of his Court, a new Order of Knighthood, called the Knights of the *Quiver;* The form and manner of whose Creation is as followeth.

First, *The Herald made this ensuing Proclamation.*

The High and Mighty Prince, Lucius Elius Pulcher etc, Knight of the Honourable Order of the Quiver, and Soveraign of the same, doth straitly charge and command that all Councellors, Lords, Knights, and all other Officers and Gentlemen of worth in the Highness Court, do personally appear at the rising of the fair Star of Venus, before his Excellency, in this his great Hall, to attend the Creation of the new Order of the Honourable Knights of the Quiver.

This Proclamation was made three several times with certain convenient distances, Before the Princes coming after the sound of a parley.

Then entered the Prince, and they proceeded to dance.

Then the *Arch-flamen* took the confessions of the Knights that were to be created.

Which being ended, the Prince commanded an Herald to make a Proclamation for silence and order.

And the Herald with sound of Trumpet made a second Proclamation in these words:

The Mighty Prince D'Amours, Knight of the Honourable Order of the Quiver, and Soveraign of the same, commandeth all persons present to keep silence, and to take their due places, upon pain of his high indignation.

Then the Prince willed the Herald to call the Knights.

Who as they appeared, placed themselves at the lower end of the Stage. The first in the mid'st, and the next on his right hand, the other on the left; and the like in every respect was done by the rest, every one in his due place and order.

Whose names were:

Cavaliero: De Belta. De Campo Virili.
               De Bello Fonte. De Bono passo.
               De Campo Georgiano. De Monte Fulgente.

Then the Prince made an Excellent Oration, wherein he declared the Reasons which moved him to institute this Order, and concluded, saying, *Earle Marshal and Herald, Bring hither those Knights to receive the Order.*

Whereupon the *Earle Marshal* and *Herald* brought them one by one, the *Earle Marshal* holding him by the right hand, and the *Herald* by the left, with three solemn Congies and placed them afore the State, three on the one side, and three on the other.

Then the Herald delivered to the Prince a book, upon which they were to take their Oaths.

Which the Prince opening and looking therein, said, *Well, Ovid de arte amandi!* and commanded the Herald to read the Articles of the Order.

Then the Herald read the Articles, which were as followeth.

1. *That no Knight that is married at eighteen years old in his Fathers life time, shall be admitted to this Order, unless he have extraordinary gifts of Nature or Art.*

2. Item, *that every Knight of this Order shall still be well horsed and well armed, and have those things in readiness which Ladies desire, as the Launce for the Ring, and such like; and shall twice a week at the least Tilt and Turine [sic] for Ladies, shewing them all their cunning in Arms when they lust or command.*

3. Item, *that no Knight shall carry any Arrow in his Quiver, unless the head be a head of advantage, or very well steeled; and that he suffer not his Arrow heads to rust, for fear of poisoning the wounded, which is contrary to the law of Arms.*

4. Item, *it shall be lawful for any Knight to shoot Forkers (though that be a Woodmans weapon) against any weak Knight that weareth two white Feathers in his Helmet hornwise.*

5. Item, *That no Knight wear any peiced Arrows, nor that the Strenes be made of burnt wood; and that the horn wherewith they are nocked be taken from between the two great Toes of a Woman.*

6. Item, *That no Knight wearing a hanging dagger shall stab suddainly, but give fair warning to draw and make ready his weapon.*

7. Item, *That no Knight shall entertain him Mistris with talking of other men; but that once in three dayes he speak with some spice of Wit, and to the purpose twice every night if possible.*

8. Item, *That every Knight be skilful in the terms of Hawking and Hunting, and the Northern riding languages, and that he say no man is of good regard but a Watchman, of good reckoning but a Tapster, of good carriage but a porter; and that in no case he use any perfumed terms, as spirit, apprehension, resolution, accommodate, humors, complement, possessed, respective, etc.*

9. Item, *That he write not in Glass with a Cornish Diamond, nor set his own name to any ordinary invention, As,* In utramque paratus; Dum spiro spero; Amor vincit omnia; Tam Marti quam Mercurio, *and such like.*

10. Item, *That no Knight reply to another mans speech,* O good Sir, You have reason, Sir, You say well Sir, It pleaseth you to say so Sir, *nor any such like answerless answers.*

11. Item, *That all Knights of this Order be able to speak ill of Innes-a-Court-Commons.*

12. Item, *That no Knight meeting another of this Order at the Ordinary, shall ask him this question,* Are you in Commons Sir?

13. Item, *That no Knight go booted and spurred with a switcher rod to make men wrongfully suspect that he keeps a great horse, when he hath none.*

14. Item, *That he tell no news but under the name of some great Lord whom he never saw but from the Scaffold in the Tilt-yard.*

15. Item, *That riding in the street after the new* French *fashion, he salute all his Friends with an affected Cringe; and being asked where he dined, he must not say at the Tavern or the Ordinary, but at the Miter, the Mearmaid, or the Kings-head in old Fish-street.*

16. Item, *That no Knight, under the degree of an unmannerly fellow, shall take Tabacco in the presence of Ladies without especial leave, unless he have kissing Comfits ready in his britches.*

17. Item, *That no Knight shew a Ladies name in the bottom of a Letter, that is either of his own making, or else was written by the Lady to some other.*

18. Item, *That he letting fall some Tailors Bill snatch it not up in haste, and say he had hazarded the discovery of the Love of some great nameless Lady.*

19. Item, *That afore his rising in the morning he be attended with other mens servants aswell as his own, namely, the Haberdashers, the Tailors, and the Mercers.*

20. Item, *That he keep but one man apparelled by way of translation.*

21. Item, *That every Knight provide that once in a year all his Gold-lace go on Progress over his clothes.*

22. Item, *That he have the wit to mislike the fashion of his clothes before he pawn them; and that he be alwayes furnished with reasons for the convenience of every fashion.*

23. Item, *That he pawn not his Ladies grand favor nor hazard the same upon pain of displeasure and dismembring for ever.*

24. Item, *That he learn no speeches out of Playes to entertain the time; and that his Picture be not drawn in clothes transgressing the Statute of Apparrel, himself being attired out of the compass of the Statute.*

25. Item, *He shall have always the first news to carry from Nobleman to Nobleman.*

27 [sic] Item, *He shall fall into no mans Acquaintance but that he shall use him to make himself further known.*

27. Item, *No Knight being out of matter shall revenge himself upon a base Viol.*

28. Item, *If any Knight dye a Maid, being above fifteen years old, he shall not*

make any Will, or declare any heir; but shall be accounted to dye as a person intesticulate, and his goods and revenues shall be taken at the Princes pleasure.

29. Lastly, *If any Knight dye having an hundred Sons of his bawdy lawlesly begotten, those other Knights living shall present and surrender his Order to the Prince, and intreat his Excellency to bestow it upon that Son that is most like his Father, or else the same to be disposed of at the Princes pleasure.*

The Articles being ended, the Prince said to the Knights,

Are ye content to swear to all these Articles.

And they all answered, Yea, we are well content.

Then the Prince commanded the Herald to give them each one the Oath.

Then the Herald willed them each one to kneel down, and gave them the Oath, saying,

Oath. *You shall swear to do your uttermost endevor to perform all these Ordinances of their honorable Order of Knighthood: So help you Opportunity and the contents of this book.*

Then the first Knight arose up first and went near to the Prince, and kneeled down again.

And there the Prince first made him Knight with his sword, saying, Stand up *Cavaliero de Belta*, and then put the Ribbon with the Jewel of the Order about his neck. And so the rest one after another.

The first that was Knighted gave place, and the Herald led him (with thrice turning back and making solemn Congies every time) to his place.

And the like in every respect was done by all the rest.

Then sounded the Trumpets, and they fell to revelling.

The next night, all things necessary being provided for that purpose, there was an Arraignment of one *Carolus Asinius Bestia*, a discontented Lover. The manner and form of which proceeding was thus.

A formal Court being made in the Great Hall of the Temple, and the Princes Officers and Judges seated in their due order, a Cryer made *Oyes*, saying, My Lords the Princes Justices streightly charge and command all manner of persons to keep silence and hear his Highness Commission read, which was in effect as followeth.

Lucius Elius Pulcher, *etc.*

Charissimo consanguineo & Consiliario suo Domino Guidoni Que sperio de Belta

magno Camerario hospitis sui; Charissimo consanguineo & consiliario suo Domino
Eugeno Eurphilo comiti Marescalto suo; Charissimo consanguineo & consiliario
suo Alexandro Flaminio Crispo Domino de campo St. Georgiano; necnon &
dilectis & fidelibus Conciliariis suis Galfrido Cynthio de Guerra, Pharamundo
Constantio Cithereo, Praehonorabilis ordinis pharetriani militibus; Ac etiam Quinto
Cassio Aristids, capitali Justiciario suo, Lucio Severo Ulpinano, Caio Sincero
Triboniano, Quinto Mutio Philonamo, Justiclariis suis de Placitis & amandium
querelis coram ipso tenendiis assignatis salutem, Etc. *Quod cum,* Etc.

Whereas in the Kingdom of Love all things should pass with delight and without
dislike, nevertheless we are given to understand that divers and sundry persons
within our Dominions, contrary to their Loyalty, have grown not onely discontent
with the present State, but also not having Beauty and the beheasts of Love before
their eyes, have of late attempted and put into practice divers most horrible and
notorious Treasons against our Highness and Principality, State, Order and Dignity,
and to the utter subversion of our most Princely Soveraignty and Government: We
therefore, upon mature deliberation thereof had, intending the due execution of the
Laws of Love, for the further encouragement and comfort of all true, faithful, and
passionate Lovers, and the utter subversion and rooting out of our Dominions and
Territories, of the male-contented, way-ward, false, jealous, leud, wanton, dis-
sembling and disdainful persons making Love, and outward shew and shadow,
and a deceitful practice, which should be indeed inward compunction and passion
of the heart, Do by these our Letters Patents under our great Seal authorize you, of
whose Faith, Fidelity, and good service towards us we have had good, experience, to
enquire by the Oaths of good, lawful and true Lovers, and by all other good wayes
and means whatsoever convenient, of all Treasons, Misprisons and Treasons,
Insurrections, Rebellions, unlawful Congregations and Conventicles; lewd speeches
savoring more of lust then of Love, contempts, disdains, scornful looks, behaviors
and Gestures, negligences, concealments, oppressions, rowts, ryots, rapes, fellonies,
and all other Trespasses and Offences whatsoever committed contrary to our
Imperial Crown of Love and the Dignity thereof, and of our Accessaries of the
same, within these our Dominions, by what person or persons, to whom, when,
where, and in what manner the same have been committed, perpetrated and done,
attempted, devised or offered to be put in practise or execution. And also given you
full power and authority to hear and to determine the said Treasons and other
Offences aforesaid according to the laudable Laws of true Love, by vertue of these
our Letters Pattents unto you our Earle Marshal or Lord Chamberlain, Lord Saint
George, Cavaliero de Belta, and our other Councellors, and to you ____ our Lord
Chief Justice and ____ our other Justices 13, 12, 11, 10, 9, 8, 7, 6, 5, or 4 of you, of
whom we will our said Earle Marshal and the Lord Chief Justice to be two: Witness
our self at our sacred Temple of Love, in the tenth day of the frozen moneth, the first
and last year of our Raign.

The Commission ended, the Cryer said, *Long live the Prince d'*Amours.

Then Proclamation was made.

Amantius Letus Esquire, Sheriff of *Hartfordshire*, return the Princes Precept to thee
directed and delivered.

Which done, another Proclamation was made:

Lieutenant of the Tower, bring forth the Prisoners.

Which being immediately done, the Cryer said,

You good men of the grand Inquest that are impannelled, to enquire for our Soveraign Lord the Prince *d'Amours*, answer to your names ever[y] man at the first call upon pain, *Etc.*

1. *Antonius Lepidus* of *Maidenhead*, Esq.

2. *Desiderius Jocundus* of *Wishford*, Esq.

3. *Cucullus Glabrio* of *Bangbury*, Esq.

4. *Ambrosius Asper* of *Nettlebed*, Esq.

5. *Innocentuis Mario* of *Littlewithin*, Esq.

6. *Venutius Gurges* of *Hoggsnorton*, Esq.

7. *Delerius Rusticus* of *Dunstable*, Esq.

8. *Simplicius Credulus* of *Hornsby*, Esq.

9. *Bonifacius Bellus* of *Honyton*, Esq.

10. *Minutuis Graticus* of *Littleport*, Esq.

11. *Ignorantius Vituly* of *Waltham*, Esq.

12. *Flavius Petulans* of *Wenchome*.

13. *Vinius Bibulus* of *Maltsbury*.

14. *Apicius Voxax* of *Coberley*.

15. *Domingo Niger* of *Blackwall*.

16. *Licinius Calvus* of *Baldock*.

17. *Scabiosus Treipilio* of *Ichford*.

18. *Prodigus Nepos* of *Hadland*.

19. *Portius Crassus* of *Borley*.

20. *Sprusius Nitidus* of *Simpringham*.

21. *Falsidicus Nebulo* of *Knavesborow.*

22. *Andreas Incubus* of *Stoneham.*

23. *Laberius Leno* of *Bandley.*

24. *Gracilius Macer* of *Leneham.*

The full Jury appeared and every man answered to his name as he was called.

Whereupon the Indictment was read as followeth.

Com. Hartfort. Inquiratur pro praepotenti Principe, etc.

Then said the Clerk of the Crown, *Carolus Asinius Bestia*, hold up thy hand. My Masters of the Jury, look upon the prisoner.

Carolus Assinius Bestia, Thou art here indicted by the name of *Carolus Asinius Bestia* of *Dolton* in the County of *Hartfort* malecontented Esquire, That thou on feast day of Saint *Rumbald*, the first year of the Reign of the mighty Prince *d'Amours*, at *Hounsditch* in the County aforesaid, in a certain Alehouse there, called the sign of the Dogs head in the Pot, not having the due regard of Beauty before thine eyes, not the seating of true Love in thy heart, but instigated by the Acherontical, scornful and disdainful spirit of discontent, didst utter these prophane, beastly, odious, execrable, hellish, abominable, savage, heinous, horrible and traiterous speeches against the high and sacred Majesty of Love, and against the Government, Crown and Dignity of the Mighty Prince of Love thy Soveraign Leige Lord; that is to say, That the name of Love was not to be used, spoken, mouthed, or uttered by any person or persons without the word *sur reverence*; and that thou thy self hadst more often shifted thy Mistris, then thou hadst shifted thy clothes, and yet was not to be adjudged a shifter; and that none ought to be Prince of Love, but he that could conquer Love, whereas indeed Love is unconquerable. And moreover, thou art farther indicted for that thou in the first of the Dog days after Midsommer Moon was then lately passed, in the heat of thy brain, in the first year aforesaid, in Ram-Alley in the County aforesaid, in a certain house at the sign of the Daw, didst wrest, turn, pervert, misconster, and Catachrestically abuse the honest, civil, chast, pure, and incorrupt meaning of divers words following, As Standing, Members, Dealing, Trunchion, Quiver, Evidences, Weapons, Lapland, Vicegerent, and suchlike, into a wicked, wanton, lascivious and leud sense. And also thou art moreover indicted, for that thou the day and year aforesaid, of thy wicked malice forethought, and in great disdain of Love and all lovers, and to the great dishonor of his Excellencies Court, in the presence of his heroical person, having eaten of set purpose a certain contagious confection of Garlick and Assa fetida, didst nevertheless presume to Court divers fair and beautiful Ladies, and didst excuse that thy ranke noisome and pestiferous savour and exhalation by saying, Sweet Ladies, I have lately taken a new and excellent kinde of Tobacco late brought into his Excellencies Court from the North Indies.

How sayest thou, Art thou guilty of these Treasons whereof thou standest indicted, yea or no?

To which he pleaded, *Not guilty.*

How wilt thou be tryed?

He said by the Laws of Love, and an Enquest of true Lovers.

Then was the charge given to the Jury.

Preamble.

You Gentlemen that are sworn, you see I doubt not how happy this State hath been ever sithence the Scepter delivered to our renowned and Victorious Soveraign the famous Prince *d'Amours,* who being adapted by Celestial influence to advance the unspotted honor of *Venus* (that great commander of hearts and thoughts) hath by sweet laws so rightly instructed us in the steps of true Love, and by admirable discipline so carefully preserved us from all distempers of irregular Fancies, as we and none but we may justly say, We live secure from the events of Folly, strengthened from the dangers of despair, and complete in the fruits and effects of true Love.

We have by his Princely access to this Empire, exchanged our heavy Studies, that long besotted our inward senses, into a happy practise of disporting pleasures, yielding every minute renewing Joy to our vital Spirits.

Whereas before we were controulable at the nod of every doting Bencher, oppressed with the yoke of quarrelsome Cases, attired with a long doleful Robe and flat cap, and fed with thin liquor and the hinder part of a rotten Sheep; we are now become subjects and servants to this famous Prince, that lives victorious in all Nations; we are prest Soldiers under the sweet Banner of Love, where we receive every hour new encouragements in all our enterprises: We are apparrelled in Ladies Colours, that still breathes life to our reputation, and our diet is now suitable to the worth of our service.

These things are of sufficient force to draw all well disposed mindes into a resolution to maintain this triumphant State of Love against those vile Vipers of disdain that would fret it, or those corrupted Caterpillers that would Crop it.

The means to preserve it, is, by execution of our Laws, to part the Weeds from the Flowers, and sift the corn from the chaff. For which purpose ye are Jurors to present, and we judges to reform all the enormities incroachéd upon this State, either by the subtilties of foreign enemies, or the disloyalties of native subjects, or common infirmities of the people.

Offences inquirable by the Jury.

Therefore your charge is to enquire

1.   If any man do maintain, by word, writing, or overt Act, the Authority of

Benchers or utter Barristers within his Excellencies Dominions, this is high Treason.

2. If any Lady or Gentlewoman wound his Excellency in the eyes or ears, and give him not a present Favor for a remedy; or do come with an amorous intent to steal away the hearts of any his loving subjects, not leaving her own in pawn for exchange; this also is high treason.

3. If any man do amorously take any of his Excellencies sweet holds, and do not yield the same within one hour after the Proclamation made in the County Court, and before any Plea there entered of Record; this is high treason.

4. If any man bring into his Excellencies Dominions, any Book Case, Moot point, or flat cap, with an intent to utter the same to any his subjects, or do give Councel in any Suite, Title or conveyance of Law within his Excellencies Dominions; this is Premunire.

5. If any man do appeal to any Play at *Pauls, Bishopsgate,* or the *Bankes-side,* upon any sentence given in any of his Excellencies disports of Records; this is also Premunire.

6. If any subject born do depart without license out of his Excellencies Dominions, and adhere to any Lady or Gentlewoman in enmity with his Excellency, he incurreth also the Premunire.

7. If any Lady or Gentlewoman wound any of his Excellencies Subjects with looks premeditate, or precogitate distain, whereof he dieth within a year and a day, this is wilful murder.

8. If any man die for his Mistresses unkindness, he is *felo de se,* and not to be buried in Christian burial.

9. If any Lady or Gentlewoman coming to be confessed of his Excellencies Arch-flamen, be surprised by an Ambuscado, this is Sacriledge.

10. If any man do wittingly or unwittingly give his Mistris for token a Cornish Diamond in lieu of a precious stone, this is petty Larceny.

11. If any man do conceal his Love for lack of Wit or good manners, the same being found upon a Writ *de Ideota de probanda,* his Custody may be begged to supply the want for some needy Suiter.

12. If any man disswade any of his Excellencies subjects from his due obedience of Courting Ladies and Gentlewomen, or from aiding, helping, or assisting them in time of need, he is to make Fine and Ransome.

13. If any man oppose himself against any Lady or Gentlewoman upon small acquaintance and leave not his quarrel upon great intreaty, he is finable for his contempt.

14. If any man suspect his Mistris upon any kindness, by kiss, dance, looks, or congy given to her friend, this is Jealousie finable.

15. If any man deprave the books of *Ovid de Arte amandi, Euphues* and his England, Petite Pallace, or other laudable discourses of Love; this is loss of his Mistris favor for half a year.

16. If any man seek by jealous enquiries to know whether his Mistris be in love with any other, or how long she is like to love him, this is a forfeiture of all his countenance for one year, and further, to be put to silence untill he submit himself in open Sessions, and pay treble dammages for his distrust.

17. If any man ignorantly misinterpret his Mistresses looks, words, or tokens, and thereupon willingly grow discontent, he is to pay Fine and ransome, and further to live in Captivity during her pleasure.

18. If any man do speak words of defamation of any Lady or Gentlewoman, or do directly or indirectly use terms of Scurrility, or Ribawdry in any discourse, verse or Oration, he shall stand in the Pillory and lose his best ear, unless within two days he publickly signifie his unfeined repentance, and make such satisfaction as shall be enjoyned at his confession by his Excellencies Archflamen.

19. If any man that receiveth Favor of any Lady or Gentlewoman, do neglect to requite it or deserve it; he is to abjure his Excellencies Dominions.

20. If any man set up his Rest at *Primero* of purpose to drive his Mistris from the Stake while she is a loser; he is to forfeit five pound, the Moity to the Informer.

21. If any man be retained with two Mistresses at one time, concealing one from the other; he is to pay double dammages to the party grieved.

22. If any man man wear his Mistris Colours in his upper Garment before he hath served three Moneths, being under the degree of a Knight of the Quiver, he forfeiteth his Feather to the Lord of the Leet.

23. If any man withdraw his service at the first denial, or upon a double Check falleth to despair, he forfeiteth for every [blank] a penny to the poor of the Parish.

24. If any man presume of Love that is not likely, or follow with fresh suite when his Mistris is out of view, he shall not have the benefit of the Statute of *Wildfowle*, but may be taken in a day-net.

25. If above the number of two do consult to mock, floute or disgrace any Lady or Gentlewoman for any defective works of natrue, or for any laudable quality learned in *Venus* School, this is an unlawful Assembly.

26. If any Man professing Arms, to any Lady or Gentlewoman go attended with

more than his own number, being arrayed in suitable Colours, this is a Riot; If in different Colours, it is a Rout; and if the retinue depart not within an hour after Proclamation of discovery; the principal in *Bigamus* by the Statute of Apparel, and cannot have Clergy; and the Accessories knowing the Fact, are to be banished for half a year from Broken Wharf and Ram Alley.

27. If any man under pretence to sollicite for another, set in for himself; this is Covin apparent by the Rule of *Andrew Woodcocks* Cafe and punishable in the Star chamber; but if he try for both and speed for neither, the Escheator may finde him by Office upon a Writ *de Ideota probanda*; and if his companion obtain Institution, being the better Clerk, he is to be removed by *a Vi laica removenda* from disturbing the Induction; and further to be punished by the Statute of 5, for badging without license.

28. If any man mistaking his Mistris, do reverence to her Maid, he must make restitution with Interest after ten in the hundred; if he be not able, he is to forfeit his Sword and his Hangers as a Deodand to the Lord of the Soyle.

29. If any Lady or Gentlewoman put away a menial servant before his time expired, unless it be for Blasphemy or willful babling; she is to give him seven years wages before hand, to live at the Ordinary; and if he were made impotent by any Mayhem received in her service, she must be bound by Recognizance to release and relieve him during his life.

30. If any man that hath served in Campe or Garrison as a Lover, depart with a Passport, and after that wander as a Rogue to the dishonor of the Wars, he is punishable by whipping untill he be content to serve as a Porter, a Sexton, or a clerk of the Parish if he can read.

Upon these Articles you are to discharge your consciences, as the Lady *Venus* shall put into your mindes.

The charge being ended, and the Indictment to the grand Jury, they presently returned and found the Bill.

Then the Sheriff was commanded to return the petty Jury.

To whom it was said,

You good men that are impannelled between our Soveraign Lord the Prince d'Amour, *and the Prisoners at the bar, answer to your names.*

1. *Hen. Hart.*

2. *Leonard Lovewell.*

3. *Francis Finechild.*

4. *Lodowick Lovelace.*

5.   *Samuel Sweeting.*

6.   *Diggery Deering.*

7.   *Ferdinando Fines.*

8.   *Tristram True.*

9.   *Humphrey Hopewell.*

10. *Thomas Toogood.*

11. *Daniel Darling.*

12. *Simon Slie.*

Everyone of the petty Jury answered to his name, and they were sworn.

Then were the Prisoners called and held up their hands at the Bar, and were arraigned upon the former Indictment, and the petty Jury charged as before with these additions.

The charge given by the Chief Justice to the Jury

1.   If any subject naturally born, for want of Wit Court his Mistris with the Fruits of Silence, and seek to win her Favor with the seeds of his Purse; he shall be imprisoned in the Island of Ideocy, and censured by the Bishop of Saint Asses.

2.   If any man not being an inheritor of Wit, or having pawned or lost the same, hath courted his Mistris with Letters of other mens Invention, he shall be taken for the one an Asse by discent, and an impaired fool for the other.

3.   If any man masking with his Mistris hath perswaded her to Devotion, except it be to be of the family of Love; he shall be taken as a counterfeit confessor.

4.   If any man swear his fowl Mistris fair, his old Mistris young, or his crooked Mistris straight; or say that the wrinkles in her face be comely, or the want of her Teeth seemly; or that being blinde of the one eye, and squint-looked in the other, it is gracious; he shall be condemned as a forsworn Sorcerer for the one, and as a false Seducer of the Innocent, in the other.

5.   If any man kissing his hand superstitiously hath taken his Mistrisses dog by the tail, swearing her breath hath perfumed the same; he is to be punished for the first part as an Idolater, and for the second as a blasphemer.

6.   If any man kiss the seat of his Mistrisses saddle, or the stool whereon she hath sitten, he shall be taken as a vain worshipper of Idols.

7.   If any man for the Love of his Mistris hath eaten the sole of her Pantofle, the

paring of her nails, or hath drank the water wherein she washed, he shall be taken as a gluttonous devourer of silly simplicity.

8. If any of the Princes subjects swallow more Feathers of his Mistrisses favor then his descretion can digest, the tone [one?] half of him shall be taken for a Gudgeon, and the other for a Gull.

9. If any man hath unfeathered his Nest to Feather his Mistrisses Fancy, he shall be metamorphosed from a fool of the air to a beast of the field.

10. If any subject, to parcel, guilt, or imbroider his Mistris, wasteth any great Woods, whereby any Airy of Daws-nests be destroyed; he shall be taken as a Depopulator and yet remain a Daw still.

11. If any man, to furnish his Mistris, hath taken up by Exchange or Retail a Commodity of Chappinoes for her Feet, Clampes for her body, Nippers for her eye-brows, Periwigs for her head, or painting for her face, he shall be taken for a decayed Chapman in his Wit, and for a Bankerout in his discretion.

12. If any man do promise his Mistris a Bodking for her hair, and pay her with a straw, he shall be taken for a decayed Cony-catcher.

13. If any of the Princes subjects hath abused the Favor of his Mistris by the Act of dissimulation, or the Mystery of double-dealing, he shall be punished by dismembring.

14. If any man set up his Rest at *Primero* of purpose to drive his Mistris from the Stake, being a loser; he is to forfeit his Rest to the party grieved.

15. If any man seek his Mistrisses Favor by promising Mountaines, uttering of great and mighty speeches, thundering out words of Conjuration, raising any unlawful spirit, or using the aide of the wise woman of Seacole-lane, or of the Bankside, or by any other artificial mean, other then by the naked Truth, he shall be punished as a Sorcerer.

16. If any man disguisedly in the night time hath walked in the dirt before his Mistrisses window, knowing her to be asleep; he shall be enquired of as a concealed Moyle or Ass in whom there is no understanding.

17. If any man in the night time, without a good Warrant hath hunted in any of the Princes Parks, Chases, or Forrests, except it be free Warren, and shall deny the same before any of the Princes Ecclesiastical Justices, it is a Felony by the Statute of *pictis faciebus*.

18. If any man do break any house or Chamber wherein is any Lady or Gentle-woman after Sunsetting, or before Sun-rising, if the door be barred with a Busk, a Bodkin, a Garter, a Cushiner, or an Apron, this is Burglary, if he put her in fear; if not, yet is he to be punished by the Statute of Entries, at the suite onely of the party grieved.

19. If any of the Princes subjects having a Lease of his Mistrisses favour for an hour, committeth Waste in the soil, he shall lose the place wasted, and treble damages.

20. If any Lay-man be admitted by his Patroness to a Cure without charge of souls, and after, for non Residence another is inducted, and entereth *ubi ingressus non datur per legem*, he shall be removed by a *vi laica removendi*, but no restitution of possession to the first Incumbent.

21. If any man by his words, signs, letters or cyphers do disclose any favor in secret received from any Mistris; this is fellony, and if it be done in bravery, he loseth the benefit of his Clergy.

22. If any man do write any letters or verses of defamation of any Lady or Gentle-woman (except it be for dismissing her sworn servants without reward) this is Felony by the Statute of *Circumspecte agatis*.

23. If any Lady or Gentlewoman wound any of his Excellencies subjects with looks premeditated, or precogitated disdain, whereof he dieth within the year; the Prince shall have of her *annum diem & vastum* [?], and after to be executed at his pleasure.

24. If any man die with his Mistrisses unkindness, or with his jealous respect of her Favor, he is *felo de se*, and shall not be buried in Christian burial, but in the High way with a stake in his belly.

25. If any retained in service with any Lady or Gentlewoman happen to kill his Mistris with over-much kindness, this is petty Treason.

26. If any man surrender to a stranger any Fortresse won by his Excellencies own valor, or burn any vessel Royal wherein his Excellency hath any Munition, this is high Treason.

27. If any man be retained with two Mistrisses at one time, concealing the one from the other, he is to pay double damages to the party grieved.

28. If any man retained in service with any Lady or Gentlewoman by Covenant, Contract or promise, depart without licence before his years expired, and place himself elsewhere, he may be attached by any Ecclesiastical Apparitor, and enforced to serve out his time upon such ease of work and increase of Wages as the Judges shall think meet.

29. If any man by irreverent and scurrilous speeches shall prophane the immaculate Majesty of Love, or by contemptuous or reproachful words shall endeavor to bring any Obloquie or Indignity to the same, or with corrupt intent shall pervert the honest, simple, and plain meaning of any lawful or current words, and turn them to a leud and reprobate sence, this is high Treason.

30. If any man having his face of an ill aspect, or clothes of an ill fashion, shall over

loudly present himself to the offence of any Ladies eyes; or having an harsh voice shall speak over boldly in any Ladies ears, or with a violent breath shall offer himself too familiarly to any Ladies mouth, this is also high Treason.

Conclusion.

Upon these Articles you are to discharge your consciences, neither going on the left hand for Love nor Lucre, nor on the right for Fear or Favor; but keeping upright in the midway between both, as the Deity of *Cupid* with his mother *Venus*, and her handmaid *Oportunity* shall put into your Mindes.

The Prisoners pleaded not guilty to the Indictment, and put themselves upon their Peers, which are you of the Jury, who now shall hear the evidence.

Then was this evidence given against the prisoner by the Princes Atturney, saying,

The Princes Atturneys speech and evidence against the Prisoner.

I will not amplifie his crimes by the common induction of *vita anteacta*, nor rip up his faults from his infancy: onely I say that his familiars have great suspicion of his nature, knowing him from a Whelp; as the Servingman hath great confidence in his Sword which he hath bred[?] up from a Dagger. I let pass most part of his education, spent in the practice of enchantments, and penning of dangerous Speeches, able to corrupt the minds of them that had beauty without discretion; though I have been informed that there was no sign of the Maidenhead or Mermaids-head in the Town where he was born, which he had not tempted with Allurements, and Courted with Orations, like the late Injury which he offered to our Princes Excellency. For he uttered no Oration before him in his Raign which he had not acted in his Study, for his better assurance, before the sign of the Kings head which he borrowed of *John* Gent. I will onely insist upon the matter of this Indictment.

First for the words which he spake; wherein I make out,

First (for our better note) who spake it.

Then what.

Then where.

The person that spake it, had he been an ordinary man, the credit of his words had not exceeded the value of himself; but this man, being otherwise admirable for his nature, and famous in Monuments. For, what is the Elephant, visited with such wonder and great concourse of people, more than he. What is the Ram with the five horns in Fleetstreet; or the Ounce in the Strand but a Beast? For his fame in Writers, hath not *Sextus Quaterman*, in his seventh Volume of *Hempstalks* in most silent sort made mention of him. And *Remigius* the Waterman, in his Exposition upon *Thames*, pretermitted many significant speeches his praise. This man was contented to make all this admiration and commendation of himself, the balance of that reproach which he hath uttered against Love, our Prince, and his own Mistris. First for the name of Love (which all take to be most honorable) he uttered it without any Preface of great worship, saying, that the name of Love is never to be spoken without Sir *Reverence*. For what Acts or Monuments make known when Sir *Reverence* was Knighted? His other speech against the Prince, that none should be Prince of Love but he that could conquer love, being full of malice, is without Law or Reason. For in the Duke of *Buckinghams* case in the 12 of *H*. 8 he is called the Mirror of all courtesie; not that he overcame courtesie; not that he overcame courtesie, but that courtesie overcame him; and in the mirror of Knighthood, *Donsel del Phebo* is called the Knight of the Sun; not that he was above the Sun, but that the Sun was above him; and so of our Princes Title.

But to the next of his speeches against his Mistris, whose constancy and kindness he requires with disdain and ingratitude, wishing that he might shift her as often as he shifts his clothes; The ex-example [sic] whereof would draw many changes and innovations in this Kingdom. For so, by all likelihood, he would change his Mistris once in two years at least. How contrary this were to his often protestations, might appear by divers his Letters to her, found in his Study upon a late search for conjurors, suspected to cause this alteration of Weather, by vertue of a Warrant from the Lord Chief Justice; yet in one of them appears this his odious mutability and slanderous presumption against our honorable Judges of this Court; in confidence whereof he presented himself here, hoping to be delivered by corruption.

The Notes were delivered unto the Clerk of the Crown to be read, and were as followeth,

> He is but a Codshead
> That for fear of bloudshed
> In love will flinch.
> I care not who know it
> That I am a Poet
> And love a Wench.
> She dwells in an Alley
> Where I visit her daily
> If the streets be not foul;
> And over against her
> There dwelleth a Sempter,
> At the sign of the Owl.
>
> Yet would I exchange her
> But onely for danger
> Of losing the credit
> Of the speech that I utter'd
> To her when I flittered
> And was glad to read it.
> But my onely trust is
> That loves Chief Justice
> If I change will maintain it,

And that the Earl Martial
Himself will be partial
When I am arraigned.

A Passion

Cupid is blind, men say,
And yet my heart he seeth,
Which he did wound to day,
A Fig in *Cupids* teeth.

My Love she is most fair,
But yet her late disgraces
Do make me to despair;
A pox on all good faces.

Tears overflow my sight
With waves of daily weeping,
And in the restless Night
I find no ease for sleeping.

But see my weary merits
Their countenance do lack;
Come stock my vital spirits
With Claret wine and Sack.

Sweet Lady since my heart
By no means can renounce you,
One friendly look impart,
Gep Gillian, I will [?] you.

Regard my strange mishaps,
Jove, father of the Thunder,
Dart down thy Thunder Claps,
And rend her Smock asunder.

But since that all Relief
And comfort doth forsake me,
Ile kill my self for Grief,
Nay then the Divel take me.

A Compassion

Your letter I received
Bedeckt with flourisht quarters,
So women are deceived
Go hang thee in thy Garters.

My beauty, which is none,
Most fair, as you protest,
Doth make you sigh and groan;
Fie, Fie, you do but jest.

You onely would I see,
'Tis you I onely think on,
My looks as kind shall be
As the Divels over *Lincolne*.

Be not in such a plight,
No labor shall you leese,
Your service Ile requite;
Maid, cut him bread and Cheese.

If ever I do turn,
Great Queen of lightning flashes,
Send fire from heaven and burn
His Codpeece into Ashes.

Live still, I cannot miss thee,
I must enjoy thee one day,
Dear sweet come home & kiss me
Where I did sit on Sunday.

These thing[s] given in evidence, the Princes Atturney proceeded to urge the Evidence, saying,

Iniquity could not grow to this pitch but by degrees. As his steps to Treason toward our Prince were made upon abuse first of the Herald, so he ascended to this leud contempt of his Mistris from an injury done unto her Dog. For the Herald, he reported that he had robbed two Ratcatchers of their Banners, and thereof made him a Coat. For his Mistrisses Dod [dog?], this it is. Upon a time (as all things fall out in time, but his Galliard) it fortuned that he mended a hole in his stockings, or rather (as mine Author faith) repaired the Ruines which the injury of time and weather had caused, *ultra crepidam*; above his Shoo the thred hung out as the tail of his endeavors; his Mistresses Dog apprehended it, whom he in scorn spurned and called him Jew, when his name indeed was Iewel; a barbarous wrong, and a Turkish contradiction, such as I hope you my Lords, and you the Iury will justly think of. (Whereat they gave a severe Nod.) And this was no better Saints day then Saint *Rombald*. For the place, it was in *Hundsditch*; if it had been in *Hounslow*, it had been low, but not so low as a ditch. For the state and majesty, at an Alehouse; for the sign, at the Dogs head in the Pot; both which express his undaunted, though Rebellious courage.

The next matter of this Indictment is the perverting of honest speeches into unhonest meaning; which though he hath executed (for his guiltiness hath been often taxed) with this answer, that for the words they were his, but the sence was in the Audience, and every one of them brought hither a minde of his own; and so returned all the dishonesty upon the hearers construction. Yet can he not save himself with this evasion, for the imputatins of such, to the discredit of this Court, have been very common, and the offence very publike. The fault onely his, by his own confession; for he hath so crept into the service of penning some speeches, in this Princes raign, with a pernicious intent of disgracing the Government, and hath thereby so impeached the estimation of our Profession, that some are of opinion that our common Law is scarce written in an honest language. But had these speeches proceeded out of a sweet breath, or presumed lips, they had been more tolerable; but out of a throat that had swallowed Garlick, and that without any allay or qualification, having not eaten a barrel of Tar after it, nor drunk so much as one Tune of Oyl, it was rudeness more then Tartareous and Phlegetonical; and this in the presence of heroical persons, in conference with beautiful Ladies, who may be carried in publicke triumph for surviving so venomous an exhalation. For though it be not contained in the Indictment, yet I have been credibly informed, that there fell down five Sparrows dead from the top of the hall, poisoned by this contagious dampe; and the strength of it brake some fewer then fifty Panes of our glass windows. His excuse doth not extenuate, but aggravate his course behaviour; for he named it a Tabacco brought from the North Indies, to the overthrow of Navigation and utter undoing of that Traffick. This man, out of his mouth before he had used those ambiguous termes expressed in the Indictment, nor in Gracious-street, that there might have been some grace in it, nor in Mincing-lane, that there might have been modesty in it, but in Ram Alley, a place defamed a thousand and odd hundred years past by *Persius, Ile Ramale vetus vegrandi subere co[?]um.* And there, not at the sign of the Lyon, to express any noble stomach, or the sign of the Fox, to declare any good Policy, nor at the sign of the Ape, to colour it with imitation, but at the sign of the Daw, which was most base, sottish and ignominious. But I am to charge him grievously with the taking of Garlick, as a matter of petty Treason, as a case of *Horace* appears, *Parenti si quis impia favus manu senile guttur fregerit, edat cicutisium nocentius. O dura messorum Ilia!* Putting him in the same degree that hath eaten Garlick, with the man that hath broken his Fathers neck; affirming Garlick more deadly than Hemlock. And there is no *Athenian* in this company but knows that *Socrates* was poisoned with Hemlock.

If this petty Treason, if these seditious words, if these former Outrages to his Mistris and her Dog, carry not sufficient cause of condemnation, yet his most hainous Treasons against our Prince, and the mighty name and Power of Love, must make him the open example of Justice in this Realm, or animate a number of savage and untamed spirits to the like disobedience and Villany. Therefore I leave the issue of these offences, and the sequel of the common good in his punishment to the honest thoughts of the Iury, and these my Lords grave determinations.

The Evidence being given, the Iury was told that the prisoner had pleaded not guilty, and thereupon had put himself for tryal upon, *etc.* which are you. Your charge is to enquire whether he be guilty or not; if you find him guilty, then must you enquire what Goods, *etc.* he is seized of; if you find him not guilty, then must you enquire whether he fled for the same or not.

So the Iury went together, and after a short consultation among themselves, returning, gave up their Verdict that the Prisoner was guilty. And then the prisoner being told that he had indicted and arraigned, and pleaded not guilty to the indictment, and thereupon put himself for trial on, *etc*. That they notwithstanding had found him guilty. Therefore he was demanded what he could say for himself why judgement should not be given against him.

Who answered, that *he referred himself to the mercy of the Prince and that Court.*

And thereupon Iudgement was pronounced against him in these words.

Thou discontented Lover, because thou hast disdained to be true Prisoner to Love, whose imprisonment is the sweetest Liberty, The Court doth therefore award, that thou be delivered over to his Excellencies Captain of the Seraglia, *who shall commit thee close prisoner to the most loathsome Dungeon in the Fort of* Fancy, *there to remaine fasting from Favors, and feeding on Melancholy till thou hast paid thy fine and ransome, which shall be an Oration in praise of Love, and of his Excellency.*

NOTE: It should seem that one that personated jealousie, was also arraigned at the same time; for I finde this sentence pronounced against jealousie in the same scattered papers out of which I transcribed this, *viz.*

The Sentence against Iealousie.
For as much as the Laws of Love do not permit that the Kingdom of Love should by any means be polluted and defiled by shedding of blood, nor do allow any violent death, but onely the lingring and self-pleasing death for Love, whereof these guilty persons are much unworthy. The Court doth therefore award, That thou, Jealousie, the onely mover and stirrer of all intestine Sedition in this Kingdom of Love, and amongst the friends, allies, and confederates of the same, shall abjure the same Kingdom, and that within fourty dayes next ensuing this sentence, thou shalt, at the next Port convenient, take thy passage towards the Kingdom of the Amazones *beyond the high Mountain* Caucasus; *And in this thy Journey shalt not pass through the Lands, Dominions or Territories of any confederate Nation with this State; but being there arrived, shalt there remain in perpetual captivity unto* Penthesilea the Queen of that Country, where there are only women and want of men, by means of whereof the flame of jealousie being destitute of fuel, thy disordinate humor may at the last be dryed up with famine, and thy self recured of that kinde of suspicious Frenzie.

End Notes

Quotations are taken from the Penguin editions of Shakespeare's plays.

INTRODUCTION
The Detective Trail (pages 1–7)

1 *Diary of John Manningham*, ed. J. Bruce, the Camden Society, London 1868; the original is to be found in Harl. MS, British Library, No.5353, fo.III.2
2 Ibid., fo.29b.
3 Ibid., fo.98b.
4 Ibid., fo.74.
5 Ibid., fo.112b.
6 See chapter 2.
7 See p.56.
8 See p.70.
9 See pp.8 and 86.
10 His name is sometimes spelt Guilpern.
11 Public Record Office, State Papers Dom. Eliz., cclxxviii 85; quoted E.K. Chambers, *William Shakespeare: A Study of Facts and Problems*, Oxford 1930.
12 Quoted J.E. Neale, *Queen Elizabeth*, Penguin edition, London 1990, at p.387.
13 Act V, sc.2, l.31.
14 Act V, sc.4, l.99.

CHAPTER ONE
Twelfth Night or What You Will (pages 8–20)

1 Act II, sc.3, l.83.
2 Act I, sc.1, l.41.
3 Act II, sc.5 l.16.
4 Generally on this passage, see L. Hotson, *The First Night of Twelfth Night*, London 1954, pp.35 et seq.
5 Public Record Office, State Papers 78/44/352, quoted Hotson ibid., at p.62.
6 Historical Manuscripts Commission, *Third Report*, App.51b; cf. Hotson, ibid., at p.15.
7 Act I, sc.2, l.30.
8 Act II, sc.1, l.40.
9 Act III, sc.3, l.27.
10 See p.16.
11 See Hotson ibid., at pp.173 et seq.
12 Roma Archivo Storico Capitolino: Archivo Orsini, Corrispondenza di Virginio II SPQR, no.03940395.
13 Possibly hautboys.
14 1908 edition, vol.I, p.97, quoted J.B. Williamson, *The Temple*, London 1923 at pp.101–2.
15 A Study of Dramatic Form and its Relation to Social Custom, Princeton 1959.

16 Barber deals with misrule in chapter 3.
17 Act II, sc.2, l.22.
18 Barber deals with *A Midsummer Night's Dream* in chapter 6.
19 See introduction to Arden edition of *Twelfth Night*, ed. J.M. Lothian and T.W. Craik, London 1983, p.lvi.
20 Barber deals with *Twelfth Night* in chapter 10.
21 Act III, sc.4, l.56.
22 Act IV, sc.2, l.21
23 Act III, sc.4, l.141.
24 Act II, sc.3, l.85 and 119.
25 Act III, sc.4, l.15.
26 Act IV, sc.1, l.26.
27 Act I, sc.4, l.1.
28 Ibid., l.41.
29 Act I, sc.5, l.151.
30 Act II, sc.2, ll.36 et seq.
31 Act II, sc.4, l.119.
32 Act V, sc.1, l.318.
33 Act III, sc.2, l.7.
34 Act V, sc.2, l.2130.
35 Generally on Marston, see P.J. Finkelpearl, *John Marston of the Middle Temple*, Cambridge, Massachusetts 1969
36 Act III, sc.4, l.328.
37 L.55.
38 Act II, sc.2, l.325.
39 Act II, sc.5, l.38.
40 The principal source for this section is S.G. Culliford, *William Strachey*, Charlottesville 1965.

41 His name does not appear in the admissions register, but in his *History of Travaile*, published in 1611, he describes himself as a member, and he is named as such in a deed in 1605.
42 Ashmolean MSS, No.781, fo.135.
43 There is an account of this action in C.W. Wallace, *Children of the Chapel at Blackfriars*, Nebraska University Studies, vol.8., 1908. Some of the original is transcribed in F.G. Fleay, *A Chronicle History of the London Stage 1559–1642*, London 1890.
44 There are quotations from it in a later action *Kirkham v Painter*, in 1612, quoted in Fleay, ibid.
45 J.O. Halliwell, *Dramatic Records: A Collection Respecting the Office of Master of the Revels, a Curious Paper of the Time of Queen Elizabeth*, London 1872.
46 Public Record Office, C24/327.
47 William's mother was dead; his stepmother remarried into a different family; his sister Marie married a captain in the Queen's service called Clement Turner.
48 *Oxford English Dictionary*.
49 See p.16 and n.38.
50 A.L. Rowse, *My View of Shakespeare*, London 1996, p.94.

CHAPTER TWO
Mad Days (pages 21–36)

1 Plays were performed in the afternoons.
2 The principal source for this chapter is J.B. Williamson, *The Temple*, London 1923.
3 Ibid., p.115.
4 *Diary of John Manningham*, ed. J. Bruce, Camden Society, London 1868, fo.316. Fleetwood was the son of a former Recorder of London.
5 *Dyer's Reports*, 1586.
6 *De Laudibus Legum Angliae*, cap.XCVIII; trans. S.B. Chrimes, Cambridge Studies in English Legal History, Cambridge 1942.
7 F.W. Maitland, *English Law and the Renaissance*, Cambridge 1901, at p.27.

8 Cf. Maitland, ibid., p.8.

9 Justinian was the emperor who introduced the legal code that still forms the basis of most continental law.

10 Cf. Maitland, ibid., p.20 and n.40.

11 J. Stow, *Annals of England*, London 1592, 1615 edition, p.631, quoted Maitland, ibid., n.52.

12 Generally on Middle Temple Hall, see Michael Murray, *Middle Temple Hall, An Architectural Appreciation*, London 1991.

13 Williamson, ibid., p.229.

14 Ibid., p.231.

15 Act IV, sc.2, ll.33 et seq.

16 G.M. Trevelyan, *English Social History*, Cambridge 1925, pp.158 et seq.

17 Williamson, ibid., p.221 and Middle Temple admission registers.

18 Ibid., p.238.

19 *Dictionary of National Biography*.

20 A.W. Green, *The Inns of Court and Early English Drama*, New Haven, Connecticut 1931, pp.161–2.

21 Finkelpearl, *John Marston of the Middle Temple*, Cambridge, Massachusetts 1969, p.11.

22 One of the preparatory or Chancery Inns; it was situated close to the site of the modern Royal Courts of Justice.

23 Prostitutes.

24 Act III, sc.2, l.11.

25 Williamson, ibid., pp.205 et seq.

26 Dine in Hall.

27 Middle Temple Records; quoted Finkelpearl, ibid., at p.11.

28 Quoted Finkelpearl, ibid., at p.205.

29 *The Poems of Sir John Davies*, ed. R. Kreuger, Oxford 1975.

30 Act II, sc.5, l.9.

31 This was in 1629; in Elizabethan times theatres only opened once a week.

32 Where cockfighting took place.

33 The Blackfriars Theatre, originally adapted by Burbage.

34 The principal source for this section is A.W. Green, ibid.

35 Finkelpearl, ibid., at p.6.

36 Carey Conley, *First English Translation of the Classics*.

37 *Gesta Grayorum*, 1594, ed. D. Bland, Liverpool 1968, pp.30–1 and Green, ibid., p.80.

38 Williamson, ibid., pp.103 and 349.

39 Generally on Serjeants, see J. Baker, *The Order of Serjeants at Law*, Selden Society, Supplementary Series, No.5, London 1984.

40 Judges travelled round the country on assize to try cases: they were empowered to act by letters patent and commissions of oyer, terminer and general gaol delivery. On occasion Serjeants also acted on such commissions as deputy judges.

41 A conveyancer – one who transfers land.

42 Fee simple was the highest title to land, equivalent to modern freehold.

43 *De Laudibus*, ibid., Cap I.

44 The original is in the Middle Temple Library – see also Williamson, ibid., pp.350–1, and W. Dugdale, *Origines Juridicales*, 3rd edition, London 1680.

45 Act I, sc.3, ll.120 et seq.

46 Public Record Office, Rolls Chapel CCLXXXVII (Ref. SP12/287 (12)).

47 *Diary of John Manningham*, ibid., lst February 1601/2.

48 See introduction to *The Poems of Sir John Davies*, ibid., at p.xxxviii.

49 Lincoln's Inn Records, February Revels, 1568.

50 British Library, Lansd. MS, No.108, fo.63r.

CHAPTER THREE
Temple Connections (pages 37–46)

1 Act III, sc.2, l.13.
2 Act III, sc.4, l.134.
3 Act I, sc.5, l.124.
4 Act IV, sc.1, l.32.
5 Act III, sc.4, l.147.
6 E. Sams, *The Real Shakespeare*, London 1995, pp.40 and 41.
7 Act V, sc.2, l.31.
8 Most of the information in this section is taken from a note written by Christopher Whitfield and preserved in the Warwick County Records Office. See also by the same author *Notes and Queries*, 211, 1966, 446. Thanks are due to Jack Lyes in Bristol and Jane Beever in Warwick for help on the background to the Greene family. There is a copy of Greene's diary in the Shakespeare Birthplace Records Office, shelf ref.BRU/13/26A.
9 There were Greenes in Snitterfield – Gabriel and his wife – but they were the same generation as Thomas Greene alias Shakespeare.
10 On the Quineys, see S. Schoenbaum, *Shakespeare's Lives*, Oxford 1991.
11 Act II, sc.5, l.133.
12 Act I, sc.1, l.19. And see p.111.
13 Act V, sc.1, ll.1 et seq.
14 Act V, sc.1, l.96
15 1, *Plowden's Reports*, 253.

CHAPTER FOUR
The Greasy Pole (pages 47–59)

1 *The Poems of Sir John Davies*, ed. R. Kreuger, Oxford 1975.
2 Act III, sc.3.
3 Preface.
4 Act III, sc.7, l.24.
5 Act I, sc.5, l.266.
6 Act I, sc.3, l.20.
7 Act I, sc.3, l.103.
8 Act I, sc.3, l.48.
9 Act I, sc.5, l.157.
10 Sir T. Smith, *De Republica Anglorum*, ed. L. Alston, Cambridge 1906, pp.31–46b.
11 Act I, sc.3, ll.85 et seq.
12 D.M. Palliser, *The Age of Elizabeth: England Under the Later Tudors 1547–1603*, London 1992, p.287.
13 Ibid., p.280.
14 *Annals of England*, London 1592, 1615 edition, fo.58.
15 Act I, sc.1, l.3.
16 See S. Schoenbaum, *Shakespeare's Lives*, Oxford 1991, pp.68 et seq.
17 Act V, sc.1, l.29.
18 The information for this section comes from Mark Eccles, *Shakespeare in Warwickshire*, Madison, Wisconsin 1961; S. Schoenbaum, *William Shakespeare, A Compact Documentary Life*, Oxford 1975 and 1987, and S. Schoenbaum, *Shakespeare's Lives*, Oxford 1991; E.K. Chambers, *William Shakespeare, A Study of Facts and Problems*, Oxford 1930; E. Sams, *The Real Shakespeare*, London 1995.
19 Schoenbaum, *Shakespeare's Lives*, ibid., p.7.
20 E.A. Fripp, *Shakespeare, Artist and Man*, London 1938, vol.I, p.79.
21 Act III, sc.1, l.11.
22 Eccles, ibid., p.39.
23 Ibid., p.31.
24 E.A. Fripp, *Minutes and Accounts of the Corporation of Stratford upon Avon 1553–1620*, Stratford upon Avon 1926.
25 Act II, sc.3, l.1.

26 Cf. J. Thompson, *Shakespeare and the Classics*, London 1952, and T.W. Baldwin, *Shakespere's Small Latine and Lesse Greek*, Urbana 1944.

27 C.W. Scott Giles, *Shakespeare's Heraldry*, London 1950, p.27.

28 Cf. Schoenbaum, *Shakespeare's Lives*, ibid., p.14.

29 *Diary of John Manningham*, ed. Bruce, Camden Society, London 1868, fo.10.

30 Ibid., fo.46.

31 Ibid., fo.97.

32 See introduction, ibid.

33 Records of the Mercers' Company.

34 Now a government research laboratory: most of the Elizabethan house has been destroyed.

35 *Diary of John Manningham*, ibid., fo.13b.

36 Act II, sc.5, l.38.

37 Jezebel is one of the most hated women in the Old Testament; in the book of Kings she is described as a bitter opponent of Elijah and a promoter of the false god Baal.

38 Act II, sc.5, l.140.

39 Act II, sc.3, l.110.

40 General sources on the Shurleys of Isfield are: E.P. Shirley, *Stemmata Shirleiana*, London 1841; F.W.T. Attree, *Notes of Post Mortem Inquisitions taken in Sussex*, London 1912.

41 Ernest Straker, *Wealden Iron*, London 1931.

42 Cf. *The Book of John Rouse*, issued by the Sussex Record Society, 1928.

43 See p.35.

44 2nd February 1603, *Diary of John Manningham*, ibid., fo.91.

45 Act IV, sc.4, l.41.

46 Act III, sc.2, l.27.

47 Act III, sc.2, l.74.

48 Act II, sc.5, l.173.

49 Act III, sc.4, l.272.

CHAPTER FIVE
Revellers All (pages 60–71)

1 Generally on revelling, see D. Underdown, *Revel, Riot and Rebellion*, Oxford 1985.

2 *Parker v Hooper*, Public Record Office, STAC 8/239/3.

3 See Underdown, ibid., p.46.

4 Ibid., p.95.

5 Ibid., p.95.

6 J.B. Williamson, *The Temple*, London 1923, p.109.

7 London 1562, and see Williamson, ibid., p.171.

8 Staples and Barnard's Inns were feeder Inns for Gray's Inn.

9 See Williamson, ibid., at p.245, n.1.

10 A.W. Green, *The Inns of Court and Early English Drama*, New Haven, Connecticut 1931, p.98.

11 Green, ibid., p.99, and B. Brown, *Law Sports at Gray's Inn*, London 1921, p.vii, and see *Gesta Grayorum 1594*, ed. D. Bland, Liverpool 1968, p.83.

12 See Williamson, ibid., on masques, pp.270–4, 313–14, 357–9.

13 Act I, sc.4, ll.8 et seq.

14 British Library, *Thomason Tracts*, E 1836 L, p.6; Microfiche B58.

15 See *Memoirs of Sir Benjamin Rudyerd*, J.A. Manning, London 1841, where his version is reproduced.

16 British Library, Harl. MS Nos. 1576, 556.

17 See n.14, supra; the script is reproduced in Appendix II.

18 Act II, sc.5, l.107.

19 Act I, sc.5, l.234.

20 Act II, sc.1.

21 Act I, sc.5.

22 Act II, sc.6.
23 Act I, sc.1, l.12.
24 Act I, sc.1, l.19.
25 Act V, sc.1, l.32.
26 Act II, sc.1, l.18.

27 Act II, sc.1, l.141.
28 Act IV, sc.1, l.148.
29 Act I, sc.3, l.108.
30 Ibid., l.128

CHAPTER SIX
The Mermaid Club (pages 72–84)

1 See K. Rogers, *The Mermaid and Mitre Taverns in Old London*, London 1928.
2 *Richard III*, Act V, sc.3, l.305.
3 See also L.Wagner, *London Inns and Taverns*, London 1924.
4 Act II, p.C2.
5 Act IV, p.E3 and F.
6 Act V, sc.3, l.3831: Malone Society Reprints, ed. W.W. Gregg, London 1920.
7 Act IV, sc.1, l.61: Tudor Facsimile Texts, London 1914.
8 Act I, sc.1, l.29.
9 Epigram 101.
10 Epigram 133.
11 See *Thomas Coryate*, ed. M. Strachan, London 1962.
12 Act II, sc.4.
13 See Strachan, ibid., p.302.
14 Rogers, ibid., pp.10–11.
15 L. Hotson, *Shakespeare's Sonnets Dated*, London 1949, p.76.
16 Ibid.
17 J.B. Williamson, *The Temple*, London 1923.
18 1898 edition, ii, 48.
19 Middle Temple Library Tracts, no.48.
20 Williamson, ibid., p.216.
21 See Williamson, ibid., at p.270 and A.W. Green, *The Inns of Court and Early English Drama*, New Haven, Connecticut 1931, at p.102.
22 Williamson, ibid., p.217.
23 Generally on Davies, see Williamson, ibid., p.214, and *The Poems of John Davies*, ed. R. Kreuger, Oxford 1975.

24 P.J. Finkelpearl, *John Marston of the Middle Temple*, Cambridge, Massachusetts 1969, p.49
25 See introduction to *The Poems of John Davies*, ibid., p.xxxiii.
26 Ibid.
27 Introduction to *The Poems of John Davies*, ibid., p.xxxiii. The passage is omitted from the Bruce edition of *The Diary of John Manningham* because it is too crude!
28 *The Diary of John Manningham*, ed. J. Bruce, Camden Society, London 1868, fo.127b.
29 See Introduction to *The Poems of John Davies*, ibid., p.xliv.
30 For these references, see J. Hoskyns, *Directions for Speech and Style*, ed. H. Hudson, Princeton 1935, pp.13, 22 and 23.
31 Finkelpearl, ibid., p.66.
32 1898 edition, ii, p.169.
33 M. Eccles, *Shakespeare in Warwickshire*, Madison, Wisconsin 1961, pp.138–9.
34 Finkelpearl, ibid., p.84.
35 Finkelpearl, ibid., at pp.86–7 suggests that Ruscus in *The Scourge of Villainy* is Davies.
36 Finkelpearl, ibid., at pp.221 et seq.
37 *The Poems of John Marston*, ed. A. Davenport, Liverpool 1961, at p.310.
38 At p.110.
39 See Finkelpearl, ibid., at p.220.
40 Ibid., at p.256.
41 Ibid., at p.257.
42 Ibid., at p.85.
43 *Dictionary of National Biography*.

44 P.J. Finkelpearl, *Review of English Studies*, 16 (1965), pp.396–9.
45 *Letters and Epigrams of Sir John Harrington*, ed. N. McClure, at p.319.
46 J.A. Manning, *Memoirs of Sir Benjamin Rudyerd*, London 1841.
47 Nos.121, 122, 123.
48 See A. Powell, *Aubrey and his Friends*, London 1963.

49 Ibid., p.252.
50 Act III, sc.1 l.127
51 British Library, Harl. MS No.1576/556; the book is dedicated to Lord Darcy, Viscount Colchester. Darcy held that title from 1621 to 1639 – see the Complete Peerage. Members of the Darcy family joined the Middle Temple.

CHAPTER SEVEN
What's in a Name? (pages 85–96)

1 Act I, sc.2, l.3.
2 Act V, sc.1, l.96.
3 *Oxford Classical Dictionary*.
4 L. Hotson, *The First Night of Twelfth Night*, London 1949, p.151.
5 Act III, sc.3, l.27.
6 Act V, sc.1, l.66.
7 Act III, sc.1, l.132.
8 Act III, sc.3, l.40.
9 M.J. Levith, *What's in Shakespeare's Names*, London 1978; W. Schleiner, 'Are the Names of the Serious Characters in *Twelfth Night* Meaningful?' *Shakespeare Studies*, 16, p.951, 1983; C. Lewis, '"A Fustian Riddle"; Anagrammatic Names in *Twelfth Night*', *English Language Notes*, 22, 1983.
10 Act II, sc.5, l.107.
11 Lewis, ibid.
12 C. Hibbert, *The Rise and Fall of the House of Medici*, London 1974, Penguin edition, p.115.
13 Ibid., p.114–16.
14 Ibid., p.170.
15 Ibid., p.278.
16 For the account of his visit see p.8.
17 See Hotson, ibid., p.37.
18 *The Expedition of the Florentines to Chios 1599*, P. Argenti, London 1934; and cf. Hotson, ibid., p.62.
19 Schleiner, ibid.
20 Ibid.

21 P. Hanks and F. Hodge, *A Dictionary of First Names*, Oxford 1990.
22 Act I, sc.1, l.4.
23 Act I, sc.2, l.58.
24 Hanks and Hodge, ibid.
25 Act I, sc.2, ll.36 et seq.
26 Act I, sc.5, l.202.
27 Hanks and Hodge, ibid.
28 *Oxford Classical Dictionary*.
29 Act II, sc.3, l.167.
30 *Oxford Classical Dictionary*.
31 See T.W. Baldwin, *William Shakespeare's Small Latine and Less Greeke*, Urbana 1944; also introduction to *The Poems of Sir John Davies*, ed. R. Kreuger, Oxford 1975.
32 Baldwin, ibid., i, 333; introduction to *The Poems of John Davies*, ibid.
33 J. L. Sanderson, 'Epigrams per Benjamin Rudyerd', *Review of English Studies*, vol. XVII (1966), pp.241–55.
34 *Oxford Classical Dictionary*, and Cicero, *Pro Sestrio*, l.96.
35 In *Orchestra*, Davies writes of a dance called Lavoltaes:
'A lofty jumping, or leaping round,
When arme in arme, two Dauncers are entwind,
And swirle themselves with strickt embracements bound.'
36 Quoted on p.47.

37 See p.37.
38 Act I, sc.1, l.18.

39 E.K. Chambers, *The Elizabethan Stage*, Oxford 1923, vol.I, p.170.

CHAPTER EIGHT
Sources (pages 97–107)

1 The various sources are usefully collected in G. Bullough, *Narrative and Dramatic Sources of Shakespeare*, New York 1957, pp.431 et seq.
2 Act II, sc.3, l.111.
3 Ibid., l.153.
4 Act II, sc.3, l.111.
5 Act II, sc.3, l.134.
6 On the subject of puritanism, see P. Collinson, *The Elizabethan Puritan Movement*, London 1967, and D. Underdown, *Revel, Riot and Rebellion*, Oxford 1985, pp.41 et seq.
7 Underdown, ibid., pp.47 et seq.
8 *A Sermon Made at Blandford*, quoted by Underdown, ibid., at p.47.
9 Underdown, ibid., p.175–6.
10 William Fennor, *Pasquil's Palinodra*, quoted by Underdown, ibid., p.54.
11 *Coleman v Thorpe*, Public Record Office, STAC 8/94/7.
12 See Collinson, ibid., pp.233, 280–1, 327 and 391–6.
13 Quoted E.K. Chambers, *The Elizabethan Stage*, Oxford 1923, vol.1, p.318.
14 Ibid., p.294.
15 J.B. Williamson, *The Temple*, London 1923, pp.199 et seq., and Collinson, ibid., p.294.
16 Collinson, ibid., p.341.
17 *The Diary of John Manningham*, ed. Bruce, Camden Society, London 1868, fo.76b.
18 Act I, sc.5, l.85.
19 Act II, sc.3, l.143.
20 Act II, sc.5, l.23.
21 L. Hotson, *The First Night of Twelfth Night*, London 1954, p.99.
22 *Dictionary of National Biography*.
23 Act I, sc.3, l.118.
24 Act II, sc.3, l.74.
25 See Hotson, ibid.
26 M.C. Linthicum, *Costume in the Drama of Shakespeare and his Contemporaries*, Oxford 1936, p.48; it was common for Hymen, the goddess of marriage, to be clothed in yellow.
27 Ibid., p.264.
28 Act II, sc.5, l.66.
29 Her first husband was Sir Thomas Hoby, who translated Castiglione's *The Courtier* into English. Their son, Edward, was a member of the Middle Temple.
30 Public Record Office, STAC/5/H16/2; Shakespeare knew of the Star Chamber jurisdiction on riot; cf. *The Merry Wives of Windsor*, Act I, sc.1, ll.1 et seq.
31 See introduction to *Diary of Lady Margaret*, ed. Dorothy Meads, London 1930.
32 Ibid., at pp.28–9.
33 Ibid., p.32.
34 Act II, sc.3, l.95.

CHAPTER NINE
Postcript: *Troilus and Cressida* (pages 108–11)

1 Act III, sc.1, l.48.
2 See Peter Alexander, 'Troilus and Cressida 1609', *The Library*, 9, 1928–9, 267.
3 Aldershot, 2000.
4 See introduction to the Arden edition.
5 For the Registry Entries, see S. Schoenbaum, *William Shakespeare,*

Records and Images, Oxford 1981, pp.216 et seq.
6 L. Hotson, *Shakespeare's Sonnets Dated*, London 1949, p.50.
7 L.1369.
8 Act V, sc.10, l.46.
9 Act III, sc.2, l.48.
10 Act III, sc.2, l.55.
11 L.26.

CHAPTER TEN
Skeleton Argument (pages 112–17)

1 D. Hume, *On Crimes*, Edinburgh 1797, 3rd edition, 1844, vol.II, p.384.

2 See preface to *Arden* edition, p.lvi.
3 L. Hotson, *Shakespeare v Shallow*, London 1931.

CHAPTER ELEVEN
The Original Performance (pages 118–21)

1 British Library, *Lansdowne Documents*, p.1171.
2 Reproduced in T.J. King, *Shakespearean Staging 1599–1642.*
3 Ibid., p.3.
4 Act II, sc.3, l.85.
5 Act II, sc.5, l.81.
6 Chapter 3.
7 See p.9.

8 Quoted Hotson, *The First Night of Twelfth Night*, London 1954, p.65.
9 Public Record Office, E 351 3223.
10 Platforms under the canopy.
11 Floor.
12 Public Record Office, E101/504/16, mem.8.
13 Public Record Office, AO1/2418/36.

APPENDIX I
Later Performances (pages 122–5)

1 There is an account of his performance in R. Speaight, *William Poel and the Elizabethan*

Revival, London 1954.
2 According to the *Nottingham Guardian.*

Bibliography

P. Argenti, *The Expedition of the Florentines to Chios 1599*, London 1934
F.W.T. Attree, *Notes of Post Mortem Inquisitions in Sussex*, London 1912
J. Baker, *The Order of Serjeants at Law*, Selden Society Supplementary Series, vol.5, London 1984
T.W. Baldwin, *William Shakespere's Small Latine and Less Greeke*, Urbana 1944
C.L. Barber, *Shakespeare's Festive Comedy*, Princeton 1959
F. Beaumont, *Wit Without Money*, London 1639
B. Brown, *Law Sports at Gray's Inn*, London 1921
G. Bullough, *Narrative and Dramatic Sources of Shakespeare*, New York 1957–75
J.H. Burn, *London Traders' Tokens*, London 1855
B. Castiglione, *The Courtier*, trans. Sir Thomas Hoby, London 1588
E.K. Chambers, *The Elizabethan Stage*, Oxford 1923
E.K. Chambers, *William Shakespeare, A Study of Facts and Problems*, Oxford 1930
Cicero, *Pro Sestio*
Coleman v Thorpe, Public Record Office, STAC 8/94/7
P. Collinson, *The Elizabethan Puritan Movement*, London 1967
C. Conley, *First English Translators of the Classics*, New Haven, Connecticut 1927
Thomas Coryate, ed. M. Strachan, London 1962
S.G. Culliford, *William Strachey*, Charlottesville 1965
John Davies, *The Poems*, ed. R. Kreuger, Oxford 1975
T. Dekker, *Westward Hoe*, London 1607
Dictionary of National Biography
E. Donno (ed.), *Twelfth Night*, New Cambridge Series, Cambridge 1985
W. Dugdale, *Origines Judicales*, 3rd ed., London 1680
Dyers Reports, 1513–82
M. Eccles, *Shakespeare in Warwickshire*, Madison, Wisconsin 1961
P.J. Finkelpearl, *John Marston of the Middle Temple*, Cambridge, Massachusetts 1969
P.J. Finkelpearl, *Review of English Studies*, 16 (1965), pp.396–9
F.G. Fleay, *A Chronicle History of the London Stage 1559–1642*, London 1890
John Fortescue, *De Laudibus Legum Angliae*, trans. S.B. Chrimes, Cambridge Studies in Legal History, Cambridge 1942
E.A. Fripp, *Minutes and Accounts of the Corporation of Stratford upon Avon, 1553–1620*, Stratford upon Avon 1926
E.A. Fripp, *Shakespeare, Artist and Man*, London 1938
C.W. Scott Giles, *Shakespeare's Heraldry*, London 1950
Gesta Grayorum 1594, ed. D. Bland, Liverpool 1968

E. Gilpin, *Skialethia or the Shadowe of Truth*, London 1598

A.W. Green, *The Inns of Court and Early English Drama*, New Haven, Connecticut 1931

T. Greene, *Shakespeare and the enclosure of common fields at Welcombe, being a fragment of the private diary of Thomas Greene 1614–17*, ed. C.M. Ingleby, Birmingham 1885; the original of the diary is in the Shakespeare Birthplace Records Office, shelf ref. BRU/13/26A.

J.O. Halliwell (later Halliwell-Phillips), *Dramatic Records – A Collection Respecting the Office of Master of the Revels, a Curious Paper of the Time of Queen Elizabeth*, London 1872

C. Hamilton, *In Search of Shakespeare*, London 1986

P. Hanks and F. Hodge, *A Dictionary of First Names*, Oxford 1990

Sir John Harington, *The Letters and Epigrams*, ed. N.E. McClure, Philadelphia 1930

Christopher Hibbert, *The Rise and Fall of the House of Medici*, London 1974

Hoby v Ewre, Public Record Office, STAC/5/H16/2

Diary of Lady Margaret Hoby, ed. D. Meads, London 1930

J. Hoskyns, *Directions for Speech and Style*, ed. H. Hudson, Princeton 1935

L. Hotson, *Shakespeare v Shallow*, London 1931

L. Hotson, *Shakespeare's Sonnets dated*, London 1949

L. Hotson, *The First Night of Twelfth Night*, London 1954

D. Hume, *Crimes*, Edinburgh 1797; 3rd edition, 1844

A.R. Humphreys (ed.), *Much Ado About Nothing*, Arden Series, London 1981

H. Jenkins (ed.), *Hamlet*, Arden Series, London 1982

B. Jonson, *Bartholomew Fair*, ed. Duncan, Edinburgh 1972

B. Jonson, *Epigrams*, London 1640

B. Jonson, *Cynthia's Revels*, London 1601, ed. Judson, New Haven, Connecticut 1912

M.J. Levith, *What's in Shakespeare's Names*, London and Sydney 1978

C. Lewis, ' "A Fustian Riddle"; Anagrammatic Names in *Twelfth Night*', *English Language Notes*, 22, 1983

M.C. Linthicum, *Costume in the Drama of Shakespeare and his Contemporaries*, Oxford 1936

J.M. Lothian and T.W. Craik (eds.), *Twelfth Night*, Arden Series, London 1983

M.M. Mahood (ed.), *Twelfth Night*, New Penguin Shakespeare, London 1968

F. Maitland, *English Law and the Renaissance*, Cambridge 1901

J.A. Manning, *Memoirs of Sir Benjamin Rudyerd, containing his speeches and poems*, London 1841

J. Manningham, *Diary*, ed. J. Bruce, Camden Society, London 1868; British Museum Harl. MS 5353, fo.III

J. Marston, *Antonio and Mellida*, London c.1601

J. Marston, *Antonio's Revenge*, London c.1601

J. Marston, *The Dutch Curtezan*, London c.1605

J. Marston, *Eastward Hoe*, London c.1604

J. Marston, *The Fawne*, London 1606

J. Marston, *The Malcontent*, London c.1604

J. Marston, *Sophonisba*, London 1606

J. Marston, *The Scourge of Villainy*, London c.1598

J. Marston, *What You Will*, London c.1601

Mercers' Company Records
Middle Temple Bench Book
Middle Temple Admissions
T. Middleton, *The Five Gallants*, London 1606
M. Murray, *Middle Temple Hall, An Architectural Appreciation*, London 1991
J.E. Neale, *Queen Elizabeth*, Penguin ed., London 1990
Oxford Classical Dictionary
D.M. Palliser, *The Age of Elizabeth: England Under the Later Tudors 1547–1603*, London 1992
Parker v Hooper, Public Record Office, STAC 8/239/3
Plowden's Cases 1550–1580
A. Powell, *Aubrey and his Friends*, London 1963
K. Rogers, *The Mermaid and Mitre Taverns in Old London*, London 1928
Roma Archivo Storico Capitolino: Archivo Orsini, Corrispondenza di Virginio II SPQR, no.03940395
A.L. Rowse, *My View of Shakespeare*, London 1996
E. Sams, *The Real Shakespeare*, London 1995
J.L. Sanderson, 'Epigrams per Benjamin Rudyerd', *Review of English Studies*, vol.xvii, 1966, p.241
S. Schoenbaum, *William Shakespeare, A Compact Documentary Life*, Oxford 1977
S. Schoenbaum, *William Shakespeare, Records and Images*, Oxford 1981
S. Schoenbaum, *Shakespeare's Lives*, Oxford 1991
W. Schleiner, 'Orsino and Viola: Are the Names of Serious Characters in *Twelfth Night* Meaningful?' *Shakespeare Studies*, 16, 1983, p.951
E.P. Shirley, *Stemmata Shirleana*, London 1841
A.G.R. Smith, *Servant of the Cecils, The Life of Sir Michael Hickes*, London 1977
Sir T. Smith, *De Republica Anglorum*, ed. L. Alston, Cambridge 1906
A. Solerti, *Musica, Ballo, Drammatico alla Corte Medicea*, Florence 1905
R. Speaight, *William Poel and the Elizabethan Revival*, London 1954
J. Stow, *Annals of England*, London 1592
J. Stow, *Survey of London*, London 1603
E. Straker, *Wealden Iron*, London 1931
Thomason Tracts, E 1836 L: Microfiche B 58
E. Thompson, *Shakespeare's Handwriting*, Oxford 1916
J. Thompson, *Shakespeare and the Classics*, London 1962
G.M. Trevelyan, *English Social History*, Cambridge 1923
D. Underdown, *Revel, Riot and Rebellion*, Oxford 1985
L. Wagner, *London Inns and Taverns*, London 1924
C.W. Wallace, *Children of the Chapel at Blackfriars*, Nebraska University Studies, vol.8, 1908
C. Whitfield, *Thomas Greene*, Warwick County Record Office
G. Wilkins, *The Miseries of Enforced Marriage*, London 1607
J.B. Williamson, *The Temple*, London 1923

Index